TOURIST
and
MOTORING ATLAS

Great Britain
& Ireland

MICHELIN the world's leading manufacturer of tyres, is also a well known name in the field of tourist publications ; its annual sales of maps and guides exceed 16 million in over 70 countries.

Acting on the belief that motoring would have a great future, the Michelin brothers decided to offer the motorist a touring service, an innovative step at the turn of the century : free or inexpensive publications designed to provide information, assistance and encouragement.

At the wheel, touring, on holiday – these three aspects of travel were met by a simple response – a trio of complementary publications to be used together.

The first of these, the Red Guides, which are published annually, present a selection of hotels and restaurants, with a wide range of prices and facilities. It is, however, probably their award of the stars for good cooking that has established their international reputation ; as well as the wealth of essential touring information included in them. There are several guides covering Europe, including the Red Guide to France which alone has sold over 20 million copies to date. Readers have such faith in their reliability that the Red Guides are foremost among reference books in this field.

The role of the Michelin Green Guides is to provide tourists with information to help them explore and enjoy the countries, regions and cities of Western Europe and North America. The guides describe the sights, the countryside and picturesque routes ; they also contain maps, plans and practical information as well as illustrations and photographs which whet one's appetite for travel. There are over 70 titles covering Europe and North America, which are published in French and other European languages and are revised regularly.

"The principal mapping in this Atlas of Great Britain and Ireland is an enlargement of the 1:400 000 sheet map series covering these countries. In addition we have 14 pages of comprehensive Route Planning mapping to help you prepare your journey. There are 103 pages of mapping, 49 town plans and an index of approximately 10 000 place names. The same grid system as on the sheet maps is used in this Atlas in order that it can be used in conjunction with our Hotel and Restaurant Guides "Great Britain and Ireland" and "Ireland" and also with our Green Guides "Great Britain", "Ireland", "Scotland", "London" and "The West Country"."

It is our intention to continue our service to our readers by annually updating the information contained within the Atlas. We should welcome your comments and suggestions in order that we may take your wishes into account when preparing the next edition.

Thank you in advance. May we wish you a safe journey.

MICHELIN maps and guides
complement one another :
use them together !

Contents

Inside front cover

Key to map pages

II Michelin

IV **Distances** in Great Britain and Ireland

V **Route Planning** at a scale of 1:1 000 000

XX **Key to symbols :** English and French

1 **Key to symbols :** Welsh and Irish

2 **Great Britain** at a scale of 1:300 000

20 **Greater London** at a scale of 1:200 000

76 **Ireland** at a scale of 1:300 000

104 **Key to town plan symbols**

105 **Index of place names :** Great Britain

136 **Index of place names :** Ireland

Channel Tunnel
115 Folkestone Terminal
116 Calais Terminal

Inside back cover

Shipping Services

Plans of cities and principal towns

105 Aberdeen
106 Bath
137 Belfast
136 Belfast area
106 Birmingham
107 Birmingham area
108 Blackpool
108 Bournemouth
108 Bradford
109 Brighton
109 Bristol
110 Cambridge
110 Canterbury
110 Cardiff/ Caerdydd
110 Carlisle

111 Chester
138 Cork/Corcaigh
111 Coventry
112 Derby
112 Dover
140 Dublin/ Baile Átha Cliath
139 Dublin area
113 Dundee
113 Durham
114 Edinburgh
113 Edinburgh area
114 Exeter
118 Glasgow
117 Glasgow area
119 Ipswich

119 Kingston upon Hull
122 Leeds
122 Leeds area
123 Leicester
131 Limerick/ Luimneach
123 Lincoln
124 Liverpool
123 Liverpool area
120 London
142 Londonderry
126 Manchester
125 Manchester area
127 Newcastle upon Tyne

127 Norwich
128 Nottingham
128 Oxford
129 Plymouth
129 Portsmouth
131 Sheffield
131 Southampton
132 Stoke on Trent
132 Stoke on Trent area
132 Stratford upon Avon
132 Sunderland
133 Swansea/Abertawe
134 Winchester
134 Wolverhampton
135 York

Distances in Great Britain and Ireland

All distances are quoted in miles and kilometres.

miles in red

kilometres in blue

The distances quoted are not necessarily the shortest but have been based on the roads which afford the best driving conditions and are therefore the most practical.

Example:

Oxford – Killarney:

Oxford – Fishguard	214 m.	or	344 km.
+ **Rosslare – Killarney**	157 m.	or	252 km.
	371 m.	or	596 km.

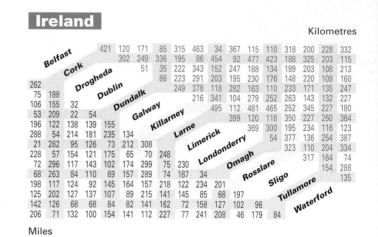

Ireland

Kilometres

```
Belfast    421 120 171  85 315 463  34 367 115 110 318 200 228 332
Cork            302 249 336 195  86 454  92 477 423 188 325 203 115
Drogheda             51  35 222 343 152 247 188 134 199 203 108 213
Dublin                   86 223 291 203 195 230 176 148 220 109 160
Dundalk                      249 378 118 282 163 110 233 171 135 247
Galway                           216 341 104 279 252 263 143 132 227
Killarney                            495 112 481 465 252 345 227 180
Larne                                    399 120 118 350 227 260 364
Limerick                                     369 300 195 234 116 123
Londonderry                                       54 377 136 254 387
Omagh                                                 323 110 204 334
Rosslare                                                  317 164  74
Sligo                                                         154 288
Tullamore                                                        135
Waterford
```

```
262                 Belfast
 75 188             Cork
106 155  32         Drogheda
 53 209  22  54     Dublin
196 122 138 139 155 Dundalk
288  54 214 181 235 134 Galway
 21 282  95 126  73 212 308 Killarney
228  57 154 121 175  65  70 248 Larne
 72 296 117 143 102 174 299  75 230 Limerick
 68 263  84 110  69 157 289  74 187  34 Londonderry
198 117 124  92 145 164 157 218 122 234 201 Omagh
125 202 127 137 107  89 215 141 145  85  68 197 Rosslare
142 126  68  68  84  82 141 162  72 158 127 102  96 Sligo
206  71 132 100 154 141 112 227  77 241 208  46 179  84 Tullamore
```

Miles

Great Britain

Kilometres

```
Aberdeen    692 962 826 750 858 368 940 108 197 947 851 238 870 739 577 173 300 520 573 880 566 438 367 776 787 632 286 803 1126 1013 936 907 375 849 357
Birmingham      268 143 158 175 327 324 584 477 264 299 482 279 266 232 737 766 196 165 186 145 290 337  92 265  85 627 109  443  330 242 213 494 234 920
Brighton            257 195 308 598 170 856 739 272 481 753 208 538 434 1008 1037 427 437  89 417 521 568 208 274 316 898 172  454  341  77  98 766 367 1192
Bristol                 245  73 461 319 718 611 124 246 616 335 400 381 871 900 344 299 197 279 439 485 184 352 234 760 120  304  191 152 121 628 131 1054
Cambridge                   296 427 195 642 550 373 469 582 107 416 236 806 866 247 315  92 269 332 379  87 108 145 727 132  555  442 222 216 594 355 990
Cardiff                         493 370 750 643 181 180 648 387 363 413 903 932 376 270 249 311 471 517 236 403 266 792 171  361  248 218 186 660  65 1086
Carlisle                            642 261 154 581 486 158 548 373 254 413 442 197 207 514 200 154  96 410 464 309 303 438 761  648  571 542 170 483 597
Dover                                   833 741 396 543 798 208 582 427 997 1082 457 481 120 461 523 569 238 274 347 894 279  578  465 229 230 810 429 1181
Dundee                                       89 839 743 124 763 631 469 205 281 412 465 772 458 330 259 668 679 524 189 696 1018 905 828 799 260 741 389
Edinburgh                                        732 637  73 671 524 377 254 330 320 358 641 351 238 167 537 587 432 198 589  912  799 721 692 210 634 437
Exeter                                               355 736 435 521 501 991 1020 465 420 298 400 559 606 315 477 354 881 250  180   73 208 174 749 240 1175
Fishguard                                                641 560 267 466 896 925 377 267 422 311 479 525 409 516 477 359 786  344  534 421 391 360 653 118 1079
Glasgow                                                     703 528 409 276 288 352 362 669 355 309 249 565 619 464 148 593  916  803 726 697 135 639 460
Harwich                                                         537 315 927 987 367 436 139 390 453 499 212 110 266 847  222  617 504 267 278 715 445 1111
Holyhead                                                            353 783 812 265 154 454 198 366 413 349 485 289 673  377  700 587 510 481 541 299 967
Hull                                                                    634 693  99 212 324 158 143 206 232 248 157 554  287  681 568 419 390 422 471 817
Inverness                                                                   129 576 617 924 610 495 424 820 843 689 183 848 1171 1058 981 952 413 894 186
Kyle of Lochalsh                                                                636 646 953 639 571 500 849 903 748 201 877 1200 1087 1010 981 449 923 279
Leeds                                                                            123 329  70 102 149 225 284 120 497 279  644  531 412 383 364 435 760
Liverpool                                                                            353  57 225 271 248 363 179 507 276  599  486 409 380 375 276 801
London                                                                                    333 423 470 110 185 218 814  89  480  367 128 140 682 307 1108
Manchester                                                                                    171 218 228 306 117 500 256  579  466 389 360 308 794
Middlesbrough                                                                                      67 319 369 215 434 374  739  626 506 477 321 529 678
Newcastle                                                                                             366 416 261 363 420 785  672  553 524 262 576 607
Northampton                                                                                              194 114 710  72  434  381 204 175 578 294 1004
Norwich                                                                                                      196 764 239  659  546 325 320 631 462 1027
Nottingham                                                                                                       609 169  534  421 301 272 477 324 872
Oban                                                                                                                 738 1061  948 871 841 280 783 369
Oxford                                                                                                                    429  316 136 107 607 230 1033
Penzance                                                                                                                        125  390 356 928 420 1355
Plymouth                                                                                                                            277 243 815 307 1242
Portsmouth                                                                                                                              34 739 308 1166
Southampton                                                                                                                                710 245 1137
Stranraer                                                                                                                                     651 596
Swansea                                                                                                                                          1077
Thurso
```

```
430                     Aberdeen
599 167                 Birmingham
514  89 160             Brighton
466  99 121 152         Bristol
534 109 191  45 184     Cambridge
229 203 371 286 265 306 Cardiff
585 202 106 198 121 230 399 Carlisle
 68 363 531 447 399 466 162 518 Dover
123 297 459 380 342 400  96 460  56 Dundee
589 164 169  77 232 113 361 246 522 455 Edinburgh
529 186 299 153 292 112 302 338 462 396 221 Exeter
148 300 468 383 362 403  98 496  77  46 458 398 Fishguard
541 174 130 209  67 240 341 129 474 417 271 348 437 Glasgow
459 166 334 249 259 226 232 362 392 326 324 166 329 334 Harwich
359 145 270 237 147 257 158 265 292 235 312 290 255 196 220 Holyhead
108 458 626 541 501 561 257 620 128 158 616 557 172 576 487 394 Hull
187 476 644 559 538 579 275 672 175 205 634 575 179 613 505 431  81 Inverness
323 122 266 214 153 234 122 284 256 199 289 235 219 229 165  61 358 395 Kyle of Lochalsh
356 103 271 186 196 168 129 299 289 223 261 166 225 271  96 132 384 402  77 Leeds
547 116  55 123  57 155 320  75 480 398 185 263 416  80 282 201 575 593 205 219 Liverpool
352  90 258 174 167 194 125 287 285 218 249 193 242 123  99 44  36 207 London
272 181 324 273 207 293  96 325 205 148 348 298 192 282 228  89 308 355  64 140 263 107 Manchester
228 209 353 302 235 322  60 354 161 104 377 327 155 311 257 128 263 311  93 169 292 136  42 Middlesbrough
482  57 130 115  54 147 255 148 415 334 196 254 351 132 217 144 510 528 140 155  69 142 199 227 Newcastle
489 165 171 219  67 251 288 171 422 365 297 358 385  69 302 154 524 561 177 226 115 190 230 259 121 Northampton
393  53 197 145  90 165 192 216 326 269 220 224 289 166 180  98 428 465  75 111 136  73 134 162  71 122 Norwich
178 390 558 473 452 493 188 586 118 124 548 488  92 527 418 345 114 125 309 315 506 311 270 226 441 475 379 Nottingham
500  68 107  75  82 106 273 146 433 367 155 214 369 178 128 235 178 528 546 174 173  56 160 232 261  45 149 105 459 Oban
700 276 282 189 345 224 473 359 633 567 112 332 569 384 435 423 728 746 401 373 298 360 459 488 307 410 332 659 267 Oxford
630 206 212 119 275 154 403 289 563 497  46 262 499 314 365 353 658 676 330 302 228 290 389 418 237 339 262 589 197  78 Penzance
583 151  48  95 138 155 356 143 516 449 130 263 452 166 318 261 611 629 256 255  80 243 315 344 127 202 188 542  85 243 173 Plymouth
565 132  61  75 134 116 338 143 498 431 108 224 434 155 300 243 593 610 238 237  87 225 297 326 109 199 169 524 71 151 12  22 Portsmouth
233 307 475 391 370 410 106 504 162 131 466 406  84 445 336 262 245 431 203 127 233 424 229 200 163 359 393 296 174 376 577 507 459 441 Southampton
528 146 228  82 221  41 301 267 461 394 149  73 397 277 186 293 556 574 271 172 191 192 329 358 183 287 202 487 143 261 191 172 152 405 Stranraer
222 572 740 655 615 675 371 734 242 272 730 671 286 690 601 508 116 174 472 498 689 494 422 377 624 638 542 229 641 842 772 724 706 371 670 Swansea
```

Miles

Key to 1:1 000 000 map pages
(1 in : 16 miles)

0 10 20 30 40 miles
0 10 20 30 40 50 60 km

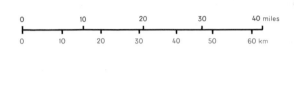

1:1 000 000 map pages

The Primary Road network in England in currently under review. Certain roads may therefore change their status during the currency of this publication.

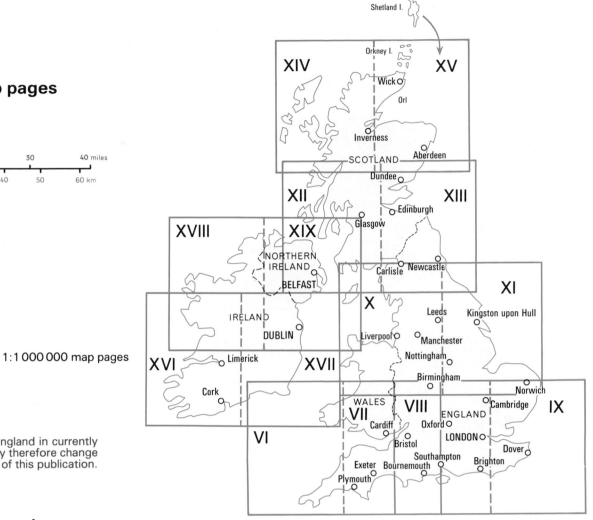

Route planning map legend

<table>
<tr><td>Road classification</td><td></td><td>Importance des routes</td><td></td></tr>
<tr><td>Motorway</td><td>M.5</td><td>Autoroute (en Grande-Bretagne, la circulation sur autoroute est gratuite)</td><td>M.5</td></tr>
<tr><td>Dual carriageway with motorway characteristics</td><td></td><td>Double chaussée de type autoroutier</td><td></td></tr>
<tr><td>Junctions : complete - limited</td><td>1 2 10</td><td>Échangeurs : complet - partiels</td><td>1 2 10</td></tr>
<tr><td>Primary route (GB) and national primary route (IRL) :</td><td></td><td>Primary route (GB) and National primary route (IRL) :</td><td></td></tr>
<tr><td>Signposting for places on motorway and primary route networks</td><td>YORK   Wells</td><td>Localités jalonnant un itinéraire autoroutier ou Primary et figurant sur la signalisation</td><td>YORK   Wells</td></tr>
<tr><td>Official road classification : primary route (GB)</td><td>A 40   A 68</td><td>Numéros des routes : Primary route (GB)</td><td>A 40   A 68</td></tr>
<tr><td>National primary and secondary route (IRL)</td><td>N 2   N 59</td><td>National primary and secondary route (IRL)</td><td>N 2   N 59</td></tr>
<tr><td>National road network :</td><td></td><td>Route de liaison nationale :</td><td></td></tr>
<tr><td>dual carriageway - 4 lanes</td><td></td><td>chaussées séparées - 4 voies</td><td></td></tr>
<tr><td>2 wide lanes - 2 lanes</td><td></td><td>2 voies larges - 2 voies</td><td></td></tr>
<tr><td>Regional road network :</td><td></td><td>Route de liaison interrégionale :</td><td></td></tr>
<tr><td>dual carriageway</td><td></td><td>chaussées séparées</td><td></td></tr>
<tr><td>2 or mote lanes - 2 narrow lanes</td><td></td><td>2 voies ou plus - 2 voies étroites</td><td></td></tr>
<tr><td>Other roads :</td><td></td><td>Autres routes :</td><td></td></tr>
<tr><td>Other selected regional road</td><td>A 258   R 335</td><td>Autre route de liaison interrégionale sélectionnée</td><td>A 258   R 335</td></tr>
<tr><td>Local road : surfaced - unsurfaced</td><td></td><td>Route locale revêtue - non revêtue</td><td></td></tr>
<tr><td>In Scotland : narrow road with passing places</td><td></td><td>En Écosse : route très étroite avec emplacements pour croisement (passing places)</td><td></td></tr>
<tr><td>Road under construction (when available : with scheduled opening date)</td><td>= = = =</td><td>Route en construction (le cas échéant : date de mise en service prévue)</td><td>= = = =</td></tr>
<tr><td>Distances (intermediate and total)</td><td></td><td>Distances (totalisées et partielles)</td><td></td></tr>
<tr><td>on motorways - on others roads</td><td>14   10</td><td>sur autoroute - sur route</td><td>14   10</td></tr>
<tr><td>in miles</td><td>24</td><td>en miles</td><td>24</td></tr>
<tr><td>in kilometres</td><td>39</td><td>en kilomètres</td><td>39</td></tr>
<tr><td>Obstacles</td><td></td><td>Obstacles</td><td></td></tr>
<tr><td>Road, bridge with toll</td><td></td><td>Route, pont à péage</td><td></td></tr>
<tr><td>Steep hill (ascent in the direction of the arrow)</td><td></td><td>Forte déclivité (montée dans le sens de la flèche)</td><td></td></tr>
<tr><td>Pass - altitude (in metres)</td><td>665</td><td>Col - altitude (en mètres)</td><td>665</td></tr>
<tr><td>Transportation</td><td></td><td>Transport</td><td></td></tr>
<tr><td>Car ferry (seasonal services : in red)</td><td></td><td>Transport des autos (liaisons saisonnières : signe rouge)</td><td></td></tr>
<tr><td>ferry</td><td>B --- B</td><td>par bac</td><td>B --- B</td></tr>
<tr><td>boat</td><td></td><td>par bateau</td><td></td></tr>
<tr><td>Airport</td><td>✈</td><td>Aéroport</td><td>✈</td></tr>
<tr><td>Important isolated sights</td><td></td><td>Curiosités importantes isolées</td><td></td></tr>
<tr><td>Ecclesiastical building - Historic house, castle - Ruins - Cave</td><td>⌐ ⋈ ∴ ∩</td><td>Édifice religieux - Château - Ruines - Grotte</td><td>⌐ ⋈ ∴ ∩</td></tr>
<tr><td>Prehistoric monument - Other sights</td><td>ᴨ ▲</td><td>Monument mégalithique - Autres curiosités</td><td>ᴨ ▲</td></tr>
<tr><td>Pleasant itinerary - National Forest Park, National park</td><td></td><td>Itinéraire agréable - Parc forestier national, parc national</td><td></td></tr>
</table>

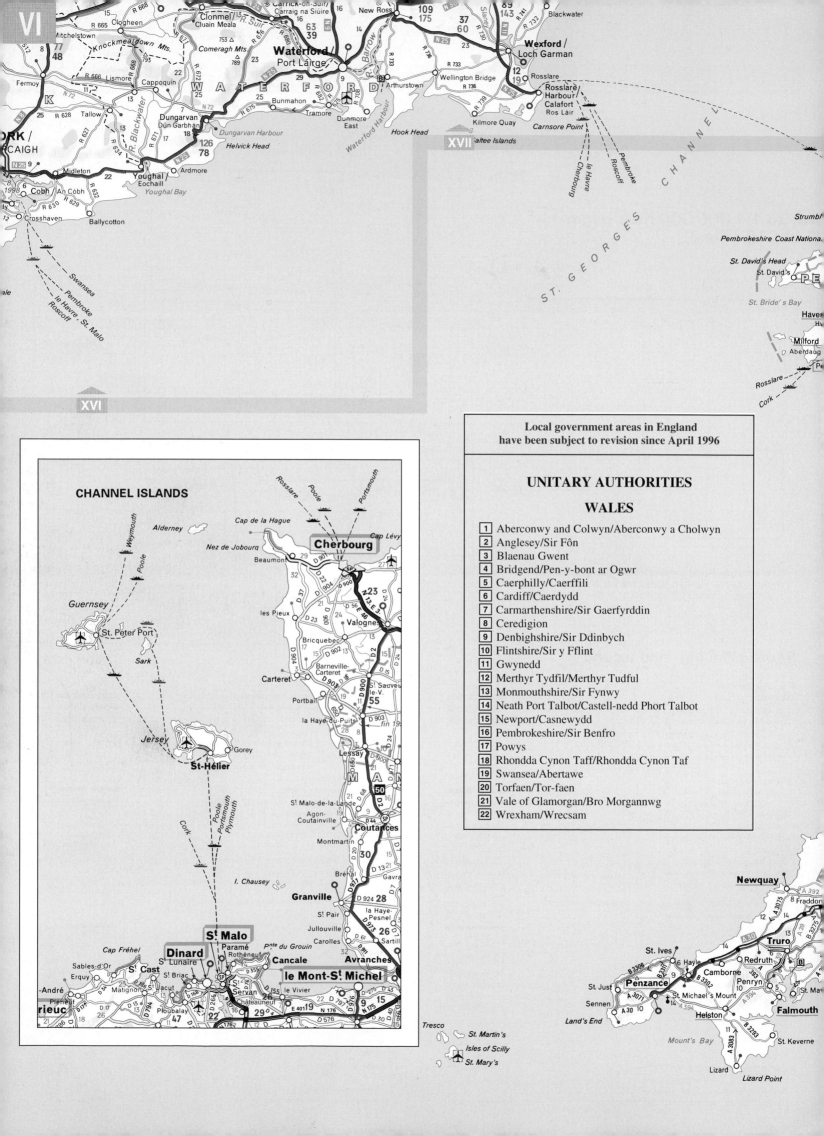

CHANNEL ISLANDS

Local government areas in England have been subject to revision since April 1996

UNITARY AUTHORITIES

WALES

1. Aberconwy and Colwyn/Aberconwy a Cholwyn
2. Anglesey/Sir Fôn
3. Blaenau Gwent
4. Bridgend/Pen-y-bont ar Ogwr
5. Caerphilly/Caerffili
6. Cardiff/Caerdydd
7. Carmarthenshire/Sir Gaerfyrddin
8. Ceredigion
9. Denbighshire/Sir Ddinbych
10. Flintshire/Sir y Fflint
11. Gwynedd
12. Merthyr Tydfil/Merthyr Tudful
13. Monmouthshire/Sir Fynwy
14. Neath Port Talbot/Castell-nedd Phort Talbot
15. Newport/Casnewydd
16. Pembrokeshire/Sir Benfro
17. Powys
18. Rhondda Cynon Taff/Rhondda Cynon Taf
19. Swansea/Abertawe
20. Torfaen/Tor-faen
21. Vale of Glamorgan/Bro Morgannwg
22. Wrexham/Wrecsam

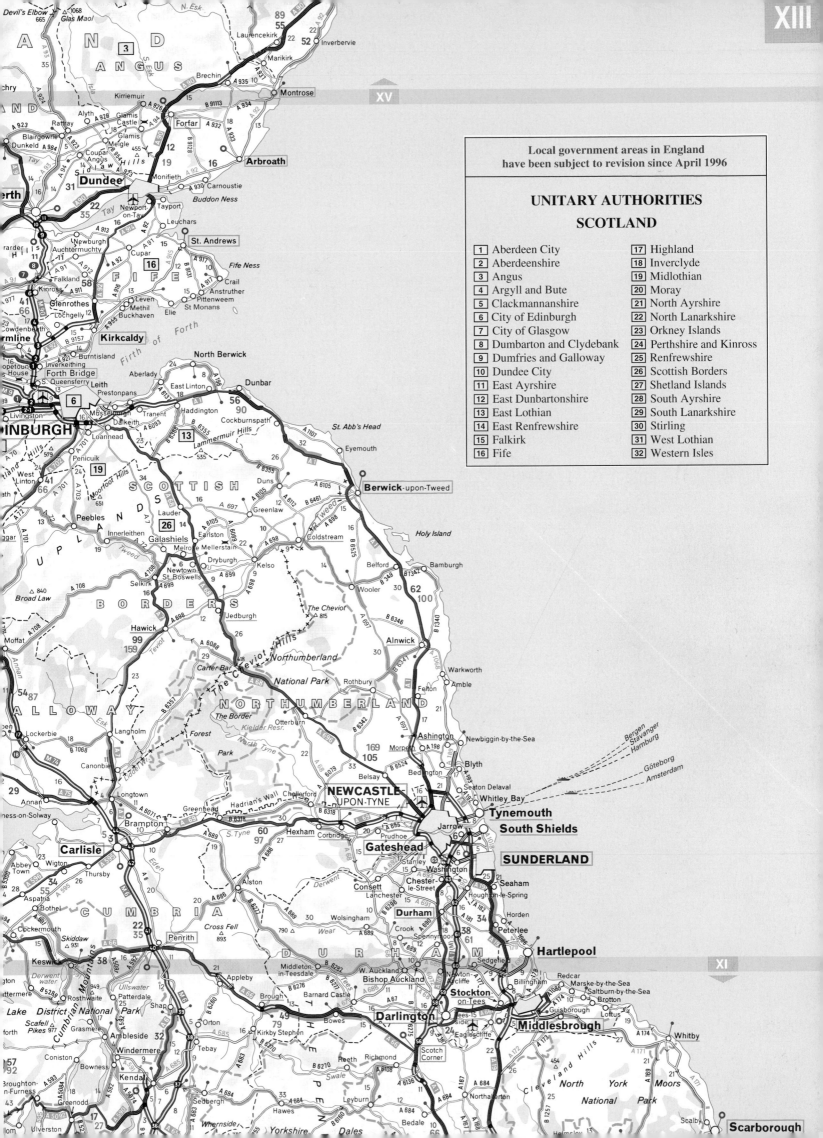

Local government areas in England
have been subject to revision since April 1996

UNITARY AUTHORITIES
SCOTLAND

1	Aberdeen City	17	Highland
2	Aberdeenshire	18	Inverclyde
3	Angus	19	Midlothian
4	Argyll and Bute	20	Moray
5	Clackmannanshire	21	North Ayrshire
6	City of Edinburgh	22	North Lanarkshire
7	City of Glasgow	23	Orkney Islands
8	Dumbarton and Clydebank	24	Perthshire and Kinross
9	Dumfries and Galloway	25	Renfrewshire
10	Dundee City	26	Scottish Borders
11	East Ayrshire	27	Shetland Islands
12	East Dunbartonshire	28	South Ayrshire
13	East Lothian	29	South Lanarkshire
14	East Renfrewshire	30	Stirling
15	Falkirk	31	West Lothian
16	Fife	32	Western Isles

Cape Wrath
Durness   Whiten Head
Kinlochbervie   A 838   20   Coldb
908 △ Foinaven   927   Tongue
Scourie   Laxford Bridge   Ben Hope
A 894   A 838   A 838
Eddrachillis   Kylestrome   Altnaharra   A 873
Bay   Ben Klibreck
A 837   19   A 894   34   39   40   961   Ber
Inchnadamph   L. Nave
Rubha Còigeach   Lochinver   998 △   A 838
Ben More Assynt   Lairg
849 △   Ledmore   A 836
Coigach   743   18   A 837   27 A 838
Ullapool   11   A 836
A 835   1084 △   A 837   31
Laide   Gruinard   Beinn Dearg   Bonar Bridge
Rubha Réidh   Bay   19
Dundonnell   12   A 835
A 832   15   29   Sgurr Mór   57   Easter
Gairloch   1062   1110   92   Ben Wyvis
A 832   980   19   1046
20   Loch Fannich   Alness   A 9176
Wester   Ross   A 9
Torridon   Liathach   Kinlochewe   Garve   Dingwall   Black Is
896 △   1054   A 896   A 832   15   26   A 832   Fortros
Shieldaig   10   Achnasheen   Contin   19   Tore
A 896   Glen Carron   Muir of Ord   A 832
24   19   1083 △   A 831   In
Lochcarron   15   A 861
Stromeferry   Cannich   A 831   A 832   B 862
Kyle of   A 890   Carn Eige   Drumnadrochit
Lochalsh   1183 △   29
Dornie   Invermoriston   Foyers   17
Eilean Donan Castle   A 887   69   33   Whitebridge
Kyleakin   Shiel Bridge   43
Kylerhea   Glenelg   A' Chràlaig   16   Fort Augustus   Monadhliath Mo
1120 △   50   80   Carn Ban   Kingus
32   Loch Quoich   Invergarry   942 △   Newtonmore
Sgurr na Ciche   13   Laggan   A 86
1040   15   25   Creag Meaghaidh   Dalwhinnie
Mallaig   40   1130 △
Loch Nevis   Spean Bridge   A 86   30   Loch Laggan
19   Loch Morar   10   A 889
Arisaig   76   Loch Arkaig   Loch Lochy   Pass of
46   Glenfinnan   Drumochte
27   A 830   Caledonian Canal   A 462
882 △   33   Loch Shiel   A 861   Fort William   Ben Nevis   Ben Alder △   1083
Ben Nevis   1148   Loch Ericht   Loch Rannoch
Kilchoan   Salen   888 △   9   Kinloch Rannoch
528 △   B 8007   Corran   Inchree   Glen Coe   33   A 846
Strontian   13   Onich
A 861   Ballachulish   Bidean   GRAM
Loch Sunart   Blackwater Resr.   nam Bian
Kentallen   1141 △   Schiehallion
Tobermory   Dervaig   Loch Linnhe   Loch Rannoch
19   B 8073   A 884   Portnacroish   A 828

Flannan I.
LEWIS
Butt of Lewis
Port of Ness
A 857
Barvas   16
A 858   A 857   12
Carloway   292 △
34   Stornoway   Broad   Portnaguran
Garynahine   Bay   Tiumpan Head
A 858   A 859   12   Eye Peninsula
THE MINCH

Hushinish   B 887   36
Clisham   Kebock Head
799 △   572 △   A 859
Tarbert   WESTERN
Toe Head   24
Harris
Leverburgh
Rodel   ISLES
Renish Point   32
North Uist   Sound of Harris   Rubha Réidh
Newtonferry
Tigharry   A 865   25   847 △
A 865   A 867   Waternish   A 855
13   347 △   Point   Staffin
Balivanich   A 865   Uig   34
Benbecula   Dunvegan   The Storr
Creagorry   Head   719 △   Rona
A 865   22   A 850   22   A 855
South Uist   Dunvegan   Portree   Sound of Raasay
SEA OF   Bracadale   52   Raasay
620 △   21   84   444 △
Daliburgh   THE HEBRIDES   Idrigill Point   A 863   9
Lochboisdale   Loch Bracadale   Sligachan   Sconser
Scalpay
SKYE   17   A 87
Sound of Barra   The Cuillins   Broadford
Barra   888   993 △   Kyleakin
383   Bayhirivagh   Canna   B 8083   10
Castlebay   14   Kylerhea
Elgol   Isleornsay
Cuillin Sound   A 851   17
Mingulay   Ardvasar   Sound of Sleat
Rhum   812 △
Eigg   Loch
Sound of Rhum   Mallaig
Muck

XII

Coll   Arinagour
Tiree   Kilchoan
Scarinish   A 848

SCOTLAND area labels: SEA OF THE HEBRIDES, The Little Minch, Sound of Monach

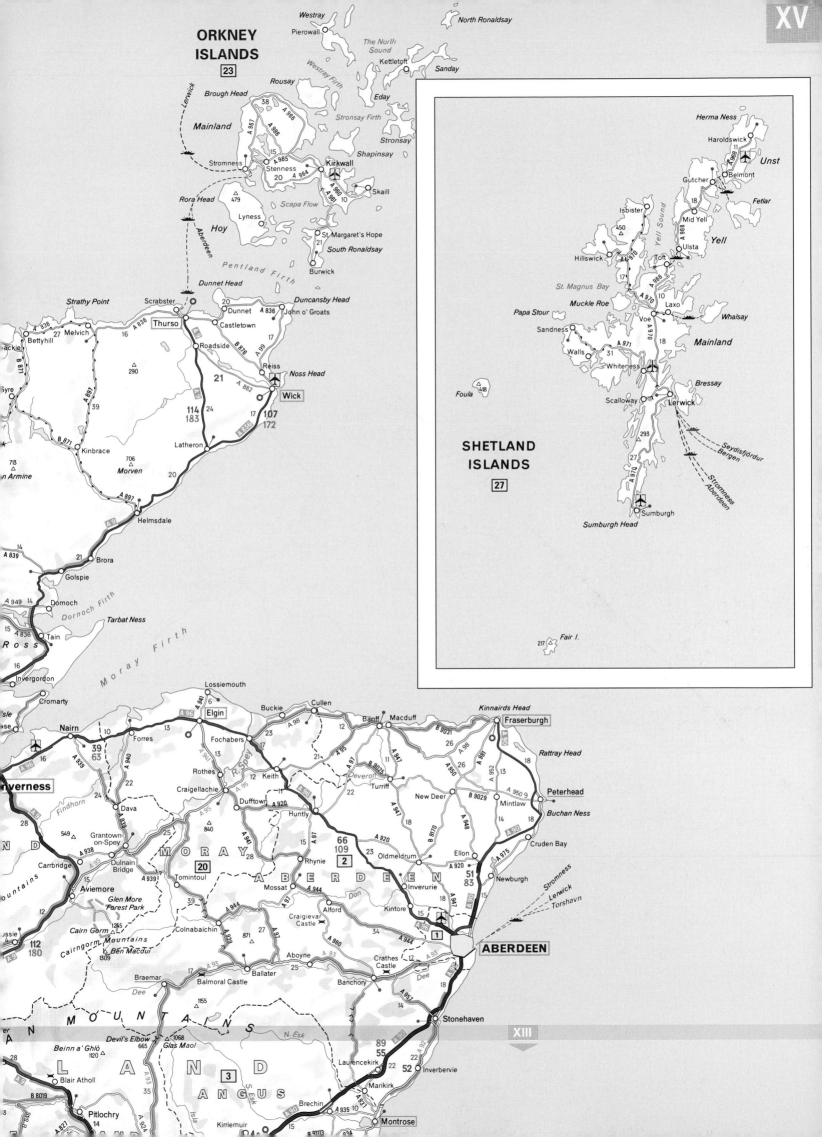

Key to map symbols — Légende

Roads — Routes

Motorway and service areas		Autoroute et aires de service
Dual carriageway with motorway characteristics		Double chaussée de type autoroutier
Junctions: complete - limited		Échangeurs : complet - partiels
Numbered junctions		Numéros d'échangeurs
Major road:		Route de liaison principale :
dual carriageway		à chaussées séparées
4 lanes - 2 wide lanes		à 4 voies - à 2 voies larges
2 lanes - 2 narrow lanes		à 2 voies - à 2 voies étroites
Regional road network		Routes de liaison régionale :
dual carriageway - 2 wide lanes		à chaussées séparées - à 2 voies larges
2 lanes - 2 narrow lanes		à 2 voies - à 2 voies étroites
Other roads: surfaced-unsurfaced		Autre route : revêtue - non revêtue
Road under construction		Route en construction
(when available: with scheduled opening date)		(le cas échéant : date de mise en service prévue)
Footpath - Long distance footpath or bridleway		Sentier - Sentier de grande randonnée ou piste cavalière
Roundabout - Pass, altitude (in metres)		Rond-point - Col, altitude (en mètres)
Distances on motorways or roads		Distances sur autoroute et route :
in miles - in kilometres		en miles - en kilomètres

Official road classification — Classement des itinéraires

United Kingdom:		Royaume-Uni :
Motorway	M 5	Autoroute
Primary route	A 38	Itinéraire principal
Other roads	A 190 B 629	Autres routes
Destination on primary route network	YORK	Localité jalonnant les itinéraires principaux
Republic of Ireland:		République d'Irlande :
Motorway	M 1	Autoroute
National primary and secondary route	N 5 N 59	Itinéraire principal
Other road	R 561	Autre route

Obstacles — Obstacles

In Scotland: narrow road with passing places	En Écosse : route très étroite avec emplacements pour croisement
Road: prohibited - subject to restrictions	Route : interdite - à circulation réglementée
Toll barrier - One-way road	Barrière de péage - Sens unique
On major and regional roads:	Sur liaisons principales et régionales :
Height limit (under 15'6'' IRL, 16'6'' GB)	Hauteur limitée (au-dessous de 15'6'' IRL, 16'6'' GB)
Weight limit (under 16t)	Charge limitée (au-dessous de 16 t)
(restrictions liable to alteration)	(Peuvent avoir été modifiées depuis la date d'édition)
Gradient:	Pentes :
(ascent in the direction of the arrow)	(les flèches dans le sens de la montée)

Railways — Voies ferrées

Standard gauge - Passenger station	Voie ferrée - Gare voyageurs
Steam railway - Industrial track	Voie touristique - industrielle
Level crossing, railway passing	Passage de la route :
under road, over road	à niveau - supérieur - inférieur
Industrial cable way - Chair lift	Transporteur industriel aérien - Télésiège

Car ferries — Transport des véhicules

Seasonal services: in red	Liaisons saisonnières : signe rouge
boat - hovercraft	par bateau - par aéroglisseur
ferry (maximum load in metric tons)	par bac (charge maximum en tonnes)
Pedestrians and cycles	Transport des piétons et cycles seulement

Towns - Administration — Localités - Administration

Ambleside

Town having a plan in the Michelin Red Guide	Localité dont le plan figure dans le Guide Rouge Michelin
Town included in the above Michelin Guide	Localité ayant des ressources sélectionnées dans ce même guide
Local government boundary (see list p. VI and XIII)	Division administrative locale (voir liste p. VI et XIII)
Scottish and Welsh borders	Limite de l'Écosse et du Pays de Galles
International border	Frontière internationale

Other symbols — Signes divers

Telecommunications mast - Lighthouse	Émetteur de télécommunication - Phare
Power station - Quarry - Mine	Centrale électrique - Carrière - Mine
Factory - Refinery	Industrie - Raffinerie
Racecourse - Caravan and camping site	Hippodrome - Camping, caravaning
Racing circuit - Pleasure boat harbour	Circuit automobile - Port de plaisance
Golf course - National Forest Park, National Park	Golf - Parc forestier national, parc national
Ireland: Fishing - Youth hostel - Greyhound racetrack	Irlande : Pêche - Auberge de jeunesse - Cynodrome
Forest walk - Country park - Cliff	Sentier signalé - Parc de loisirs - Falaise
Scenic route	Parcours pittoresque
Airport - Airfield	Aéroport - Aérodrome

Principal sights: see Michelin Guides — Principales curiosités : voir Guides Michelin

Ecclesiastical building - Ruins - Monument	Édifice religieux - Ruines - Monument
Historic house, castle	Château, manoir, palais
Prehistoric monument - Cave	Monument mégalithique - Grotte
Ireland: Celtic cross, cross slab - Round tower	Irlande : Croix celte - Tour ronde
Zoo - Nature reserve, bird sanctuary	Parc animalier, zoo - Réserve d'oiseaux
Gardens - Miscellaneous sights	Jardin, parc - Curiosités diverses
Panorama - Viewpoint	Panorama - Point de vue
Towns or places of interest, places to stay	Localités ou sites intéressants, lieux de séjour

Rye ▲
Elgol

Bóithre / Ffyrdd

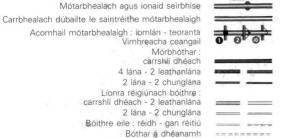

Eochair		Allwedd
Mótarbhealach agus ionaid seirbhíse		Traffordd a mannau gwasanaethu
Carrbhealach dúbailte le saintréithe mótarbhealaigh		Ffordd ddeuol â nodweddion traffordd
Acomhail mótarbhealaigh : iomlán - teoranta		Cyfnewidfeydd : wedi'i chwblhau - cyfyngedig
Vimhreacha ceangail		Rhifau'r cyffyrdd
Mórbhóthar : carrshlí dhéach		Prif ffordd gysylltu : ffordd ddeuol
4 lána - 2 leathanlána		4 lôn - 2 lôn lydan
2 lána - 2 chunglána		2 lôn - 2 lôn gul
Líonra réigiúnach bóithre : carrshlí dhéach - 2 leathanlána		Rhydwaith ffyrdd rhanbarthol : ffordd ddeuol - 2 lôn lydan
2 lána - 2 chunglána		2 lôn - 2 lôn gul
Bóithre eile : réidh - gan réitiú		Ffyrdd eraill : â wyneb - heb wyneb
Bóthar á dhéanamh		Ffordd yn cael ei hadeiladu
(an dáta oscailte sceidealta, mas eol)		(Os cyfodi yr achos : dyddiad agor disgwyliedig)
Cosán - Cosán fadsli		Llwybr troed - Llwybr hir neu lwybr ceffyl
Timpeall - Bearnas is a airde (i méadair)		Cylchfan - Bwlch a'i uchder (mewn metrau)
Faid ar mhótarshlíte, ar bóithre : i mílte - i méadair		Pellter ar ffyrdd a thraffyrdd : mewn miltiroedd - mewn kilometrau

Aicmiú oifigiúil bóithre / Dosbarthiad ffyrdd swyddogol

Eochair		Allwedd
An Ríocht Aontaithe :		Y Deyrnas Gyfunol :
Mótarshlí		Traffordd
Priomhbhealach		Prif ffordd
Bóithre eile		Ffyrdd eraill
Ceann scríbe ar ghréasán bóithre priomha		Cyrchfan ar rwydwaith y prif ffyrdd
i bPloblacht na hÉireann :		Gweriniaeth Iwerddon :
Mótarshlí		Traffordd
Priomhbhóithre agus fobhóithre náisiúnta		Prif ffordd genedlaethol a ffordd eilradd
Bóthar		Ffyrdd eraill

Constaicí / Rhwystrau

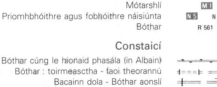

Eochair		Allwedd
Bóthar cúng le hionaid phasála (in Albain)		Yn yr Alban : ffordd gul â mannau pasio
Bóthar : toirmeasctha - faoi theorannú		Ffordd : gwaharddedig - cyfyngiadau arni
Bacainn dola - Bóthar aonslí		Rhwystr Toll - Unffordd
Ar phríomhbóithre agus ar bhóithre réigiúnacha :		Ar brif ffyrdd a ffyrdd rhanbarthol :
Teorainneacha airde (faoi 15'6'' IRL, faoi 16'6'' GB)		Terfyn uchder (llai na 15'6'' IRL, 16'6'' GB)
Teorann Mheáchain (faoi 16 t) (teorannu - inathraithe)		Terfyn pwysau (llai na 16 t) (y cyfyngiadau'n agored i gael eu newid)
Grádán : (suas treo an gha)		Graddiant (esgyn gyda'r saeth)

Iarnróid / Rheilffyrdd

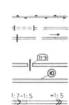

Eochair		Allwedd
Leithead caighdeánach - Staisiún paisinéirí		Lled safonol - Gorsaf deithwyr
iarnród thraein ghaile - Ráille tionsclaíoch		Rheilffordd ager - Trac diwydiannol
Crosaire comhréidh, iarnród ag dul faoi bhóthar, os cionn bóthair		Croesfan rheilffordd : rheilffordd yn croesi ffordd, o dan ffordd
Cáblashlí thionsclaíoch - Cathaoir cábla		Lein gêbl ddiwydiannol - Cadair esgyn

Longsheirbhísí / Llongau ceir

Eochair		Allwedd
Seirbhísí séasúracha : dearg		Gwasanaethau tymhorol : mewn coch
Bád - Árthach foluaineach		Ilong - Ilong hofran
Fartha (uas-ualach : tonnaí méadracha)		Fferi (llwyth uchaf : mewn tunelli metrig)
Coisithe agus lucht rothar		Teithwyr ar droed neu feic yn unig

Bailte - Riarachán / Trefi - Gweinyddiaeth

Ambleside

Eochair		Allwedd
Bailte a bhfuil a bplean in Eolaí Dearg Michelin		Trefi â map ohonynt yn Llyfr Coch Michelin
Bailte a chuimsítear san Eolaí Michelin sin		Trefi â cynhwysir yn Llyfr Michelin uchod
Teorainn Rialtais Áitiúil		Llywodraeth Leol
Teorainn na hAlban agus teorainn na Breataine Bige		Ffin Cymru, ffin yr Alban
Teorainn idirnáisiúnta		Ffin ryngwladol

Comharthaí Eile / Symbolau eraill

Eochair		Allwedd
Crann teileachumarsáide - Teach Solais		Mast telathrebu - Goleudy
Stáisiún Giniúna - Cairéal - Mianach		Gorsaf bŵer - Chwarel - Mwyngloddio
Monarcha - Scaglann		Ffatri - Purfa
Ráschúrsa - Láthair champa, láthair charbhán		Rasio Ceffylau - Leoedd i wersylla
Timpeall rásaíochta - Cuan bád aeraíochta		Rasio Cerbydau - Harbwr cychod pleser
Machaire Gailf - Páirc Fhoraoise Náisiúnta, Páirc Náisiúnta		Cwrs golff - Parc Coedwig Cenedlaethol, Parc Cenedlaethol
Éire : Iascaireacht - Brú chumann na hóige - Ráschúrsa con		Iwerdon : Pysgota - Hostel ieuenctid - Maes rasio milgwn
Siúlóid fhoraoise - Páirc thuaithe - Aill		Llwybr coedwig - Parc gwledig - Clogwyn
Bealach Aoibhinn		Ffordd dygfeydd
Aerfort - Aerpháirc		Maes awyr - Maes glanio

Príomhionaid inspéise : féach Eolaithe Michelin / Prif Olygfeydd : gweler Llyfr Michelin

Eochair		Allwedd
Foirgneamh Eaglasta - Fothrach - Séadchomhartha		Adeilag eglwysig - Adfeilion - Cofadail
Caisleán, teach stairiúil		Castell, tŷ hanesyddol
Leacht meigiliteach - Pluais		Heneb fegalithig - Ogof
Éire : Cros Cheilteach - Cloigtheach		Iwerdon : Croes Geltaidd - Twr crwn
Zú - Caomhnú nádúir, tearmannéan mara		Parc saffari, sw - Gwarchodfa natur
Gáirdíní - Amhairc éagsúla		Gerddi, parc - Golygfeydd amrywiol
Lánléargas - Cothrom Radhairc		Panorama - Golygfan
Bailte nó áiteanna inspéise baill lóistín		Trefi new fannau o ddiddordeb, mannau i aros

Rye (▲) Elgol

C   D   E

Isles of Scilly

A   B   50°

Round Island
St. Martin's
Bryher
Tresco
Hugh Town   St. Mary's
Penzance
Bishop Rocks   St. Agnes
6°20

32

Pentire Point
Padstow Bay
Trevose Head   Trevone
Constantine Bay   St. Merr
Treyarnon   Little
Porthcothan   Petherick
Park Head
Bedruthan Steps   Trenance
(△) Mawgan Porth
(△) Watergate Bay
(△ ▲) **Newquay**   Tregurrian (△)

(△) Crantock
(△) Holywell Bay   Trerice
Penhale Point   Holywell   St. Newlyn   Fraddon
Cubert   East   Summerc
Ligger or
Perran Bay   Goonhavern   Mitchell
(△) Perranporth   12   Perranzabuloe   Ladock
St. Agnes Head   (△)   Trispen   Probus
St. Agnes   Mithian   21
The Beacon   192   1¼   13
22   A 30
Porthtowan   6   **Truro** (△)
(△) Portreath   Blackwater   Kea   St Michael
Tin Streaming   Chacewater   Penkevil
Hell's Mouth   **Illogan**   (△)   Come-to-Good
Gwithian   St. Day   Ruan High
St. Ives   23 · 37   **Redruth** (△)   Lanes
(△)   Bay   **Camborne**   Gwennap   Trelissick
Zennor   Carbis   Perranarworthal   Garden   Ver
Gurnard's Head   Halsetown   Bay   Praze-an-   (△)   Feock
247   Beeble   Stithians   Mylor   Portscatho
Pendeen Watch   Hayle (△)   Bridge   St Just in Roseland
St. Erth   Leedstown (△)   **Penryn**   (△)
Penwith   252   Madron   Ludgvan   Carleen (△)   Lamanva   St. Mawes
Cape Cornwall   Trengwainton   Marazion   Relubbus   Wendron   Mawnan   **Falmouth**   Zone Point
(△) **St Just**   Sancreed   Rosudgeon   14   Breage   Sithney   Smith   Falmouth Bay
Whitesand Bay   Cross-   **Penzance**   Newlyn   **St Michael's**   Constantine   Glendurgan   Mawnan
an-Wra   Mount   Culdrose   Gweek   Helford
Sennen   St. Buryan   Mousehole   Praa   **Helston** (△)   Gillan
Longships   Lamorna   Sands   Porthleven   Mawgan   Manaccan
Land's End   Porthcurno   Cudden Point   Gunwalloe   Mawgan   Porthallow
Gwennap Head   Mount's Bay   **Lizard**   Manacle Point
Porthgwarra   Poldhu Point   11   St. Keverne
Isles of Scilly (St. Mary's)   (△) Mullion   Peninsula   (△) Coverack
Mullion Cove   Black Head
Kynance Cove   Ruan Minor
Wolf Rock   Lizard
Lizard Pt.

33

34

C   D   E

Height limit (Feet/Metres)
Hauteur limitée (Pieds/Mètres)

10' 11' 12' 13' 14' 14'6 15' 16' 16'6
3ᵐ   3ᵐ5 4ᵐ   4ᵐ4 4ᵐ5 5ᵐ

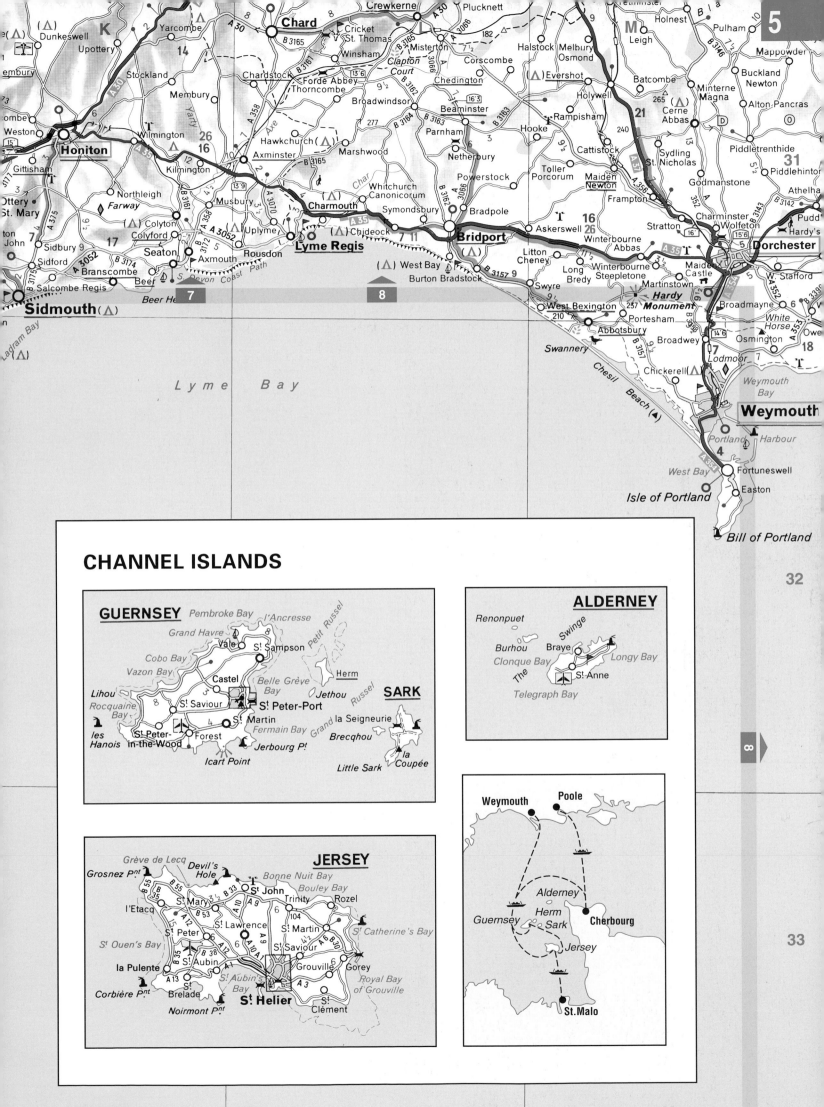

CHANNEL ISLANDS

GUERNSEY

Pembroke Bay
l'Ancresse
Grand Havre
Petit Russel
Vale
St Sampson
Cobo Bay
Herm
Vazon Bay
Castel
Belle Grève Bay
Lihou
St Saviour
Jethou
Russel
Rocquaine Bay
St Peter-Port

SARK

les Hanois
St Peter-in-the-Wood
Forest
St Martin
Fermain Bay
Grand la Seigneurie
Brecqhou
Icart Point
Jerbourg Pt
Little Sark
la Coupée

ALDERNEY

Renonpuet
Swinge
Burhou
Braye
Clonque Bay
Longy Bay
The
St Anne
Telegraph Bay

JERSEY

Grève de Lecq
Devil's Hole
Bonne Nuit Bay
Grosnez Pnt
Bouley Bay
St John
Trinity
Rozel
l'Etacq
St Mary
St Martin
St Lawrence
St Catherine's Bay
St Ouen's Bay
St Peter
St Saviour
la Pulente
St Aubin
Grouville
Gorey
Corbière Pnt
St Brelade
St Helier
Royal Bay of Grouville
Noirmont Pnt
St Clément

Weymouth
Poole
Alderney
Herm
Guernsey
Sark
Cherbourg
Jersey
St.Malo

32

33

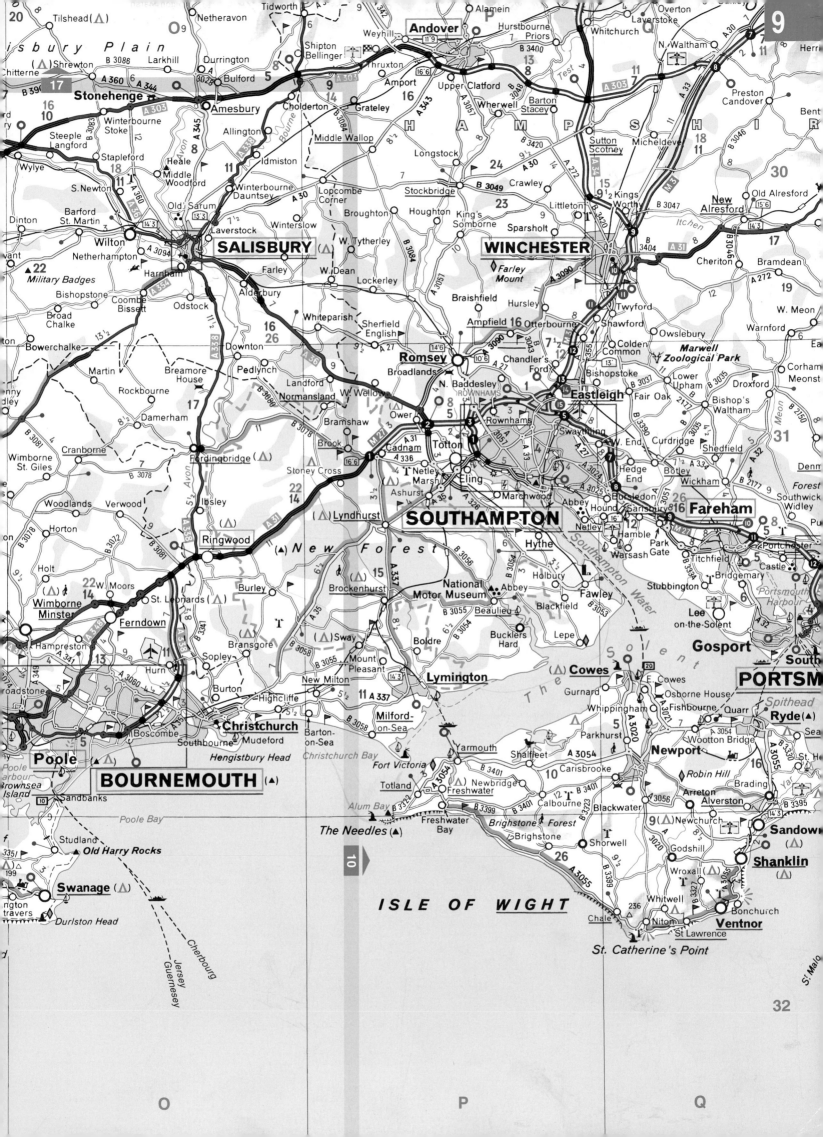

(▲) **Margate** Cliftonville
Westgate-on-Sea Foreness Point
B 205¹ Kingsgate
Herne Bay Reculver (△) **Birchington** 9 6 North Foreland
B 2205 B 205² St. Peter's
le 6 A 299 A 28 I. of Thanet 5¹₂
B 2049 4
A 28 **Broadstairs** (▲)
7¹₂ A 253 A 2050 A 256
St. Nicolas-at-Wade A 253 2
10 5 Hoath Sarre A 253
Chislet **Ramsgate** (▲ △)
rkletts Blean 11 Abbey *Pegwell Bay*
A 291 18 Pucks Gutter
B 2068 A 280 Sturry Fordwich *Stour* Oostende
Dunkerque
Richborough *Sandwich Bay*
Preston A 257 Ash 5
CANTERBURY Wingham **Sandwich** (△)
Littlebourne Woodnesborough A 258
24 A 257 Patrixbourne
39 13 Eastry
Chartham Bridge 12
Lower Hardres Aylesham 6¹₂
Barfreston A 256 13 **Deal** (▲)
Barham *The Downs*
Stelling Lydden Eythorne Ringwould
Minnis Circuit 11 Kingsdown
B 2068 A 260 (△) Martin Mill 8¹₂
Elham Lydden Whitfield St. Margaret's-at-Cliffe
Swingfield 9 A 258 *St. Margaret's Bay*
Lees Lyminge Alkham A 256 *South Foreland*
dge Stanford Acrise A 20 A 2011 **DOVER**
Place 1
B 2065 A 261 Terminal 8
11a 12 13 Capel-le-Ferne 13
6 Sandgate *The Warren* (△)
Hythe 10 **FOLKESTONE** *E. Wear Bay*
(▲ △)

S T R A I T   O F   D O V E R

Channel Tunnel

CALAIS

Dymchurch
Mary's Bay Blériot-Plage
stone-on-Sea Sangatte D 940 19.5
stone-on-Sea *Cap Blanc-Nez* Coquelles 13 14 17
(134) 114 12 5 3
d-on-Sea 90 D 243E 11 Terminal
26 D 243E
42 Escalles D 246
Dungeness 11 D 127
Wissant 17 9
D 244
Cap Gris-Nez St. Inglevert A 16-E 402 Guînes
(50) 163 8 D 244
D 191 D 127
7 D 231
Audresselles 6.5 D 238 15 168
D 191 D 191E **PAS - DE - CALAIS**
Ambleteuse 10.5 D 238 D 127 31
9 6 120
Wimereux 14 8 D 238 Herbingh
D 233 11
6 Colembert
BOULOGNE- 3 32 N 42 D 233 Belle
S-MER St Martin D 254 D 238
la Capelle N 42 D 127 N 42
lès Boulogne D 254 Selle
7 4 D 341
le Portel 15 Crémarest
D 119 5 8 Wirwignes D 254E
Equihen-Plage Pont-de- Desvres
Briques

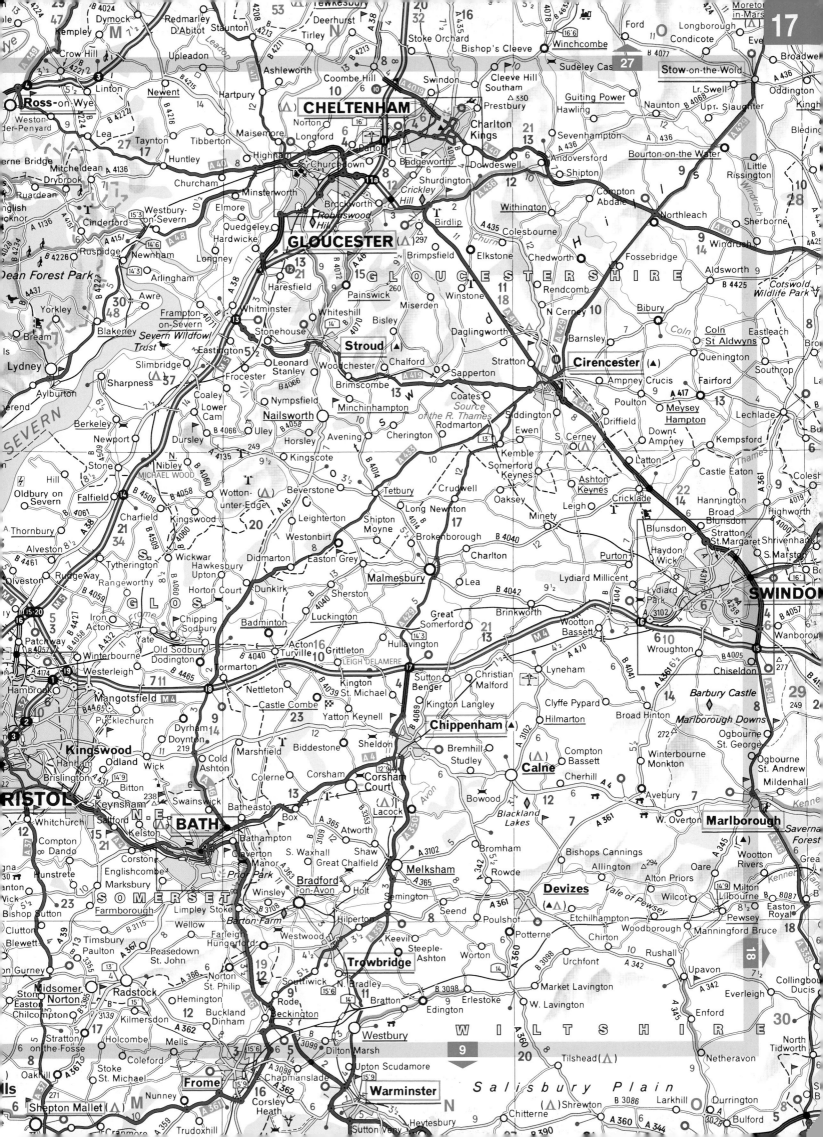

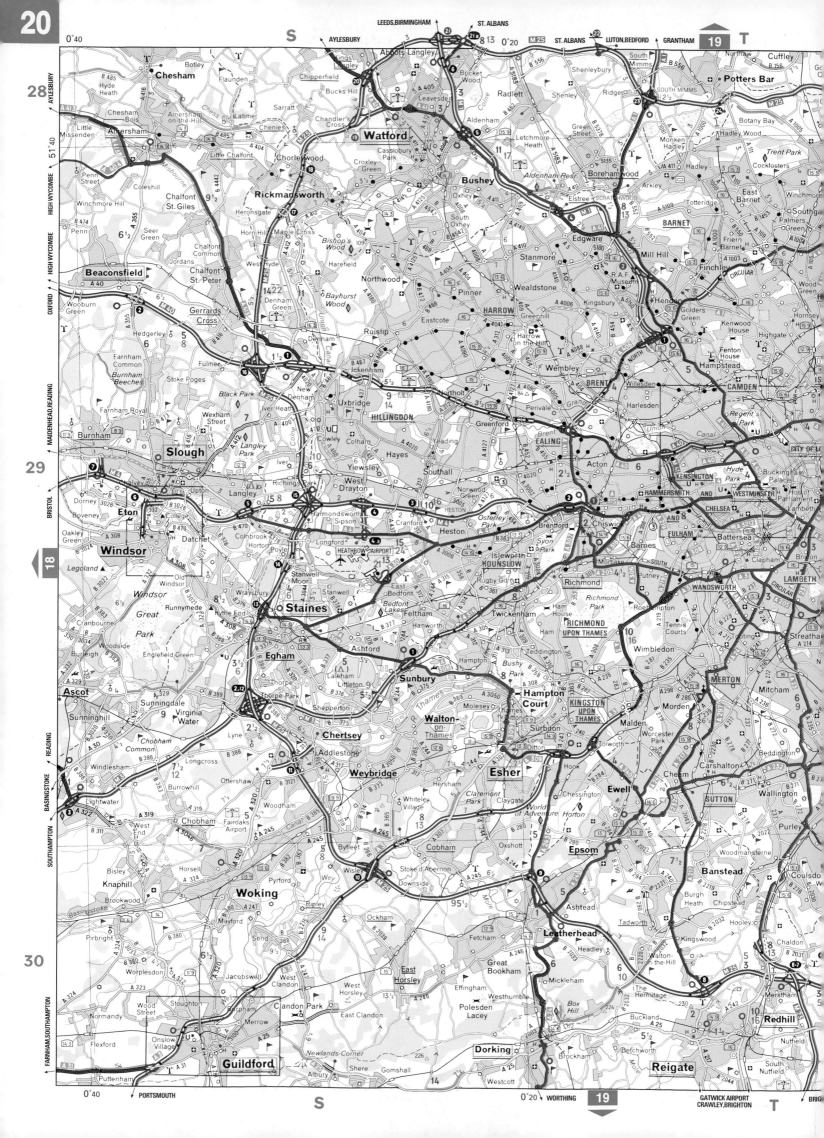

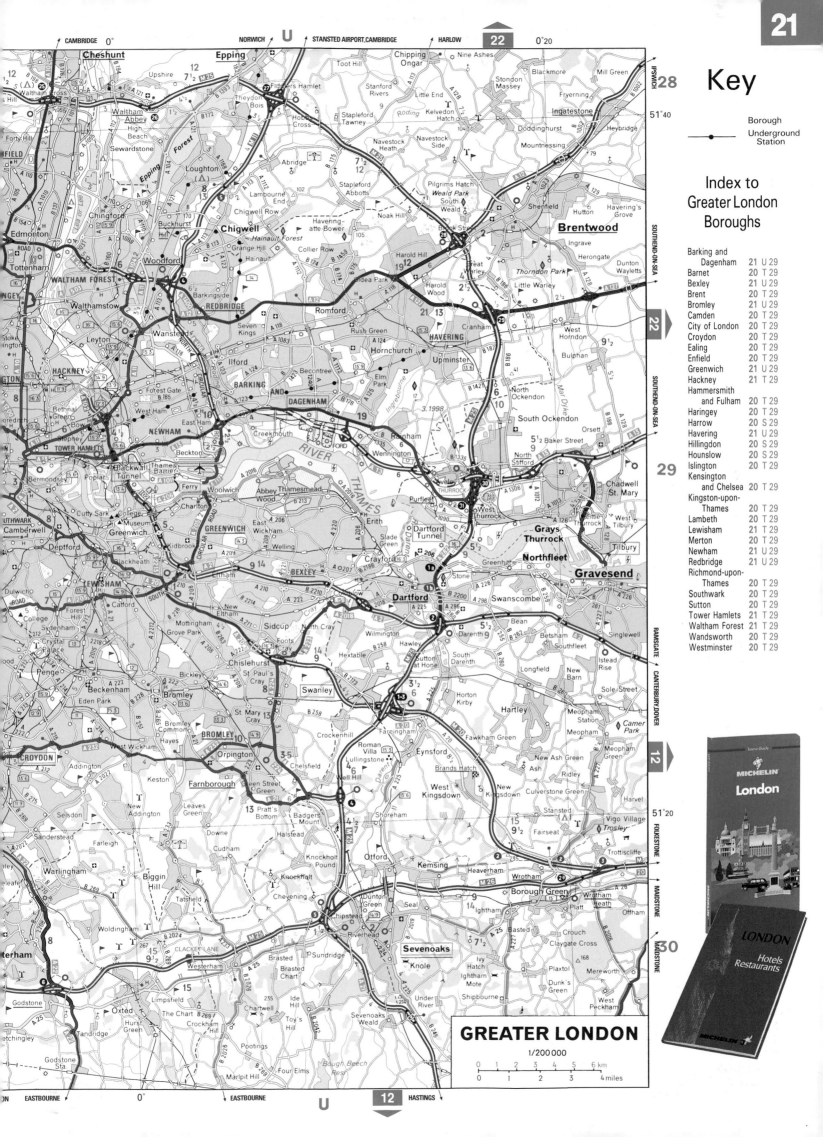

Key

Borough
● Underground Station

Index to Greater London Boroughs

GREATER LONDON

1/200 000

0 1 2 3 4 5 6 km
0   1   2   3   4 miles

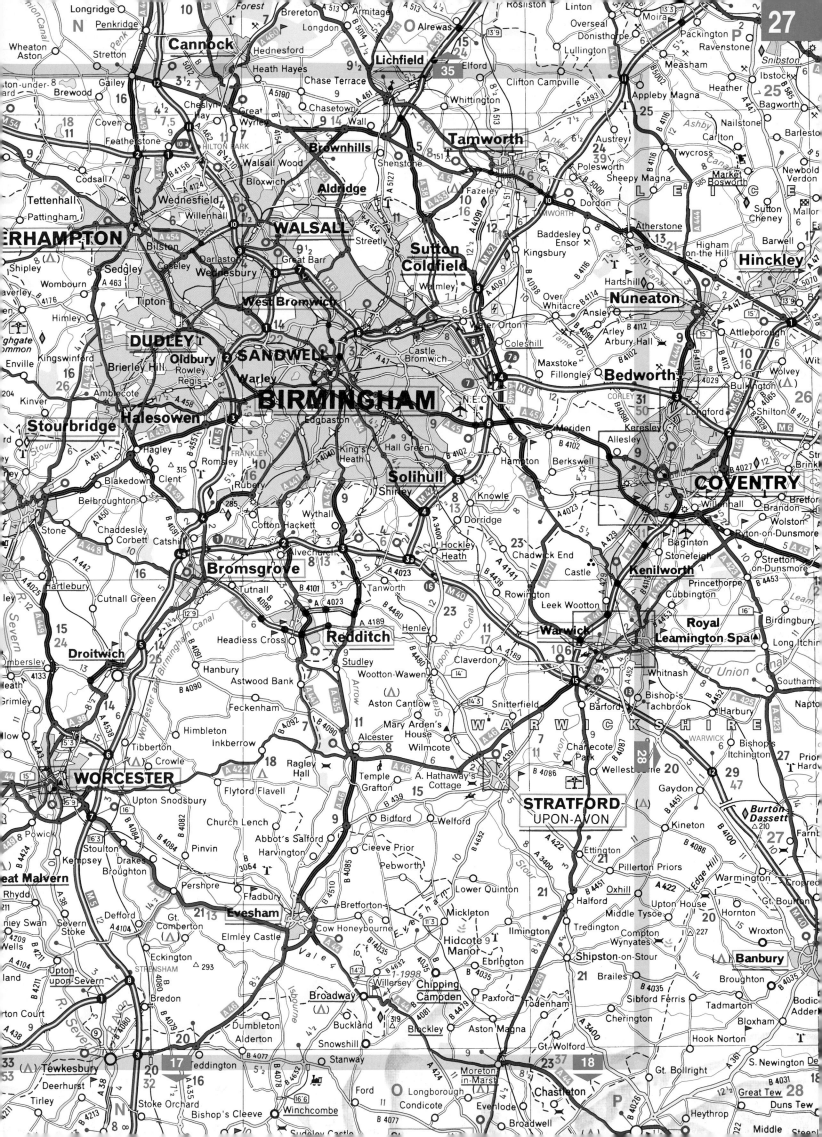

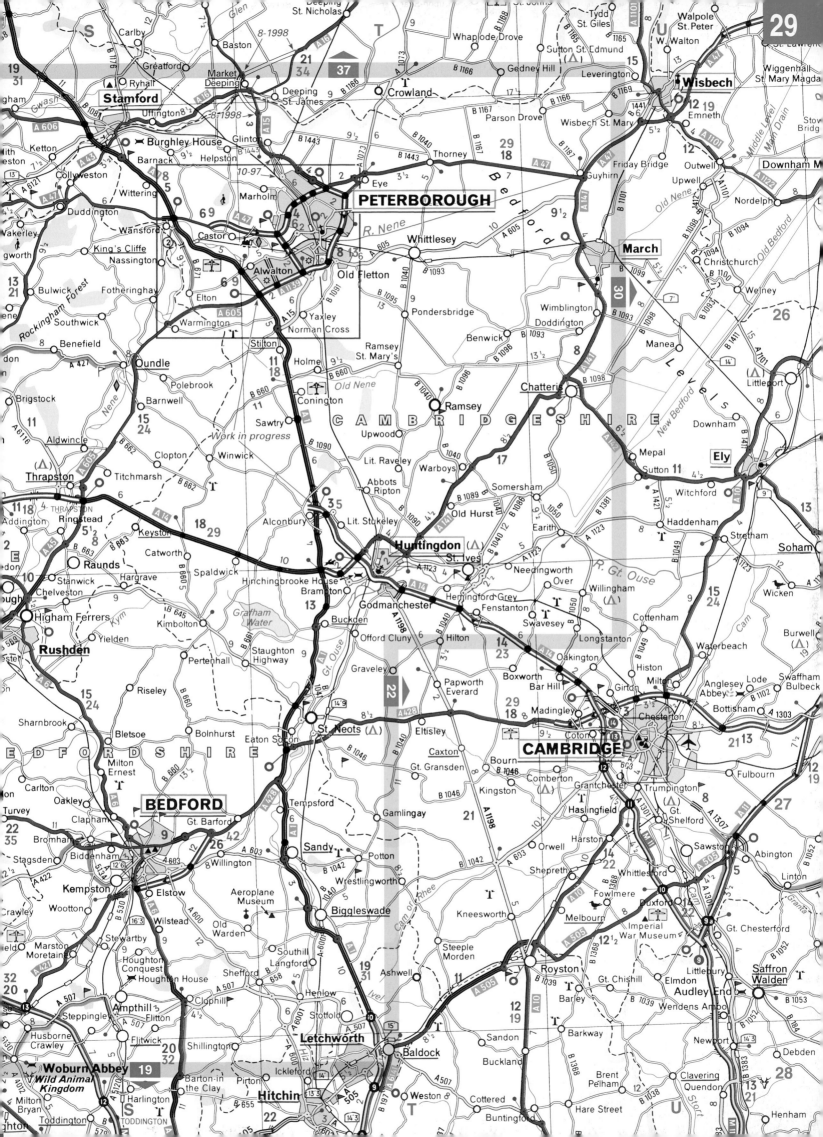

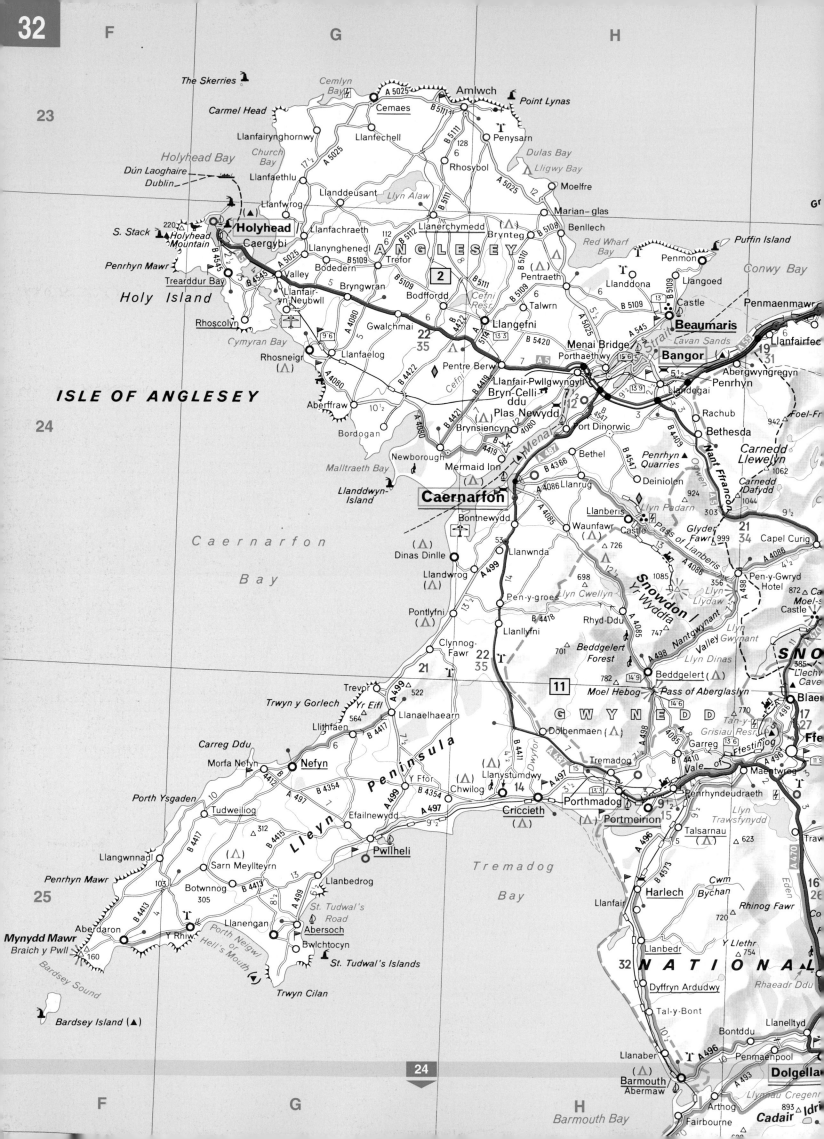

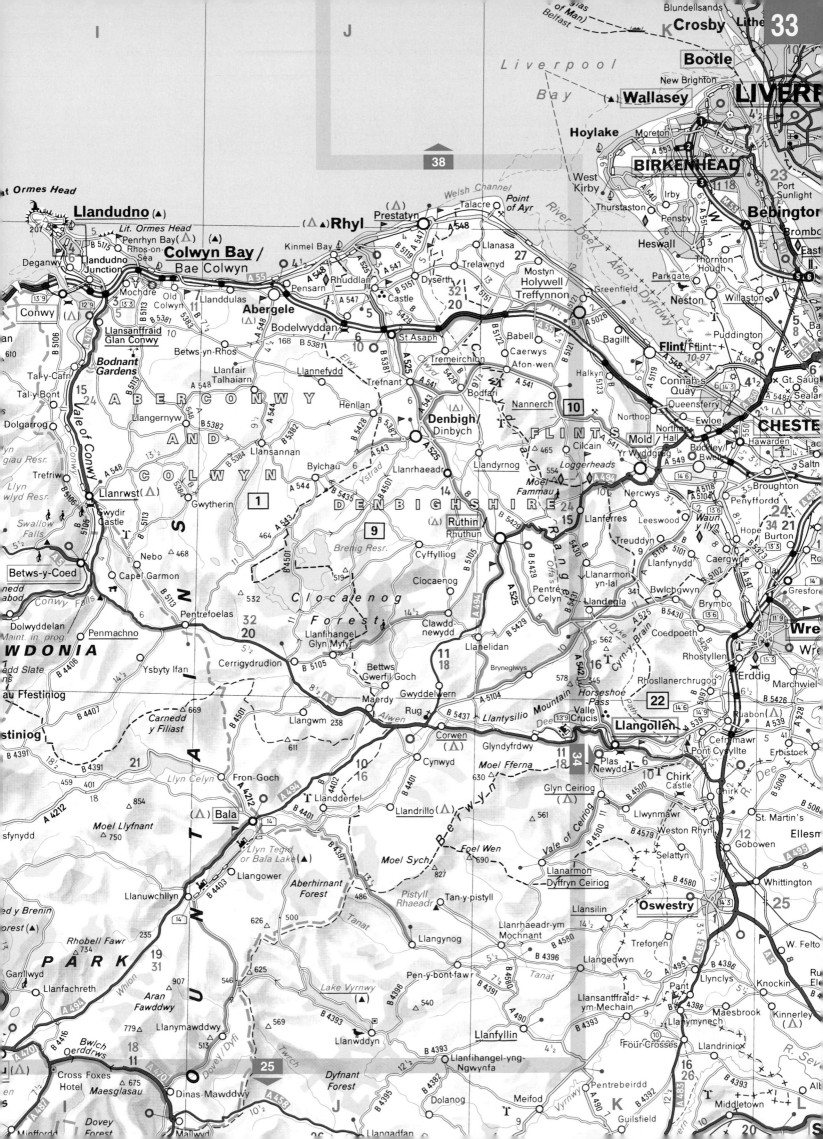

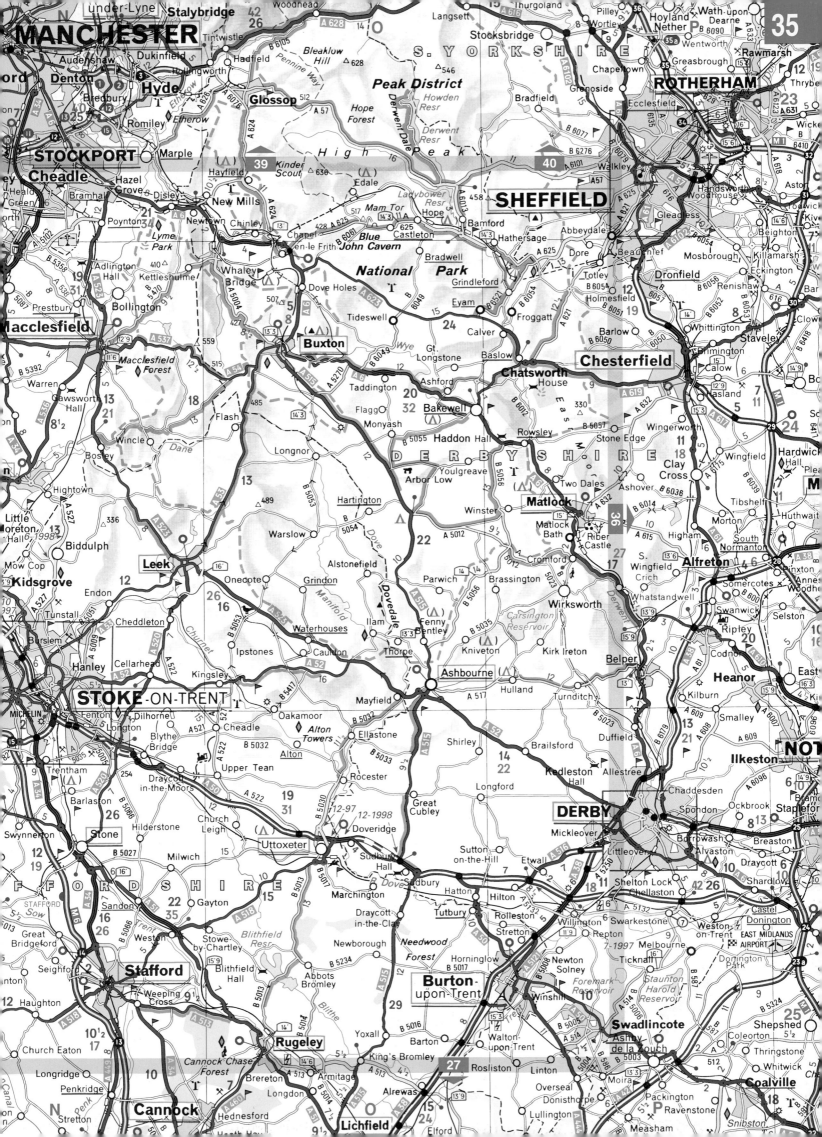

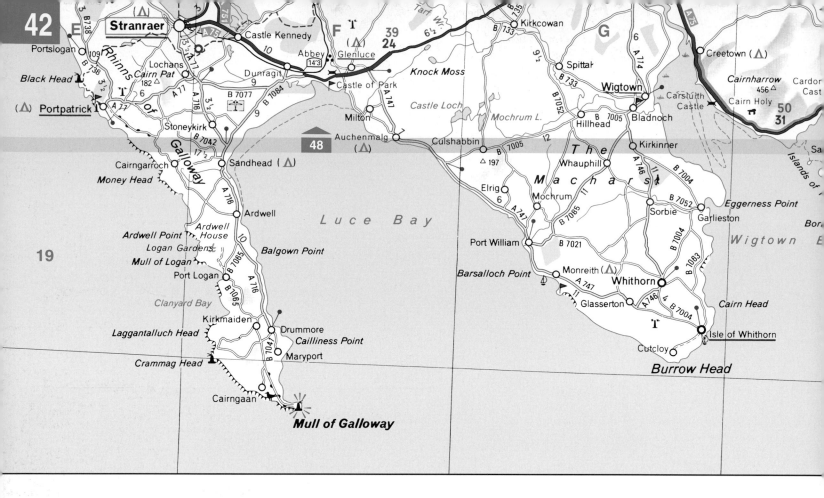

Map 1 (top)

E ‧ **F** ‧ **G**

Portslogan

Stranraer
Castle Kennedy
Lochans
Cairn Pat 182△
Dunragit
Abbey
Glenluce 14'3
39
24
Black Head
Rhinns
Portpatrick
(△)
Stoneykirk
Galloway
B 7042
Cairngarroch
Sandhead (△)
Money Head
Milton
Auchenmalg
(△)
Castle of Park
Knock Moss
Castle Loch
Culshabbin
197
Kirkcowan
Spittal
Wigtown
Hillhead
Bladnoch
Kirkinner
Whauphill
The
Machars
Elrig
Mochrum
Sorbie
Garlieston
Eggerness Point
Creetown (△)
Cairnharrow 456△
Cairn Holy
50
31

48

Ardwell
Ardwell Point
Ardwell House
Logan Gardens
Mull of Logan
Port Logan
Clanyard Bay
Kirkmaiden
Laggantalluch Head
Crammag Head
Cairngaan
Mull of Galloway

19

Luce Bay
Balgown Point
Drummore
Cailliness Point
Maryport

Port William
Barsalloch Point
Monreith (△)
Whithorn
Glasserton
Cutcloy
Isle of Whithorn
Cairn Head
Burrow Head
Wigtown B

Map 2 (bottom)

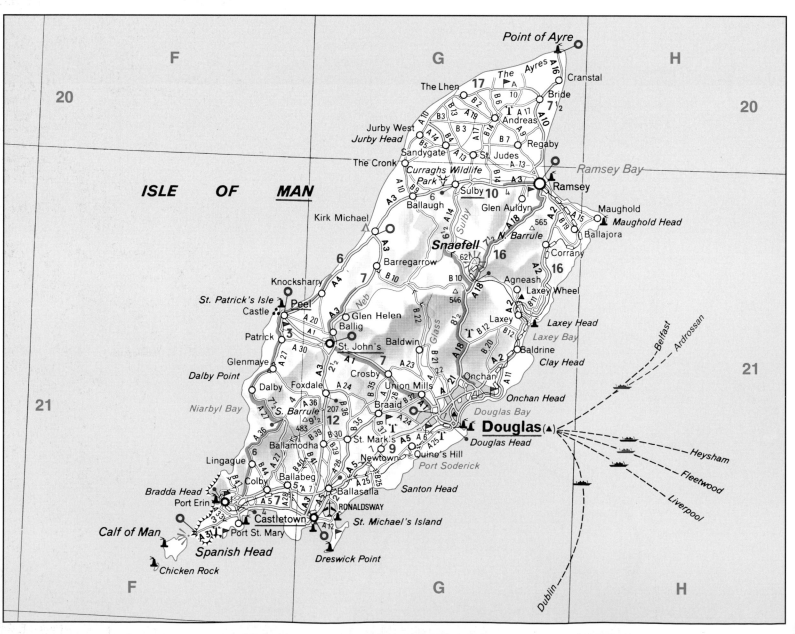

F ‧ **G** ‧ **H**

20 ‧ **20**

Point of Ayre
The Ayres
The Lhen
17
Cranstal
Bride
7
Jurby West
Jurby Head
Andreas
Regaby
Sandygate
St. Judes
The Cronk
Curraghs Wildlife Park
Ramsey Bay
Sulby
10
Ramsey
ISLE OF MAN
Ballaugh
Glen Auldyn
Maughold
Maughold Head
Kirk Michael
N. Barrule
Ballajora
Snaefell
16
Corrany
6
Barregarrow
Agneash
Knocksharry
7
Laxey Wheel
St. Patrick's Isle
Peel
Castle
Glen Helen
Ballig
Laxey
Laxey Head
Patrick
3
St. John's
Baldwin
Laxey Bay
Glenmaye
Dalby Point
Crosby
Baldrine
Dalby
Foxdale
Union Mills
Clay Head
Niarbyl Bay
S. Barrule
207
12
483
Braaid
Onchan
Onchan Head
Ballamodha
St. Mark's
9
Ballabeg
Newtown
Quine's Hill
Port Soderick
Douglas (△)
Douglas Bay
Douglas Head
Lingague
Colby
Ballasalla
Santon Head
Bradda Head
Port Erin
Castletown
Ronaldsway
St. Michael's Island
Calf of Man
Port St. Mary
Spanish Head
Dreswick Point
Chicken Rock

Belfast
Ardrossan
Heysham
Fleetwood
Liverpool
Dublin

21 ‧ **21**

Glengap H

A762 A745 Dalbeattie
B736 A75 Bridge of Dee B793
366 Forest Miefield Ringford 6 of Dee B738
Gatehouse of Fleet
Twynholm A755 Tongland Gelston Palnackie
Kirkcudbright (Δ) Orchardton Tower
Knockbrex St. Mary's Isle A711
Borgue Dundrennan
Ross Townhead
Lit. Ross

Abbey Head

569

Carsethorn
Caulkerbush Kirkbean
Arbigland
Southerness Southerness Point

SOLWAY FIRTH

Skinburness
Silloth (Δ)

Cardurnock

Moricambe Bay
Newton A
B 5302

Waver

19

Beckfoot Abbey Town
Mawbray Waverton
Westnewton B 5300
Allonby Aspatria 34 55

Allonby Bay

Crosby Plumbland
Maryport Gilcrux Bothel
Dearham
Flimby Broughton Moor A 594
Broughton Cockermouth (Δ)
Seaton Brigham
Workington (Δ) Gt. Clifton 12 A 66 Embleton
8 13 9 13 Greysouthen
Harrington Dean A 5086
Distington Ullock
Lowca Moresby 247
Parton Lamplugh Loweswater
Whitehaven Frizington B 5294 Cleator Moor
St. Bees Head 6 10 Ennerdale Bridge
(Δ) St. Bees Egremont
Beckermet Calder Bridge Copeland Forest
Gosforth Strands
Seascale Santon Bridge
Holmrook Eskdale Green Boot
Drigg
Ravenglass Muncaster Ulpha
(Δ)

Selker Bay 43 69 Bootle

Silecroft Millom
Haverigg

H I J K

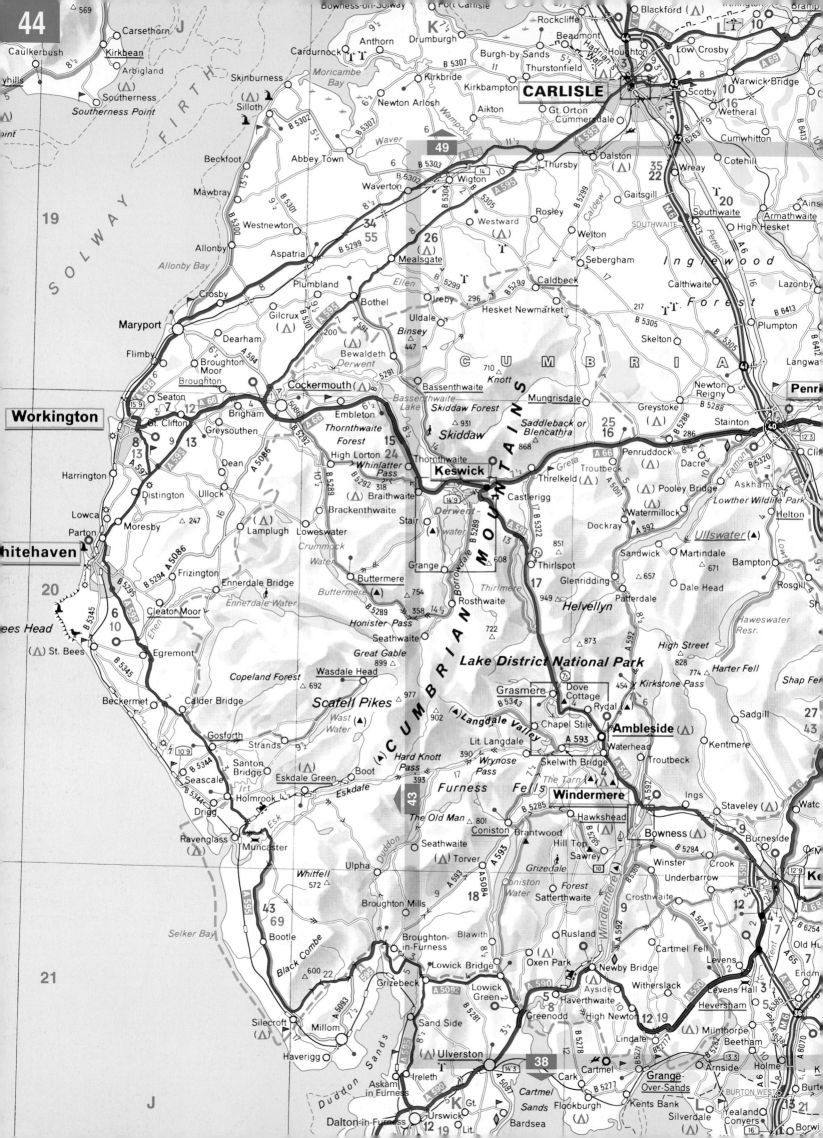

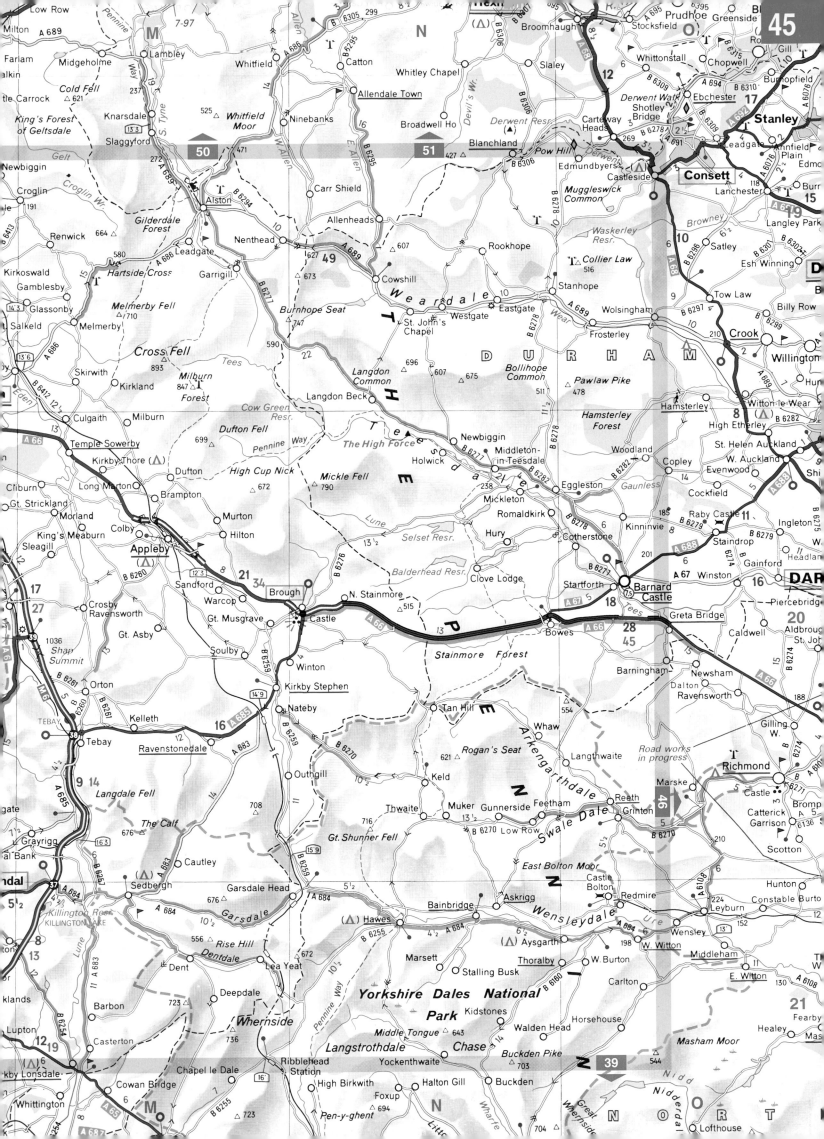

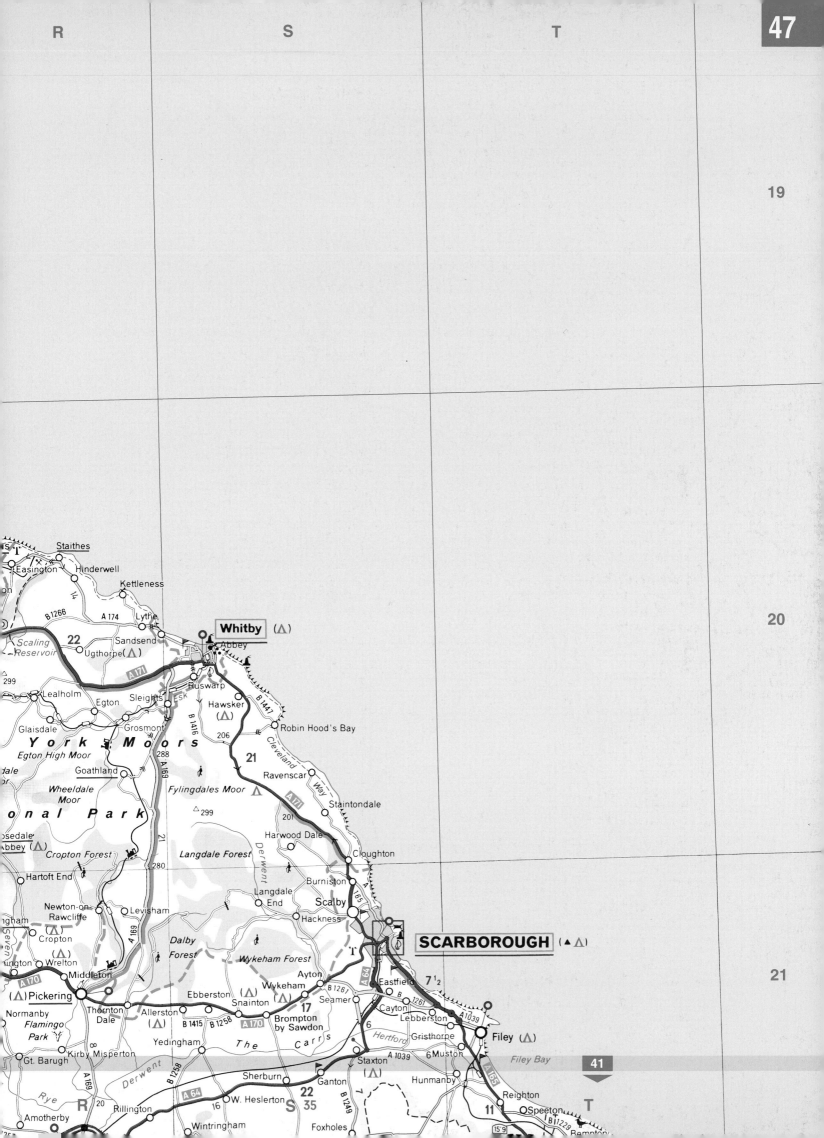

Staithes
Easington
Hinderwell
Kettleness
B 1266
A 174
Lythe
Scaling
Reservoir
22
Sandsend
Ugthorpe (Δ)
Whitby (Δ)
Abbey
A 171
Ruswarp
299
Lealholm
Egton
Sleights
Esk
Hawsker (Δ)
B 1447
Glaisdale
Grosmont
206
Robin Hood's Bay
Y o r k   M o o r s
Egton High Moor
288
21
Cleveland
Ravenscar
Goathland
A 169
Wheeldale
Moor
Fylingdales Moor (Δ)
Way
Staintondale
n a l   P a r k
Δ 299
A 171
201
osedale
bbey (Δ)
Cropton Forest
Langdale Forest
Harwood Dale
Cloughton
280
Hartoft End
Derwent
Burniston
Langdale
End
A 165
Newton-on-
Rawcliffe
Levisham
Scalby
gham
Cropton
Hackness
SCARBOROUGH (▲ Δ)
(Δ)
Dalby
Forest
ington
Wrelton
Wykeham Forest
Ayton
A 64
Eastfield
T
7½
A 170
Middleton
Wykeham
B 1261
Seamer
B
1261
(Δ)
Pickering
Ebberston (Δ)
(Δ)
Snainton
17
Cayton
Lebberston
A 1039
Normanby
Thornton
Dale
(Δ)
Allerston
(Δ)
B 1415
B 1258
A 170
Brompton
by Sawdon
6
Hertford
Gristhorpe
Filey (Δ)
Flamingo
Park
Yedingham
T h e   C a r r s
6 Muston
Kirby Misperton
Derwent
Staxton
A 1039
Filey Bay
Gt. Barugh
A 169
Sherburn
Ganton
(Δ)
Hunmanby
A 165
Rye
R
20
Rillington
16
W. Heslerton
22
35
B 1249
11
Reighton
T
Amotherby
Wintringham
Foxholes
Speeton
B 1229
B 1258
A 64
S

41

15·9

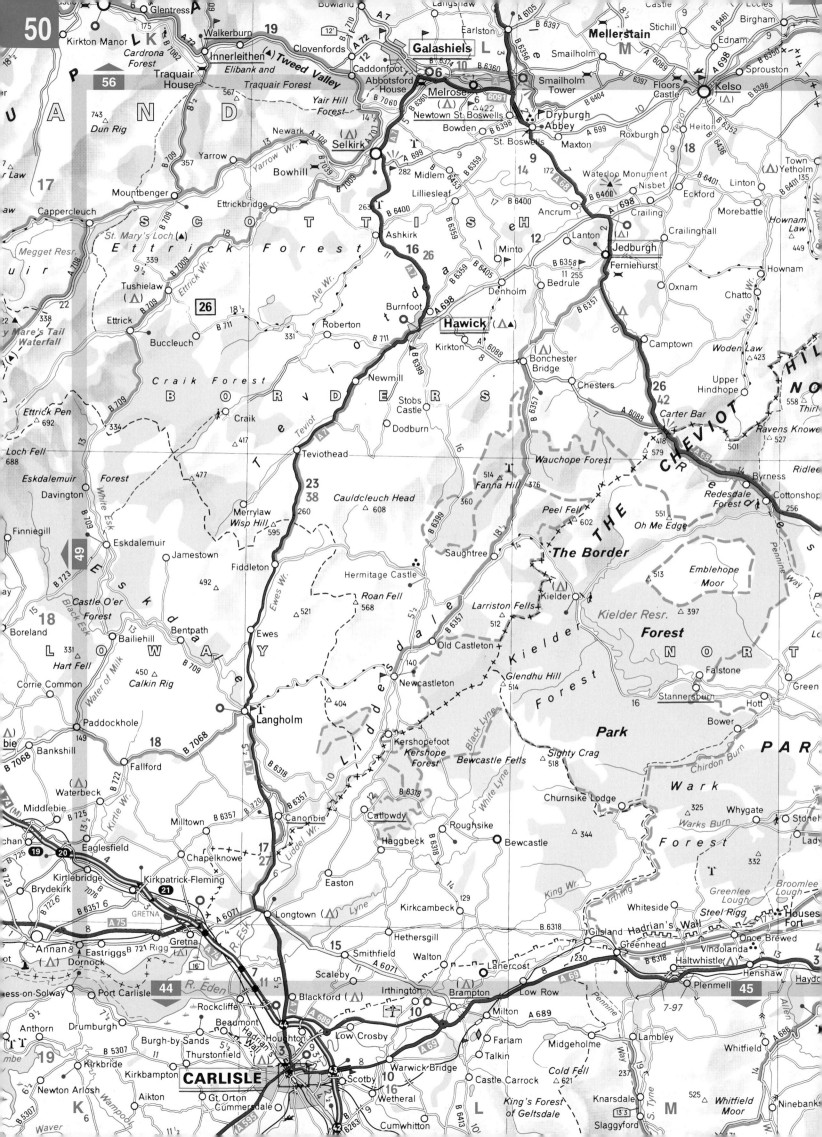

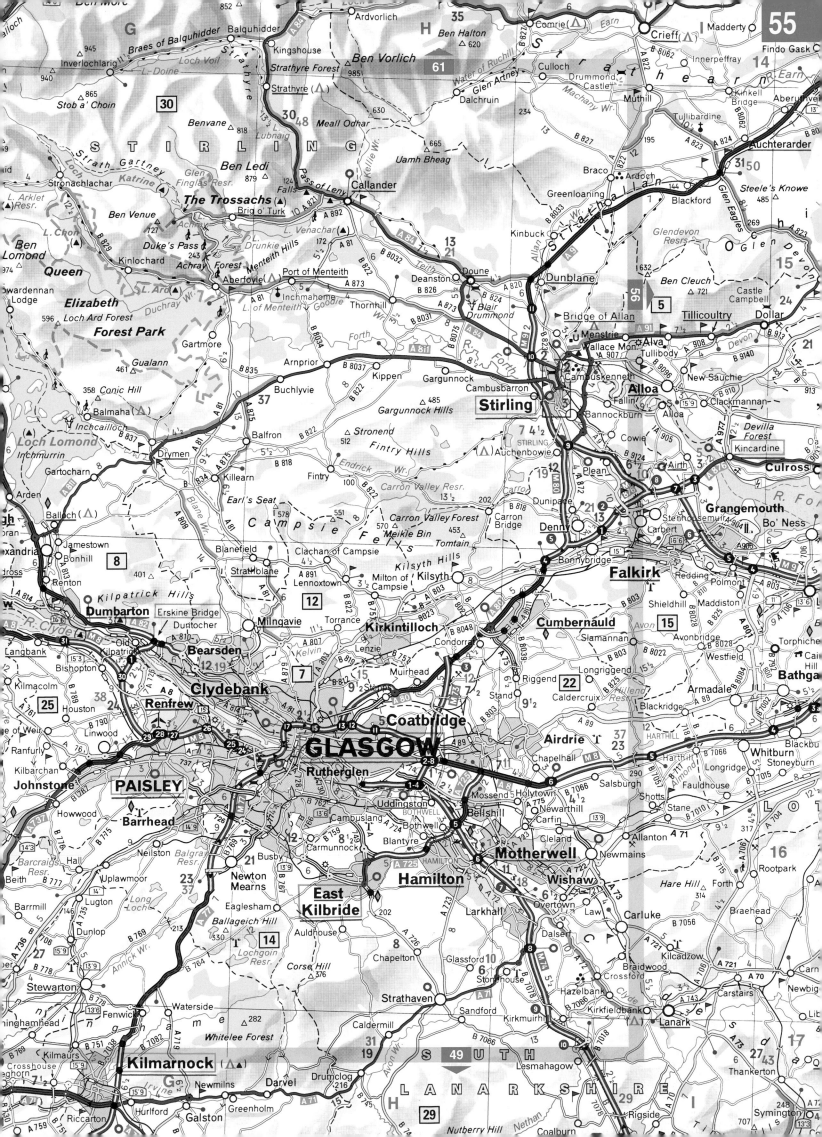

X

Doirlinn Head

Borve

Heaval

△333

△888

△383

Ersary

Bruernish Point

Y

Z

Oigh-sgeir

Caolis

Castlebay

△102

Vatersay

△190

64

Vatersay

Muldoanich

Floday

Sound of Sandray

13

Lingay

207

Sandray

Sound of Pabbay

Pabbay

△171

Rosinish

Sound of Mingulay

△273

Mingulay

Sounds of Berneray

Berneray

Barra Head

H
E
B
R
I
D
E
S

Ballyhaugh

Arileod

Calgary Point

Crossapol
Bay

Gunna

Urvaig

Rubha Dubh

14

Hough Skerries

Clachan-Mór

Balephetrish
Bay

B 8069

3 ½

Caoles

Rubha Chraiginis

119 △Ballevullin

B
8068

4 ½

Gott
Bay

Kenovay

Soa

Scarinish

Middleton

B
8065

2 ½

1 ½

B 8065 ½

Tiree

3

Crossapoll

Hynish Bay

Balephuil

B 8065

3

B
8067
B8066

Balemartine

2 ½

Rinn Thorbhais

Hynish

Balephuil Bay

I
N
N
E
R

Skerryvore

X

Y

Z

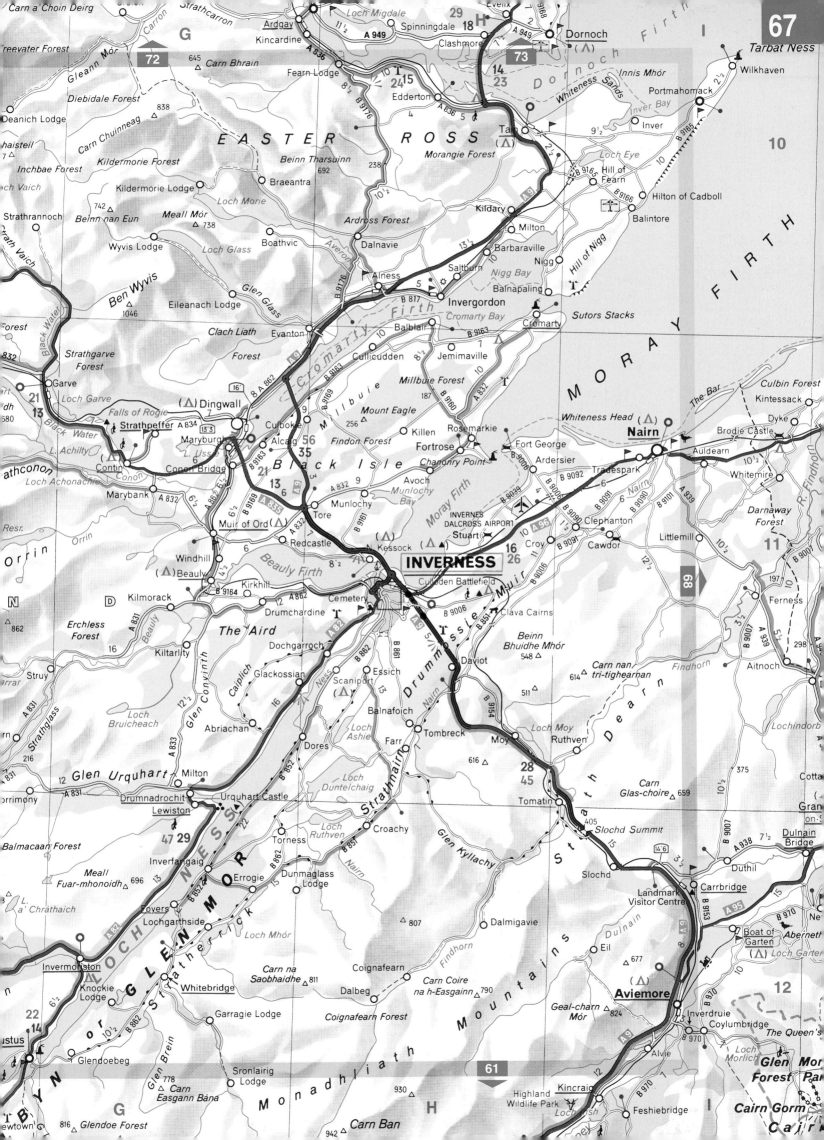

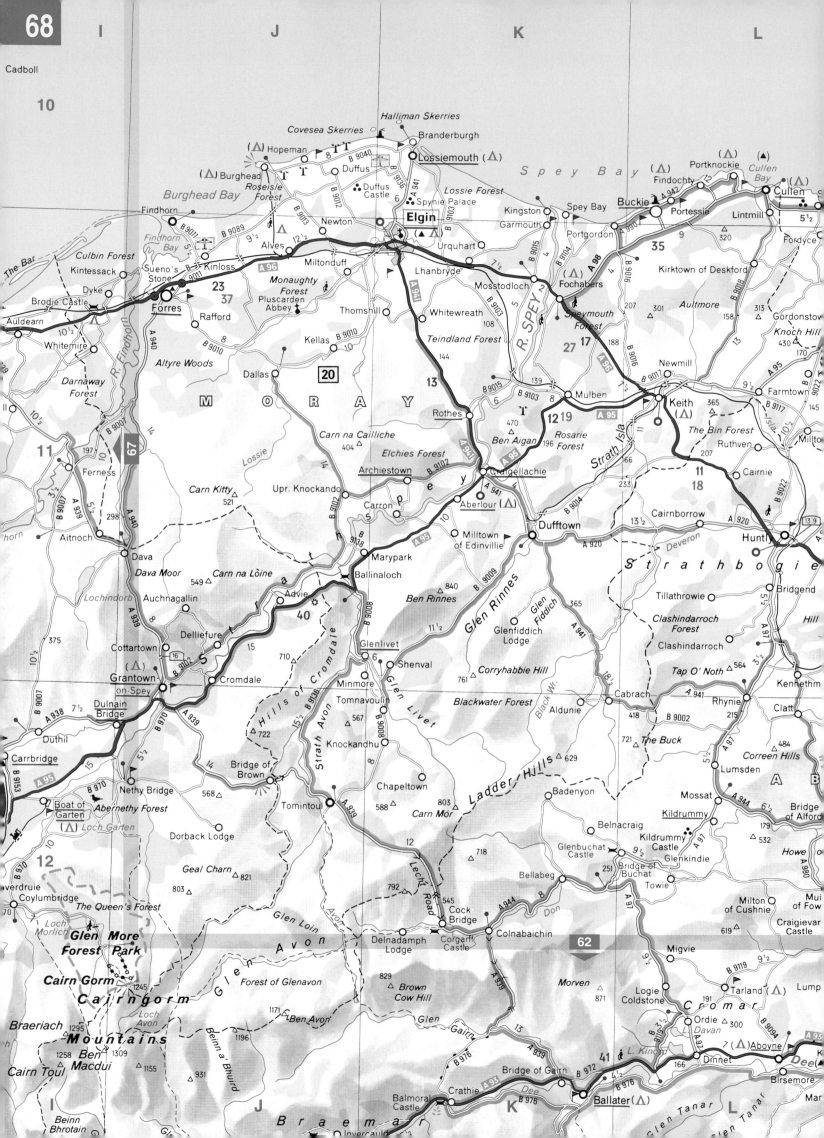

8

9

10

OUTER HEBRIDES

Y
Z
A

ISLE OF LEWIS AND HARRIS

Galson
Borve
Shader
Barvas
Arnol
Bragar
50
Shawbost
L. Urrahag
28
Garenin
Carloway
Loch Breivat
Dun Carloway Broch
261
Beinn Mholach
292
L. Laxavat Ard
A 857
110
Col
Little Bernera
Tobson
A 858
12
Gallan Head
West Loch Roag
Tong
Aird Uig
Valtos
Pabay Mór
Breaclete
Great Bernera
8½
Newmarket
205
Miavaig
Vuia Mór
Eilean Kearstay
Breasclete
T
Timsgarry
Floday
Callanish
Stornoway
Camas Uig
Uig
Crulivig
Garynahine
A 858
13½
A 859
Mangersta
Standing Stones
13
B 8011
B 8059
112
Achmore
L. Orasay
7
B 897
Islivig
574
Enaclete
B 8011
LEWIS
Leurbost
9
Aird Brenish
L. nam Falcag
Crossbost
Ranish
Brenish
L. Grunavat
20
Loch Airigh na h-Airde
8½
Laxay
Keose
Barkin Isles
Mealasta I.
L. Trealaval
Balallan
Eilean Chaluim Chille
281
Kershader
Cromore
Kearstay
Morsgail Forest
Loch Langavat
L. Erisort
B 8060
Eilean Th
Scarp
308
Arivruaich
L. Sgibacleit
Marvig
303
36
Seaforth Head
Glenside
Gasker
Hushinish
Tirga Mór
Stulaval
492
A 859
Park or Pairc
Gravir
L. Odhairn
Kebo
Hushinish Point
B 887
679
579
17½
217
401
Eishken
Lemreway
B 8060
Forest of Harris
Meavaig
Ardvourlie
Seaforth Island
572
Loch Shell or Loch Sealg
Amhuinnsuidhe
13
Clisham
Beinn Mhór
Eilean Iubhard
Taransay Glorigs
Meavaig
799
Crionaig
371
467
HARRIS
Soay Mór
North Harris
Maaruig
Loch Seaforth
Taransay
West Loch Tarbert
Rhenigidale
267
Isay
Ardhasaig
L. Claidh
L. Bhrollum
WESTERN ISLES
506
3
Tarbert
Loch Trollamarig
Sound of Shiant
Luskentyre
Kyles Scalpay
Eilean Mór a'Bhàigh
334
Scotasay
Toe Head
South Harris Forest
Scalpay
Coppay
24
16½
A 859
Shiant Islands
Shillay
Borve
Scarista
Drinnishadder
Scalpay
104
365
East Loch Tarbert
Pabbay
398
Grosebay
Northton
L. Langavat
Manish
Stockinish I.
Brenish Point
196
Ensay
14
Spuir
Leverburgh
Finsbay
65
Boreray
93
460
A 859
Berneray
Killegray
3
12½
Borve
Langay
Gilsay
Rodel
Renish Point
Sgeir nam Maol
Groay
Fladda-chùain
Eilean

Butt of Lewis

B

Eoropie
Port of Ness
Habost
B 8015
Skigersta
Cross
Dell
Ness

Loch Langavat

248
△
Muirneag

Tolsta
Tolsta Head

B 895

Gress

Back

12 ¹⁄₂

Tiumpan Head
Portnaguran

Broad Bay
(▲)
Melbost 12
Garrabost
Knock
Bayble
Eye Peninsula

Chicken Head

aidh

Head

huire

B

Troday

C

T H E   M I N C H

8

Handa Isla

Up

Eddrachillis Bay

Point of Stoer

Culkein
Eilean Chrona
Oldany

Clashnessie
Stoer
L. Crocach
Clachtoll
B 869
9

Achmelvich
A 837
Baddidarach
Inv
Soyea Island
L. Inver
Loc
A' Chleit
Kirkaig Point
Inverkirkaig
Eilean Mór

Rubha Cóigeach
Enard Bay
11 ¹⁄₂
Fior
Loch Sion

Rubha Mór
Reiff
Brae of Achnahaird
Badnagyle
Eilean Mullagrach
6
Altandhu
L. Osgaig
Stac Polla
613 △
Isle Ristol
Polbain
L. Bad a' Ghail
Glas-leac Mór
L.-Lúrgain
Tanera Mór
Achiltibuie
Tanera Beg
Badenscallie
Summer Is.
Horse I.
Culnacraig
Ben
△ 743
Eilean Dubh
Achduart
Coig
Priest Island
Càrn nan Sgeir
I. Martin
Bottle I.
Stra

Greenstone Point
Cailleach Head
Annat Bay

Opinan
Rubha Beag
Scoraig
Little Loch Broom
Mellon Udrigle
Stattic Point
Badluarach
Beinn Ghobhlach
△ 635
Gob a' Gheodha
Gruinard Island
Mungasdale
Allt na h-Airbhe
Eilean Furadh Mór
Achgarve
Badralach
Rubha Réidh
Mellon Charles
Laide
A 832
Badcaul
10 Blarna
Cove
66
Coast
Gruinard Bay
Camusnagaul
Aultbea
767
T
△ 296
L. a' Bhaid-
Luachraich
Dundonnell
An Cuaidh
I. of Ewe
B 8057
B 8021
Inverasdale
9
L. Fada
An Teallach
Melvaig
△ 1062
Midtown
Loch Ewe
Inverewe Gardens
Tournaig
(△)
Loch na Sealga
N. Erradale
Poolewe
9 ¹⁄₂
6
Fisherfield Forest
908
Dundonnel

72

C

D

E

ORKNEY ISLANDS

7

Hoy

Lyness

Fara

360

B 9047

Flotta

Flotta

A 96

Water Sound

Burray

Causeway

L

M

St. Margaret's Hope

Herston

B 4043

Langhorpe

Bow

B 9044

Grim Ness

A 9042

B 9047

Wateringhouse

Hurliness

Switha

Sound of Hoxa

A 961

118

South

Ronaldsay

Tor Ness

Cantick Head

South Walls

Swona

Burwick

Cleat

Old Head

B 9041

Brough Ness

Pentland Firth

Langaton Point

Island of Stroma

Nethertown

Pentland Skerries

Uppertown

51

Dunnet Head

Scarfskerry

St. John's Point

Gills

Duncansby Head

Brough

20

A 836

11½

John o' Groats (△)

St. John's Loch

Mey

Canisbay

2

Holborn

Head

(△) *Dunnet Bay*

Dunnet

Barrock

124

Skirza

*Thurso

Bay*

A 836

Castletown

(△)

Loch Heilen

13½

Freswick

Skirza Head

Freswick Bay

Thurso (△)

5½

141

B 876

Slickly

A 99

6

7½

Auckengill

B 874

Roadside

Bower

Lyth

Sortat

17

B 874

Myrelandhorn

Keiss

Halkirk

7

L. Scarmclate

4½

B 870

8½

*Sinclair's

Bay*

Olgrinmore

Loch Watten

B 876

Reiss

Noss Head

8

Banniskirk

Spittal

A 882

Watten

B 874

Girnigoe and Sinclair

5½

Mybster

B 870

8

Staxigoe

B 870

21

Haster

Wick

North Head

Badlipster

Tannach

South Head

44

71

13

Loch Hempriggs

Thrumster

A 99

Grey Cairns

of Camster

212

12½

Sarclet

211

Ulbster

60

37

287

Hill o' Many Stanes

Houstry

Lybster

Latheron

4½

W. Clyth

A 9

Forse

Janetstown

A 9

Dunbeath

20

Berriedale

orgue

9

◀ 73

J

K

Inset map

4°20

3°

J

Sule Skerry

K

L

5

Stack Skerry

Mull Head

Bow Head

Noup Head

Papa Westra

Pierowall

3°20

Westray

1691

B 9066

*The Nor

Sound*

Midbea

Rapness

Westray Firth

Calfsound

Eday

6

(△) Brough of Birsay

Rousay

Wasbister

Egilsay

Back

101

Brough Head

250

B 9064

Brinyan

Wyre

**Kitchener

Memorial**

Birsay

A 966

9½

Gurness

Broch

Stronsay

Twatt

Georth

B 9057

Gairsay

B 9058

Firth

Skara Brae

Dounby

221

Balfour

Sandgarth

Yesnaby

A 961

L. of Harray

8½

Shapin.

Maes

Howe

A 966

Finstown

Rennibister

Mainland

Ring of

Brodgar

A 965

Wideford

Hill Cairn

Kirkwall

Stromness

44

Stenness

268

A 960

B

Graemsay

A 964

Orphir

10

A 961

Monéss

15½

St. Mary's

Cava

Lamb

Holm

**Old Man of

Hoy**

479

Fara

Scapa Flow

Rose Ness

Rora Head

Rackwick

Lyness

Flotta

Causeway

Burray

Causeway

Hoy

B 9047

St. Margaret's Hope

*Lenwick

Aberdeen*

Tor Ness

South Walls

A 961

118

South Ronal.

Burwick

Old Head

Pentland   Firth

Pentland Skerrie

Dunnet Head

Stroma

7

B 855

Scarfskerry

Gills

Duncansby Head

Scrabster

(△) Dunnet

A 836

Thurso

(△)

14½

John o' Groats (△)

Castletown

J

5½

K

A 9

L

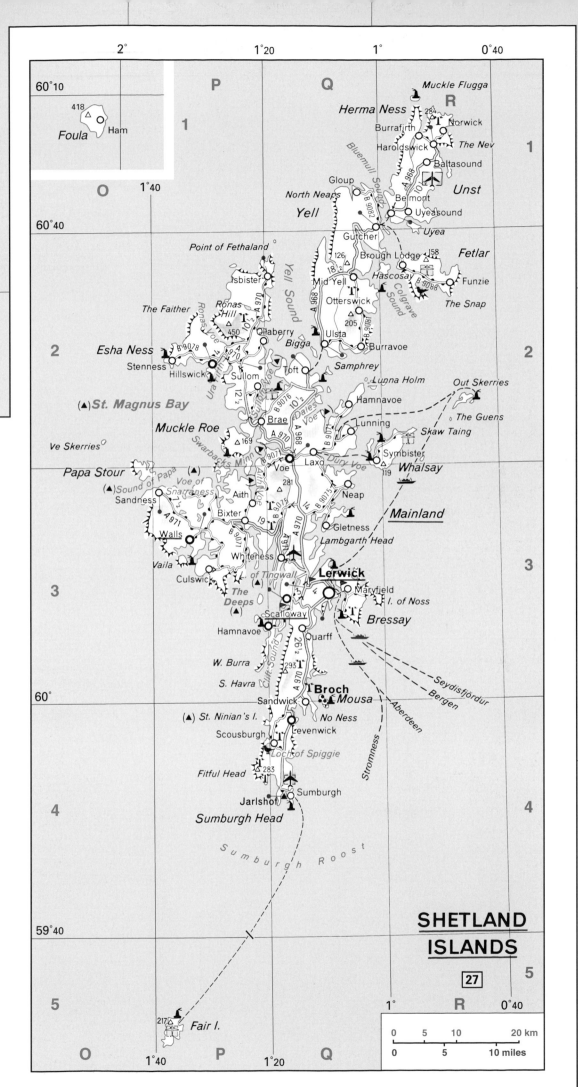

SHETLAND
ISLANDS

27

ORKNEY
ISLANDS

23

M

| 5 | 10 | 20 km |

| 5 | | 10 miles |

A

B

9

10

Tullig Po...

Feeard

Bridge　Moneen

Kilbaha　R 487

(71)　3½　*Kilbaha*

Loop Head　*Bay*　Ki...

MOUTH　OF

THE　SHANNO...

Ballynaskree...

Dreenagh

Kerry Head　218　5½

△

Ca...

Glenderry　5　R 55...

(△) Ballyheige　Ler...

Ballyheige Bay　Banna

Akeragh

R 551　Banna

The Seven Hogs or　*Barrow*

Magharee Islands　Ardfert

Illauntannig　*Harbour*

Rough Point

Fahamore　Chapeltown

Brandon Point　Kilshannig　Spa

11

Brandon Head　*Brandon Bay*　(△) Fenit

Brandon /　*Tralee Bay*　(△▲) **Tra...**

Cé Bhréanainn　*Tr...*

Brandon Creek　Ballyquin ( )　*Lough Gill*　Castlegregory (△)　Blennervil...

Ballydavid Head　**Brandon**　9　R 560

Mountain　**Strand** Killmey　*Derrymore I...*

Tiduff　△ 951　Kilcummin　9½

Feohanagh　Cloghane　Stradbally　N 86

5　1½　Aughacasla　Derrymore

Smerwick　*Smerwick*　*Feohanagh*　Ballyduff　**Beenoskee**　Camp

Sybil Head　*Harbour*　Ballydavid　825 △　T 68　Derrymore

Murreagh　5　Ballinloghig　**D　I　N　G**　△ 825　850 *Baurtregaum*

Ballyferriter　Kilmalkedar　△ 623　*L. Slat*　594 △　Caherconree　△

Baile an Fheirtéaraigh　Gallarus Oratory　456 △　616 △　**L E**　N 86　Slieve Mish Mou...

Clogher Head　(△)　5　Connor Lougher

Ballineanig　Ballynana　*Owenascaul*　White Gate

Inishtooskert　R 559　31　10½　Cross Roads

Milltown　**76**　Aughils

Dunquin　Ventry　R 559　**Dingle /**　Lispole /　Anascaul　R 561　Castlen...

Blasket Islands / (▲)　Dún Chaoin　*An Daingean*　Lios Póil　4½　Inch

Na Blascaodaí　516 △ **Mount Eagle**　R 559　*Dingle*　N 86　11　Inch

Beehive　*Harb...*　Castle...

Great Blasket　Huts　*Ventry*　*Castlemaine*

Island　R 559　10½　*Harbour*　Milltow...

...raght Island　*Harbour*　Doonmanagh　Inch

Parkmore Pt.　Castle　Cromane　Knockaunnaglashy

Bull's Head　Minard Head　Killorgli...

Inishnabro　A　B　Illaunstookagh　Tullig　Cill Orgla...

Inishvickillane

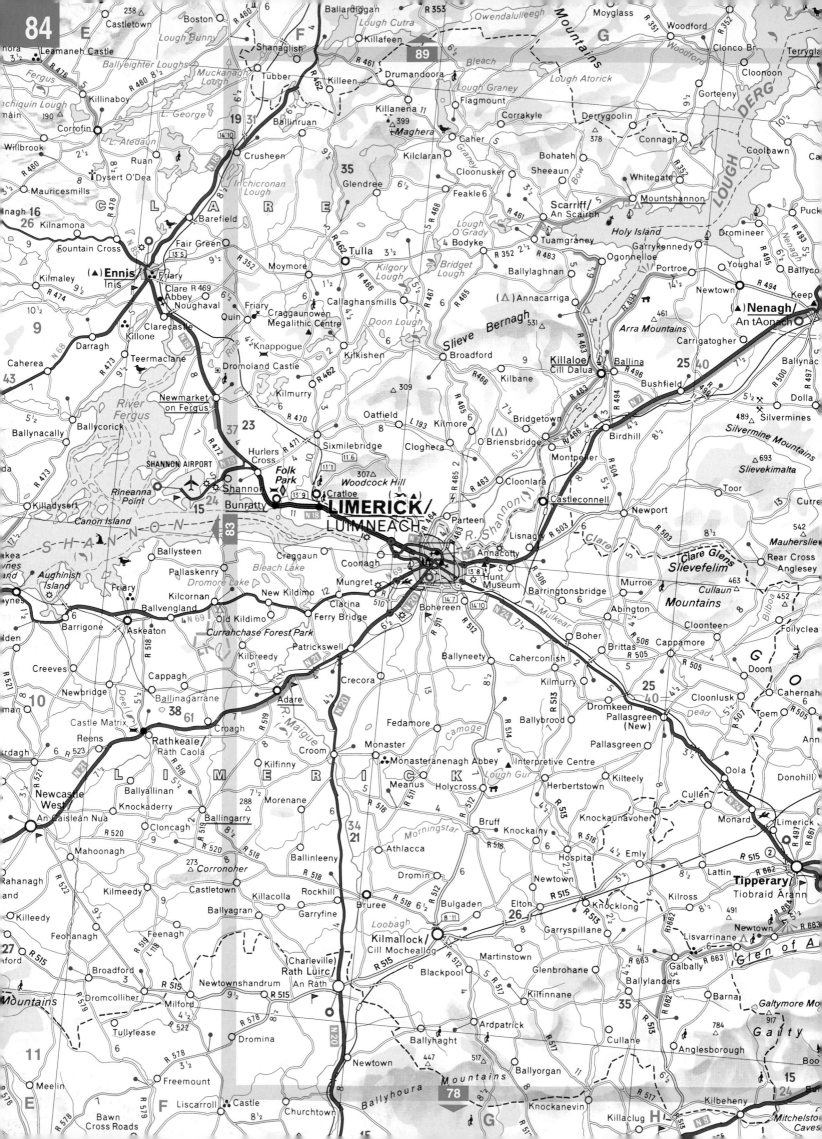

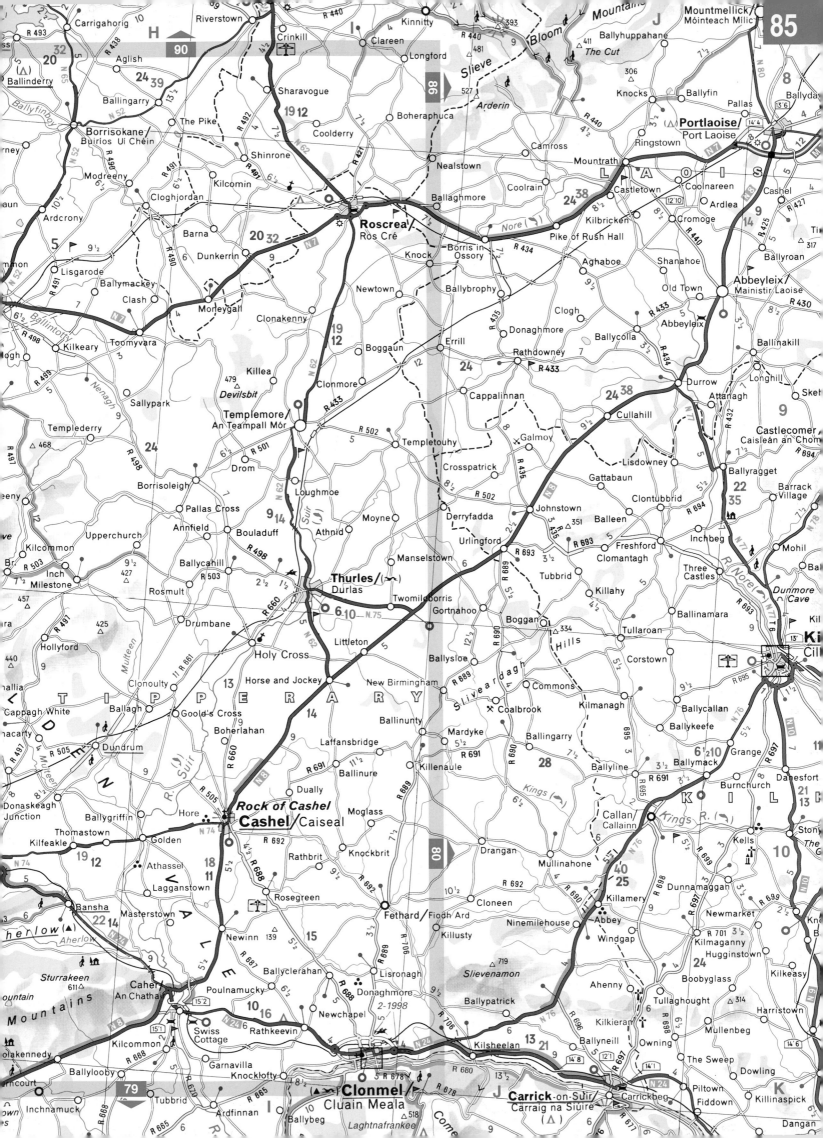

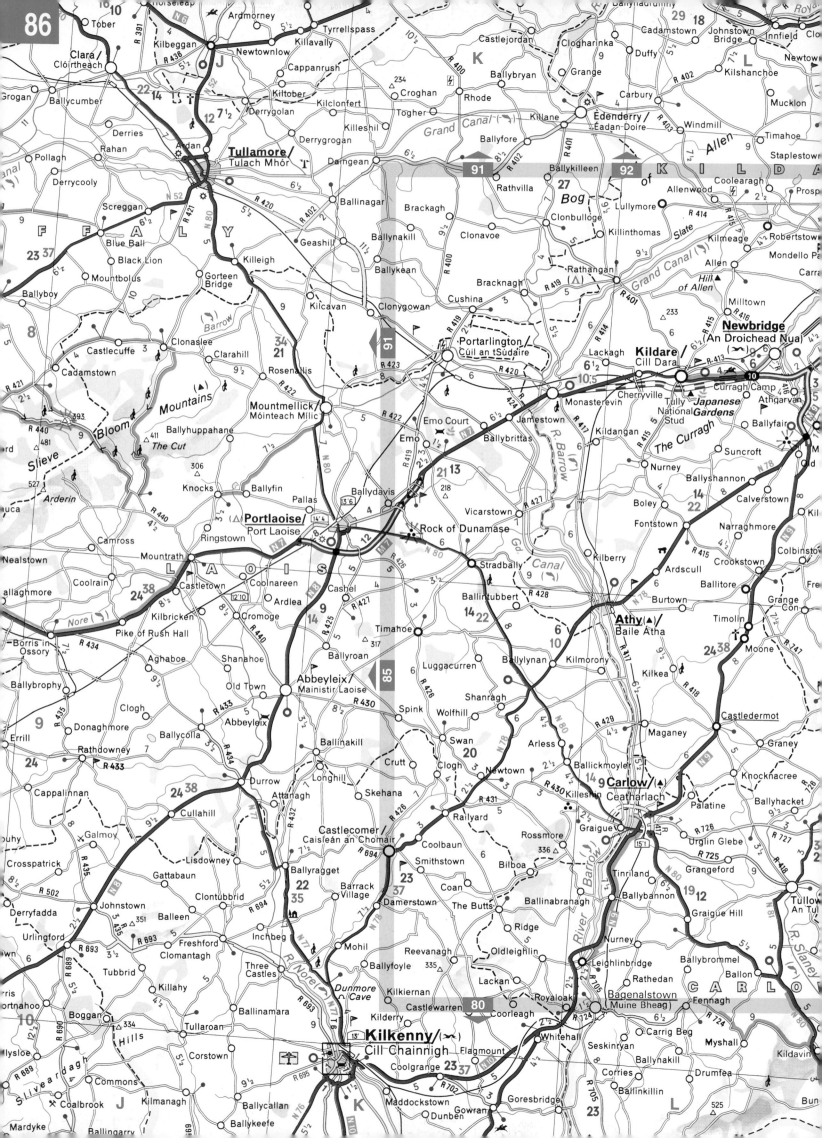

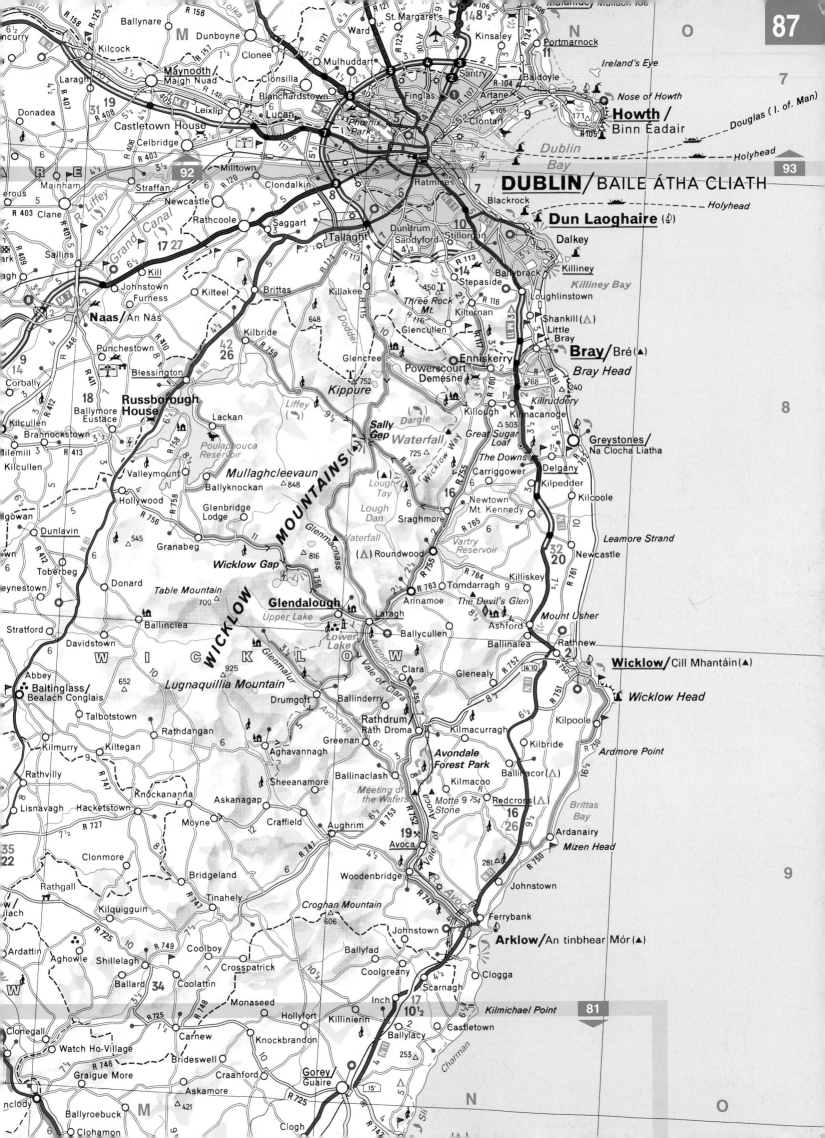

B   C   D

Stags of Broad Haven

Benwee Head

Erris Head   *Kid Island*   Portacloy

Eagle Island   *Broad Haven*   232   Carrowteige /   Porturlin /   *Belderg*
    Aghadoon   *Rinroe Point*   Ceathrú Thaidhg   Port Durlainne   305   *Glinsk*   *Harbour*

Annagh Head   138   Ross Port   340   Belderrig /
    Corclogh   Knocknalina   266   8½   Béal Deirg
    6   Inver   Pollatomish   *Maumak*   379 △
    R 313   Belmullet /   Annie Brady   *Benmore*   31
Inishglora   Béal an Mhuirthead   Knocknalower   Bridge   △ 351

Corraun Point   An Geata Mór   4½   R 314   Barnatra /   Glenamoy /   R 314
    7   Bunnahowen /   Bárr na Trá   Gleann na Múaidhe
Mullet Peninsula   Drumreagh   Bun na hAbhna   3   Bellanaboy Bridge

Trawmore   240   *Carrowmore Lake*   *Glenamoy*
Inishkea North   *Bay*   6½   7½   331   Sheskin
    Elly Bay   12   Gortmore   *Slieve Fyagh*
Inishkea South   *Doolough Point*   Srahmore   Attavally   *Doobehy*
    R 313   Aghleam   Tristia   R 313   Bangor   Largan   8½   *o Owenny*
    105   6½   Dooyork   7   367   *Lough Dahyba*
Black Rock   Fallmore   **Blacksod**   Geesala /   7½   N 59   *Muing*   42 26
    Point   Gaoth Saile   Bellacorick
Duvillaun More   *Duvillaun Beg*   **Blacksod**   *Tullaghan*   N 59   R 312
    Doohooma   *Bay*   Shranamanragh Br.   *Owenduff (*   *Tarsaghaunmore*   **Slieve Car**   Deel Bridge

Saddle Head   *Ridge Point*   *Fahy Lough*   Doona   720   *N e p h n*   Keenagh
    Slievemore   N 59   *Nephin Beg*   387
    △ 671   Valley   Ballycroy   628   *Bunaveela*
Achill Head   Croaghaun   (Λ) Doogort   *Lough*
    △ 667   Dooagh   River   *Inishbiggle*   Castlehill   Bellagarvaun   *B e g*
    R 319   Keel   3   *Annagh*   Srahduggaun   628   *Derreen*
Moyteoge Head   Keem Strand   Bunacurry   *Island*   **Glennamong**   698 △   *Birreencorragh*
    Cathedral Rocks   Cashel   Salia   Claggan   63   712 △   *R a n g e*
(Λ) ACHILL ISLAND   △ 464   39   Srahmore   588
    Dooega Head   Knockmore   Achill   581 △
Dooega / Dumha Éige   △ 340   Achill Sound / Gob an Choire   △ 382   *Cloondaff*
    Derreen   Belfarsad   36   Mulrany /   *Beltr*
Bills Rocks   *Ashleam Bay*   **Corraun**   An Mhala Raithní   *Lough*
    Cloghmore   Corraun Hill   Rosturk   11½   *Furnace*   R 317
An Chloich Mhóir   Glassillaun   521   **Peninsula**   Carrigahowley   *Lough*   Burrishoole
Achillbeg Island   Dooghbeg   8   *Newport Bay*   Newport /   R 311
    Bolinglanna   Baile Uí Fhiacháin

Clare Island   Ballytoohy   *Island More*   Kilmeena   7½   *Clogher*
    △ 461   *C L E W   B A Y*   Carraholly   N 59
    Wesport Bay   Westport Quay   Westport House   11 18
Inishturk   *Old Head*   Leckanvy   Murrisk   **Westport /** Cathai   N 5
    Roonah Quay   Kilsallagh   Killadangan   (Λ)
    Emlagh Point   Louisburgh   R 335   763   12'6   Mace
Caher Island   4½   8   **Croagh**   Knappagh   5½
    Formoyle   **Patrick**   Aghagower   Killaval
    Mullagh   *Owenwee*   Liscarney   Cordarragh
    Roonah Lough   *Lough Nacorra*   336   *Boha*
    Silver Strand   *Carrownisky*   R 335   *Moher*   N 59
    Bridge   Killadoon   Cregganbaun   *Bunowen*   *Lough*   Carrowkennedy
    Kinnadoohy   Glenkeen Br.   Owenmore Bridge   393 △

Inishbofin   88   *Doo Lough*   **Sheeffry**
ishshark   *Tonakeera Point*   **Pass**   **Hills**   *Croaghrimbeg*
    Crump Island   **Mweelrea Mountains**   761   Erriff Bridge
Bofin   *Rinvyle Point*   817 △   *Doo*   Delphi   66 41
    Rinvyle Castle   Ardnagreevagh   Rinvyle (Λ)   *Lough*   700 △ Ben Gorm   **Maumtrasna**
    Cashleen   356   Gowlaun   *Killary Harbour*   648 △ Devilsmother   671 △   Cappanacreha   *Partry Mount*
    Cashel   12   Tully Cross   600   Salrock   R 335   Trean   9½
Cleggan Bay   *Ballynakill Harbour*   Culfin   N 59   *Glennacroyagh*

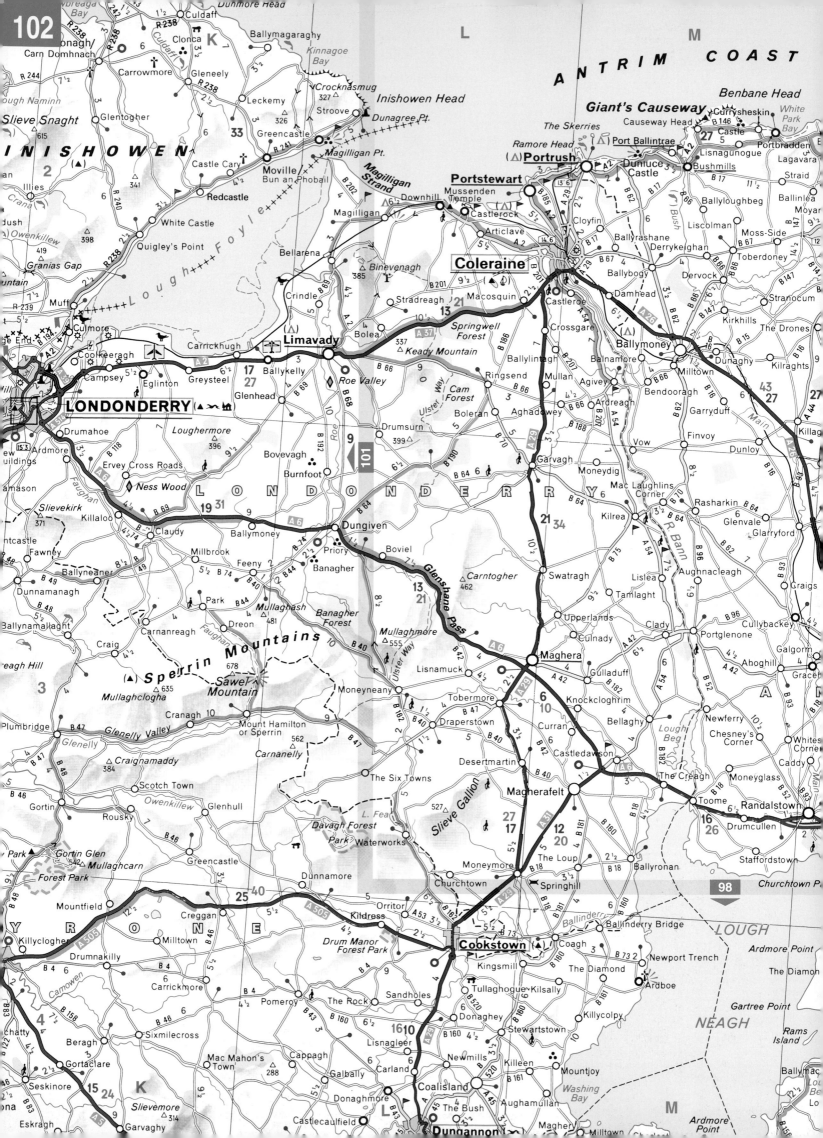

How to use this index

Stonehaven   **63** N13

Page number

Map co-ordinate common
to all Michelin publications

County abbreviations

ENGLAND

Avon ....Avon
Bedfordshire...........................Beds.
Berkshire ....Berks.
Buckinghamshire..................Bucks.
Cambridgeshire ....Cambs.
Cheshire ....Cheshire
Cleveland ....Cleveland
Cornwall............................Cornwall
Cumbria ....Cumbria
Derbyshire...............................Derbs.
Devon ....Devon
Dorset......................................Dorset
Durham..................................Durham
East Sussex................East Sussex
Essex...Essex
Gloucestershire ....Glos.
Greater Manchester......Gtr. Man.
Hampshire.............................Hants.
Hereford and
   Worcester ....Heref. and Worc.
Hertfordshire ....Herts.
Humberside ....Humberside
Isle of Wight........................I. O. W.
Kent..Kent
Lancashire ....Lancs.
Leicestershire...........................Leics.
Lincolnshire...........................Lincs.
Merseyside ....Merseyside
Norfolk...................................Norfolk
Northamptonshire........Northants.
Northumberland ....Northumb.
North Yorkshire........North Yorks.
Nottinghamshire ....Notts.
Oxfordshire ....Oxon.
Shropshire..............................Salop
Somerset ....Somerset
South Yorkshire.......South Yorks.
Staffordshire.......................Staffs.
Suffolk....................................Suffolk
Surrey.....................................Surrey
Tyne and Wear.....Tyne and Wear
Warwickshire ....Warw.
West Midlands.......West Midlands
West Sussex.............West Sussex
West Yorkshire ....West Yorks.
Wiltshire..................................Wilts.

Symbols on townplans

Roads

Motorway, dual carriageway
Major thoroughfare
Street: Unsuitable for traffic, subject to restrictions - Pedestrian
Shopping street - Car park
Car ferry - Lever bridge

Sights - Hotels - Restaurants
(See Michelin Red Guide)

Place of interest and its main entrance
Cathedral - Church or chapel
Reference letter locating a sight
Reference letter locating a hotel or a restaurant

Various signs

Tourist information centre - Hospital
Cathedral - Church - Cemetery
Garden, park, wood - Stadium
Golf course: visitors unrestricted - restricted
Public building located by letter:
Local government Offices - Town Hall
Police (Headquarters) - Museum
Theatre - University, polytechnics
Main post office with poste restante, telephone
Underground station

London

Borough - Area
Borough boundary - Area boundary
Underground station

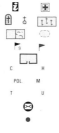

Comnarthaí ar phleanna bailte

Bóithre

Mótarbhealach, carrbhealach dúbailte
Priomh-thrébhealach - Bóthar aonslí
Sráid : neamhoiriúnach do thrácht, ach í stáit speisialta - coisithe
Sráid siopadóireacha - Carrchlós
Bád fartha feithiclí - Droichead starrmhaidí

Ionaid inspéise - Óstáin - Bialanna
(Féach Eolaí Dearg Michelin)

Ionad inspéise agus an priomhbhealach isteach
Ardeaglais - Eaglais nó séipéal
Ionad inspéise curtha in iúl le litir thagartha
Óstán nó bialann curtha in iúl le litir thagartha

Comharthaí Éagsúla

Ionad eolais turasóireachta - Ospidéal
Ardeaglais - Eaglais - Reilig
Gairdín, páirc, coill - Staidiam
Galfchúrsa : gan bac ar chuairteoirí - cuairteoirí faoi theorannú
Foirgneamh poiblí curtha in iúl le litir thagartha :
Oifigí rialtais áitiúil - Halla baile
Póitíní (ceanncheathrú) - Músaem
Amharclann - Ollscoil, polaiteicnicí
Príomhoifig phoist le poste restante, teileafón
Stáisiún traenach faoi thalamh

Londain

Buirg - Limistéar
Teorainn bhuirge - Teorainn limistéir
Stáisiún traenach faoi thalamh

Légende des plans de ville

Voirie

Autoroute, route à chaussées séparées
Grandes voies de circulation - Sens unique
Rue impraticable, réglementée - Rue piétonne
Rue commerçante - Parc de stationnement
Bac pour autos - Pont mobile

Curiosités - Hôtels - Restaurants
(Voir le Guide Rouge Michelin)

Bâtiment intéressant et entrée principale
Cathédrale - Église ou chapelle
Lettre identifiant une curiosité
Lettre identifiant un hôtel ou un restaurant

Signes divers

Information touristique - Hôpital
Cathédrale - Église - Cimetière
Jardin, parc, bois - Stade
Golf : Ouvert à tous - Réservé
Bâtiment public repéré par une lettre :
Administration du comté - Hôtel de Ville
Police (commissariat central) - Musée
Théâtre - Université, grande école
Bureau principal de poste restante, téléphone
Station de métro

Londres

Nom d'arrondissement - de quartier
Limite d'arrondissement - de quartier
Station de métro

Symbolau ar gynlluniau'r trefi

Ffyrdd

Traffordd, ffordd ddeuol
Prif ffordd drwodd - Unffordd
Stryd : Anaddas i draffig, cyfyngedig - Cerddwr
Stryd siopa - Parc ceir
Fferi geir - Pont liferi

Golygfeydd - Gwestai - Tai bwyta
(Gweler Llyfr Coch Michelin)

Man diddorol a'i brif fynedfa
Eglwys Gadeiriol - Eglwys neu gapel
Llythyren gyfeirio sy'n dynodi golygfa
Llythyren gyfeirio sy'n dynodi gwesty neu dŷ bwyta

Arwyddion amrywiol

Canolfan croeso - Ysbyty
Eglwys Gadeiriol - Eglwys - Mynwent
Gardd, parc, coedwig - Stadiwm
Cwrs golff : dim cyfyngiad ar ymwelwyr - cyfyngiad ar ymwelwyr
Adeilad cyhoeddus a ddynodir gan lythyren :
Swyddfeydd llywodraeth leol - Neuadd y Dref
Yr Heddlu (pencadlys) - Amgueddfa
Theatr - Prifysgol, Colegau Politechnig
Prif swyddfa bost gyda poste restante, ffôn
Gorsaf danddaearol

Llundain

Bwrdeistref - Ardal
Ffin Bwrdeistref - Ffin yr Ardal
Gorsaf danddaearol

Great Britain

A

Abbas Combe 8 M 30
Abberley 26 M 27
Abbey 13 X 30
Abbey Dore 26 L 28
Abbey Town 44 K 19
Abbeydale 35 P 23
Abbeystead 38 L 22
Abbots Bromley 35 O 25
Abbots Langley 20 S 28
Abbotsbury 8 M 32
Abbotsford House 50 L 17
Abbotskerswell 4 J 32
Aberaeron 24 H 27
Aberaman 16 J 28
Aberangell 25 I 25
Abercarn 16 K 29
Aberchirder 69 M 11
Abercynon 16 J 29
Aberdare/Aberdâr 16 J 28
Aberdaron 32 F 25
Aberdaugleddau/ Milford Haven 14 E 28
Aberdeen 69 N 12
Aberdour 56 K 15
Aberdour Bay 69 N 10
Aberdovey/ Aberdyfi 24 H 26
Abereiddy 14 E 28
Aberfeldy 61 I 14
Aberffraw 32 G 24
Aberford 40 P 22
Aberfoyle 55 G 15
Abergavenny/ Y-Fenni 16 K 28
Abergele 33 J 24
Abergwaun/ Fishguard 14 F 28
Abergwesyn 25 I 27
Abergwyngregyn 32 H 24
Abergynolwyn 24 I 26
Aberhonddu/ Brecon 25 J 28
Aberlady 56 L 15
Aberlemno 62 L 13
Aberlour 68 K 11
Abermaw/ Barmouth 32 H 25
Abernethy 56 K 15
Aberpennar/ Mountain Ash 16 J 28
Aberporth 24 G 27
Abersoch 32 G 25
Abersychan 16 K 28
Abertawe/Swansea 15 I 29
Aberteifi/Cardigan 24 G 27
Abertillery 16 K 28
Aberuthven 55 J 15
Aberystwyth 24 H 26
Abingdon 18 Q 28
Abinger Common 19 S 30
Abington (South Lanarkshire) 49 I 17
Abington (Cambs.) 29 U 27
Aboyne 62 L 12
Abridge 21 U 29
Accrington 39 M 22
Achallader 60 F 14
Achanalt 66 F 11
Achaphubuil 60 E 13
Acharn 61 H 14
Achavanich 73 J 8
Achiltibuie 72 D 9
Achmelvich 72 E 9
Achmore 66 D 11
Achnasheen 66 E 11
Achnashellach Forest 66 E 11
Achray (Loch) 55 G 15
Achriesgill 72 F 8
Acklington 51 P 18
Ackworth 40 P 23
Acle 31 Y 26
Acomb 51 N 19
Acrise Place 13 X 30
Acton Turville 17 N 29
Adderbury 28 Q 27
Addingham 39 O 22
Addlestone 20 S 29
Adlington 38 M 23
Adlington Hall 35 N 24
Advie 68 J 11
Adwick-le-Street 40 Q 23
Ae (Forest of) 49 J 18
Affric (Glen) 66 F 12
Afon Dyfrdwy/ Dee (River) 33 K 24
Ailort (Loch) 59 C 13
Ailsa Craig 48 E 18
Ainort (Loch) 65 B 12
Ainsdale 38 K 23
Ainwick 51 O 17
Aird (The) 67 G 11
Airdrie 55 I 16
Airigh na h-Airde (Loch) 70 Z 9
Airth 55 I 15
A La Ronde 4 J 32
Albourne 11 T 31
Albrighton 27 N 26
Albyn or Mor (Glen) 60 F 12
Alcester 27 O 27
Alconbury 29 T 26
Aldbourne 18 P 29
Aldbrough 41 T 22
Aldbury 19 S 28
Alde (River) 23 Y 27
Aldeburgh 23 Y 27
Aldenham 20 S 28
Alderley Edge 35 N 24
Alderney (Channel I.) 5
Aldershot 19 R 30
Aldridge 27 O 26
Aldringham 23 Y 27
Aldwick 10 R 31
Alexandria 55 G 16
Alfold Crossways 11 S 30
Alford (Aberdeenshire) 69 L 12
Alford (Lincs.) 37 U 24
Alfreton 35 P 24
Alfrick 26 M 27
Alfriston 12 U 31
Aline (Loch) 59 C 14
Alkborough 40 S 22
Alkham 13 X 30
Allendale Town 45 N 19
Allerston 47 S 21
Alligin Shuas 66 D 11
Alloa 55 I 15
Alloway 48 G 17
All Stretton 26 L 26
Alltan Fhèarna (Loch an) 73 H 9
Almond (Glen) 61 I 14
Almondbank 62 J 14
Almondsbury 17 M 29
Alness 67 H 10
Alnmouth 51 P 17
Alnwick 51 O 17
Alpheton 22 W 27
Alphington 4 J 31
Alpraham 34 M 24
Alrewas 35 O 25
Alsager 34 N 24
Alsh (Loch) 66 D 12
Alston 45 M 19
Alswear 6 I 31
Altarnun 3 G 32
Altnacealgach 72 F 9
Altnaharra 72 G 9
Alton (Hants.) 10 R 30
Alton (Staffs.) 35 O 25
Alton Towers 35 O 25
Altrincham 34 M 23
Alum Bay 9 P 31
Alva 55 I 15
Alvechurch 27 O 26
Alvediston 8 N 30
Alves 68 J 11
Alvie 67 I 12
Alyth 62 K 14
Amberley 11 S 31
Amble 51 P 18
Amblecote 27 N 26
Ambleside 44 L 20
Amersham 19 S 28
Amesbury 9 O 30
Amlwch 32 G 23
Ammanford/ Rhydaman 15 I 28
Ampleforth 46 Q 21
Ampthill 29 S 27
Amroth 14 G 28
An Riabhachan 66 E 11
An Socach 62 J 13
An Teallach 66 E 10
Ancroft 57 O 16
Andover 18 P 30
Andoversford 17 O 28
Andreas 42 G 20
Angle 14 E 28
Anglesey (Isle of) 32 F 24
Anglesey Abbey 29 U 27
Angmering 11 S 31
Annan 50 K 19
Annan (River) 49 J 17
Annat 66 D 11
Annat Bay 72 E 10
Annbank Station 48 G 17
Anne Hathaway's Cottage 27 O 27
Annfield Plain 46 O 19
Anstey 28 Q 25
Anston 36 Q 23
Anstruther 56 L 15
Antony House 3 H 32
Appin 60 E 14
Appleby 45 M 20
Appleby Magna 27 P 25
Appledore (Devon) 6 H 30
Appledore (Kent) 12 W 30
Appleford 18 Q 29
Aran Fawddwy 33 I 25
Arber Low 35 O 24
Arberth/Narberth 14 F 28
Arbirlot 63 M 14
Arbroath 63 M 14
Arbury Hall 27 P 26
Archiestown 68 K 11
Ard (Loch) 55 G 15
Ardarroch 66 D 11
Ardcharnich 66 E 10
Ardechive 60 E 13
Ardeonaig 61 H 14
Ardersier 67 H 11
Ardfern 54 D 15
Ardgay 67 G 10
Ardgour 60 D 13
Ardingly 11 T 30
Ardivachar 64 X 11
Ardleigh 23 W 28
Ardlui 54 F 15
Ardlussa 52 C 15
Ardmore Point 65 A 11
Ardnamurchan 59 B 13
Ardnave Point 52 B 16
Ardrishaig 54 D 15
Ardrossan 54 F 17
Ardvasar 65 C 12
Ardverikie Forest 61 G 13
Argyll 54 D 15
Argyll Forest Park 54 F 15
Arienas (Loch) 59 C 14
Arinagour 59 A 14
Arisaig 59 C 13
Arivruaich 70 Z 9
Arkaig (Loch) 60 E 13
Arkengarthdale 45 O 20
Arklet (Loch) 55 G 15
Arlingham 17 M 28
Arlington Court 6 I 30
Armadale (West Lothian) 55 I 16
Armadale Bay 65 C 12
Armadale (Highland) 73 H 8
Armitage 35 O 25
Armthorpe 40 Q 23
Arncliffe 39 N 21
Arncott 18 Q 28
Arnesby 28 Q 26
Arnisdale 66 D 12
Arnol 70 A 8
Arnold 36 Q 25
Arnside 44 L 21
Aros 59 B 14
Arran (Isle of) 53 E 17
Arreton 10 Q 31
Arrochar 54 F 15
Arun 11 S 31
Arundel 11 S 31
Ascot 20 R 29
Ascott House 19 R 28
Ascrib Islands 65 A 11
Asfordby 36 R 25
Ash (Kent) 13 X 30
Ash (Surrey) 19 R 30
Ash Mill 7 I 31
Ashbourne 35 O 24
Ashburton 4 I 32
Ashbury 17 P 29
Ashby de la Zouch 35 P 25
Ashcott 8 L 30
Ashford (Derbs.) 35 O 24
Ashford (Kent) 12 W 30
Ashford (Surrey) 20 S 29
Ashie (Loch) 67 H 11
Ashingdon 22 W 29
Ashington (Northumb.) 51 P 18
Ashington (West Sussex) 11 S 31
Ashover 35 P 24
Ashperton 26 M 27
Ashtead 21 T 30
Ashton-in-Makerfield 38 M 23
Ashton Keynes 17 O 29
Ashton-under-Lyne 39 N 23
Ashton-upon-Mersey 39 M 23
Ashwell 29 T 27
Askam in Furness 44 K 21
Askern 40 Q 23
Askernish 64 X 12
Askerswell 8 L 31
Askham 44 L 20
Askrigg 45 N 21
Aspatria 44 K 19
Aspley Guise 29 S 27
Assynt (Loch) 72 E 9
Aston 36 Q 23
Aston Clinton 19 R 28
Aston Rowant 18 R 28
Aston Tirrold 18 Q 29
Astwood Bank 27 O 27
Atcham 26 L 25
Athelhampton Hall 8 N 31
Athelney 7 L 30
Atherington 6 H 31
Atherstone 27 P 26
Atherton 38 M 23
Atholl (Forest of) 61 H 13
Attleborough 30 X 26
Auchenblae 63 M 13
Auchencairn 43 I 19
Auchinleck 48 H 17
Auchleven 69 M 12
Auchnagatt 69 N 11
Auchterarder 55 I 15
Auchterderran 56 K 15
Auchterhouse 62 K 14
Auchtermuchty 56 K 15
Auchtertyre 66 D 12
Auckengill 74 K 8
Audenshaw 39 N 23
Audlem 34 M 25
Audley 34 N 24
Audley End 29 U 27
Aughton (Lancs.) 38 L 23
Aughton (South Yorks.) 40 Q 23
Auldearn 67 I 11
Auldhouse 55 H 16
Aultbea 66 D 10
Aust 16 M 29
Austwick 39 M 21
Avebury 17 O 29
Aveley 21 U 29
Avening 17 N 28
Aveton Gifford 4 I 33
Aviemore 67 I 12
Avoch 67 H 11
Avon (Glen) 62 J 12
Avon (River) 9 O 31
Avon (River) (Wilts.) 09 O 31
Avon (River) (R. Severn) 27 Q 26
Avonbridge 55 I 16
Avonmouth 16 L 29
Awe (Loch) 54 E 15
Awliscombe 7 K 31
Awre 17 M 28
Axbridge 16 L 30
Axminster 8 L 31
Axmouth 5 K 31
Aylesbury 18 R 28
Aylesford 12 V 30
Aylesham 13 X 30
Aylsham 31 X 25
Aymestrey 26 L 27
Aynho 28 Q 28
Ayr 48 G 17
Aysgarth 45 O 21
Ayton 47 S 21

B

Bà (Loch) 59 C 14
Babbacombe Bay 4 J 32
Backaland 75 L 6
Backwater Reservoir 62 K 13
Baconsthorpe 31 X 25
Bacton 31 Y 25
Bacup 39 N 22
Bad a' Ghaill (Loch) 72 E 9
Bad an Sgalaig (Loch) 66 D 10
Badachro 66 C 10
Badanloch (Loch) 73 H 9
Badcaul 66 D 10
Baddidarach 72 E 9
Badenoch 61 H 13
Badluarach 72 D 10
Badminton 17 N 29
Badrallach 66 E 10
Bae Colwyn/ Colwyn Bay 33 I 24
Bagh nam Faoileann 64 Y 11
Bagillt 33 K 24
Bagshot 19 R 29
Baile Mór 59 A 15
Bainbridge 45 N 21
Bainton 41 S 22
Bakewell 35 O 24
Bala 33 J 25
Balallan 70 A 9
Balbeggie 62 J 14
Balblair 67 H 10
Balcary Point 43 I 19
Balchrick 72 E 8
Balcombe 11 T 30
Balderton 36 R 24
Baldock 29 T 28
Balemartine 58 Z 14
Balephetrish Bay 58 Z 14
Balephuil Bay 58 Z 14
Baleshare 64 X 11
Balfour 74 L 6
Balfron 55 H 15
Balintore 67 I 10
Balivanich 64 X 11
Ballabeg 42 F 21
Ballachulish 60 E 13
Ballantrae 48 E 18
Ballasalla 42 G 21
Ballater 62 K 12
Ballaugh 42 G 21
Ballingry 56 K 15
Balmaha 55 G 15
Balmedie 69 N 12
Balmoral Castle 62 K 12

ABERDEEN

Bon Accord Centre Y
George Street Y
St Nicholas Centre Y 29
St Nicholas Street YZ 30
Trinity Centre Z
Union Street Z

Broad Street Y 6
Castle Street Y 7
College Street Z 9
Craigie Loanings Y 12
Denburn Road Y 14
East North Street Y 16
Great Southern Road Z 18
Guild Street Z 19
Justice Street Y 21
Millburn Street Z 23
Rosemount Terrace Y 25
Rosemount Viaduct Y 26
St. Andrew Street Y 28
School Hill YZ 32
South Esplanade West Z 33
South Mount Street Y 34
Springbank Terrace Z 35
Spring Garden Y 36
Trinity Quay Z 37
Union Terrace Z 39
Upperkirkgate Y 40
Victoria Street Z 42
Waverley Place Z 43
Wellington Place Z 45
Wellington Road Z 47
Woolmanhill Y 48

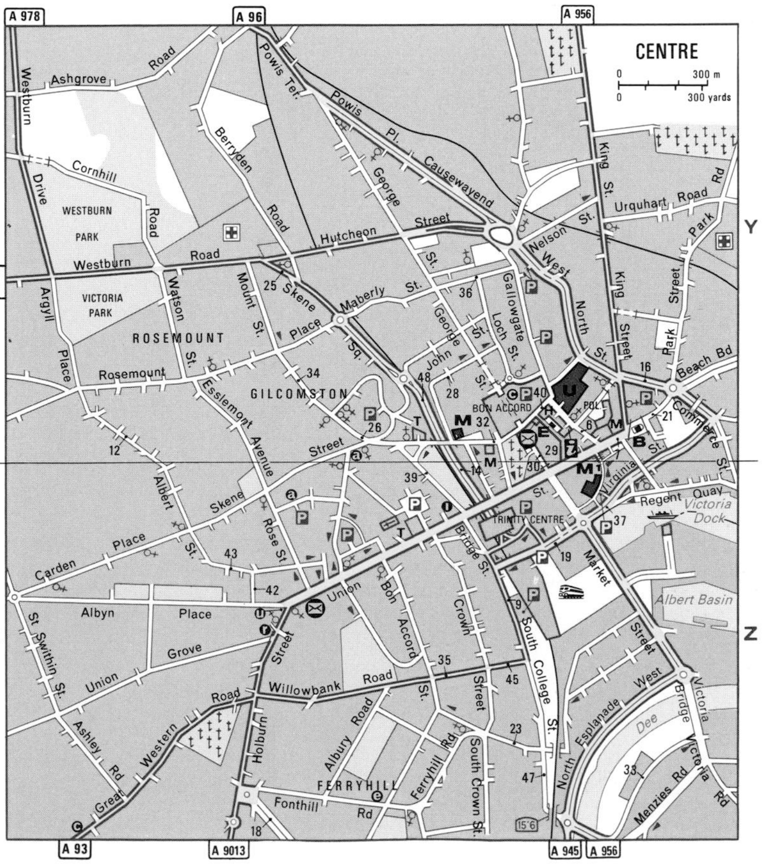

BATH
CENTRE

Gay Street . . . . **AV**
Green Street . . . . **BV** 21
Milsom Street . . . . **BV**
New Bond Street . . . . **BV** 31

Ambury . . . . **BX** 2
Argyle Street . . . . **BV** 3
Bennett Street . . . . **AV** 4
Bridge Street . . . . **BVX** 6
Broad Quay . . . . **BX** 7
Chapel Row . . . . **AVX** 9
Charles Street . . . . **AX** 10
Charlotte Street . . . . **AV** 12
Cheap Street . . . . **BX** 13
Churchill Bridge . . . . **BX** 14
Circus Place . . . . **AV** 16
Grand Parade . . . . **BX** 17
Great Stanhope
  Street . . . . **AV** 18
Guinea Lane . . . . **BV** 23
Henry Street . . . . **BX** 24
Lower Borough Walls . . . . . **BX** 26
Monmouth Place . . . . **AVX** 28
Monmouth Street . . . . **AX** 30
New Orchard Street . . . . . . **BX** 32
Nile Street . . . . **AV** 34
Northgate Street . . . . **BVX** 35
Old Bond Street . . . . **BX** 36
Orange Grove . . . . **BX** 38
Pierrepont Street . . . . **BX** 39
Quiet Street . . . . **BV** 41
Russell Street . . . . **AV** 42
Southgate Street . . . . **BX** 43
Stanley Road . . . . **BX** 45
Terrace Walk . . . . **BX** 46
Upper Borough
  Walls . . . . **BX** 48
Westgate Buildings . . . . . . **AX** 49
Westgate Street . . . . **ABX** 50
Wood Street . . . . **AV** 52
York Street . . . . **BX** 53

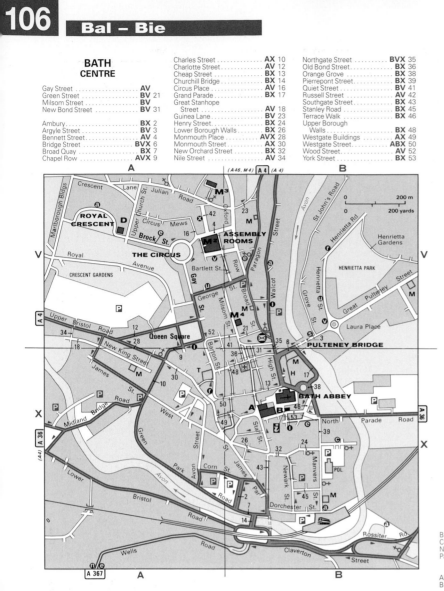

Balmullo	56	L 14	Barnby Moor			Baschurch	34	L 25
Balnakeil Bay	72	F 8	(East Riding of			Basildon (Berks.)	18	Q 29
Balvicar	54	D 15	Yorks.)	41	R 22	Basildon (Essex)	22	V 29
Bamburgh Castle	51	O 17	Barnby Dun	40	Q 23	Basingstoke	18	Q 30
Bampton			Barnby Moor			Baslow	35	P 24
(Cumbria)	44	L 20	(Notts.)	36	Q 23	Bass Rock	57	M 15
Bampton (Devon)	7	J 31	Barnet (London			Bassenthwaite	44	K 19
Bampton (Oxon.)	18	P 28	Borough)	20	T 29	Bassingham	36	S 24
Banavie	60	E 13	Barnetby-le-Wold	41	S 23	Bath	17	M 29
Banbury	28	P 27	Barnhill	68	J 11	Bathgate	55	J 16
Banchory	63	M 12	Barnoldswick	39	N 22	Batley	39	P 22
Banff	69	M 10	Barnsley	40	P 23	Battle	12	V 31
Bangor	32	H 24	Barnstaple	6	H 30	Baumber	37	T 24
Bankfoot	62	J 14	Barr	48	F 18	Bawdeswell	30	X 25
Bankhead	69	N 12	Barra	64	X 13	Bawdsey	23	Y 27
Banks	38	L 22	Barra (Sound of)	64	X 12	Bawtry	36	Q 23
Bannockburn	55	I 15	Barra Head	58	X 13	Bayble	71	B 9
Banstead	20	T 30	Barrhead	55	G 16	Bayhead	64	X 11
Banwell	16	L 30	Barrhill	48	F 18	Beachy Head	12	U 31
Bapchild	12	W 30	Barri/Barry	16	K 29	Beacon (The)	2	E 33
Bar Hill	29	U 27	Barrington Court	8	L 31	Beaconsfield	20	S 29
Barbaraville	67	H 10	Barrisdale Bay	60	D 12	Beadnell Bay	51	P 17
Barbon	45	M 21	Barrow	22	V 27	Beaford	6	H 31
Barcombe Cross	11	U 31	Barrow-in-Furness	38	K 21	Beaminster	8	L 31
Bardney	37	T 24	Barrow-upon-			Beamish Hall	46	P 19
Bardsea	38	K 21	Humber	41	S 22	Bearsden	55	G 16
Bardsey Island	32	F 25	Barrow-upon-Soar	36	Q 25	Bearsted	12	V 30
Barfreston	13	X 30	Barrowby	36	R 25	Beattock	49	J 18
Bargoed	16	K 28	Barrowford	39	N 22	Beauchief	35	P 24
Barham	13	X 30	Barry (Angus)	63	L 14	Beaulieu	9	P 31
Barking and			Barry/Barri (Vale of			Beauly	67	G 11
Dagenham			Glamorgan)	16	K 29	Beauly Firth	67	G 11
(London Borough)	21	U 29	Bartestree	26	M 27	Beaumaris	32	H 24
Barkston	36	S 25	Barton (Lancs.)	38	L 22	Beaupré Castle	16	J 29
Barkway	22	U 28	Barton (Staffs.)	35	O 25	Bebington	34	L 23
Barkwith	37	T 24	Barton in the Clay	29	S 28	Beccles	31	Y 26
Barlaston	35	N 25	Barton Mills	30	V 26	Beckingham	36	R 23
Barlborough	36	Q 24	Barton-on-Sea	9	P 31	Beckington	17	N 30
Barley	29	U 27	Barton-upon-			Beckton	21	U 29
Barmouth/			Humber	41	S 22	Bedale	46	P 21
Abermaw	32	H 25	Barvas	70	A 8	Beddgelert	32	H 24
Barmouth Bay	32	H 25	Barwell	28	P 26	Beddingham	11	U 31
Barmston	41	T 21	Barwick-			Bedford	29	S 27
Barnard Castle	45	O 20	in-Elmet	40	P 22	Bedford Levels	29	T 26
						Bedfordshire		
						(County)	29	S 27
						Bedgebury		
						Pinetum	12	V 30
						Bedlington	51	P 18
						Bedwas	16	K 29
						Bedworth	27	P 26
						Bee (Loch)	64	X 11
						Beer	5	K 31
						Beeston	36	Q 25
						Beeswing	49	I 18
						Beinn a' Ghlò	61	I 13
						Beinn a'		
						Mheadhoin	66	F 12
						Beinn Dearg		
						(Perthshire and		
						Kinross)	61	I 13
						Beinn Dearg		
						(Highland)	66	F 10
						Beinn Heasgarnich	61	G 14
						Beinn Ime	54	F 15
						Beith	55	G 16
						Belbroughton	27	N 26
						Belford	51	O 17
						Bellingham	51	N 18
						Bellshill	55	H 16
						Belmont	75	R 1
						Belnahua	52	C 15
						Belper	35	P 24
						Belsay	51	O 18
						Belton (North Lincs.)	41	R 23
						Belton House		
						(Lincs.)	36	S 25
						Belton (Norfolk)	31	Y 26
						Belvoir	36	R 25
						Bembridge	10	Q 31
						Bempton	41	T 21
						Ben Alder	61	G 13
						Ben Armine Forest	73	H 9

Ben Chonzie	61	I 14	Berriew	25	K 26
Ben Cruachan	60	E 14	Berrington Hall	26	L 27
Ben-damph Forest	66	D 11	Berrow	7	K 30
Ben Hope	72	G 8	Berry Head	4	J 32
Ben Klibreck	73	G 9	Berry Hill	16	M 28
Ben Lawers	61	H 14	Berrynarbor	6	H 30
Ben Ledi	55	H 15	Bervie Bay	63	N 13
Ben Lomond	55	G 15	Berwick-		
Ben Loyal	73	G 8	upon-Tweed	57	O 16
Ben Macdui	61	I 12	Berwyn	33	J 25
Ben More (Argyll			Bethersden	12	W 30
and Bute)	59	C 14	Bethesda	32	H 24
Ben More (Stirling)	61	G 14	Bettyhill	73	H 8
Ben More Assynt	72	F 9	Betws-y-Coed	33	I 24
Ben Nevis	60	E 13	Beverley	41	S 22
Ben Starav	60	E 14	Bewcastle	50	L 18
Ben Vorlich	55	H 14	Bewdley	26	N 26
Ben Wyvis	67	G 10	Bexhill	12	V 31
Benbecula	64	X 11	Bexley (London		
Benderloch	60	E 14	Borough)	21	U 29
Benenden	12	V 30	Beyton	21	W 27
Benfleet	22	V 29	Bhaid-Luachraich		
Benigton	37	U 25	(Loch)	66	D 10
Benington	37	U 25	Bhealaich (Loch a')	72	G 9
Benllech	32	H 24	Bhraoin (Loch a')	66	E 10
Benmore Lodge	72	F 9	Bhrollum (Loch)	70	A 10
Benson	18	Q 29	Bibury	17	O 28
Bentley	40	Q 23	Bicester	18	Q 28
Beoraid (Loch)	60	D 13	Bickington	4	I 32
Bere Alston	3	H 32	Bickleigh	7	J 31
Bere Regis	8	N 31	Bicton gardens	4	K 31
Berkeley	17	M 28	Biddenden	12	V 30
Berkhamsted	19	S 28	Biddestone	17	N 29
Berkshire (County)	18	P 29	Biddulph	35	N 24
Berneray (near			Bidean nam Bian	60	E 14
Barra)	58	X 13	Bideford	6	H 30
Berneray (near			Bidford	27	O 27
North Uist)	64	Y 10	Bieldside	69	N 12
Bernisdale	65	B 11	Bierton	19	R 28

BIRMINGHAM
CENTRE

Bull Ring Centre . . . . **KZ**
Corporation Street . . . . **KYZ**
New Street . . . . **JKZ**
Paradise Forum Shopping
  Centre . . . . **JZ**
Albert Street . . . . **KZ** 2
Bull Street . . . . **KY** 13
Dale End . . . . **KZ** 21
Hall Street . . . . **JY** 29
Holloway Circus . . . . **JZ** 32
James Watt Queensway . . . **KY** 35
Jennen's Road . . . . **KY** 36
Lancaster Circus . . . . **KY** 39
Lancaster Street . . . . **KY** 41
Masshouse Circus . . . . **KY** 43
Moor Street
  Queensway . . . . **KZ** 46
Navigation Street . . . . **JZ** 49
Newton Street . . . . **KY** 52
Paradise Circus . . . . **JZ** 56
Priory Queensway . . . . **KY** 57
St Chads Circus . . . . **JKY** 62
St Chads Ringway . . . . **KY** 63
St Martin's Circus . . . . **KZ** 64
Shadwell Street . . . . **KY** 70
Smallbrook
  Queensway . . . . **KZ** 71
Snow Hill Queensway . . . . **KY** 73
Summer Row . . . . **JY** 77
Temple Row . . . . **KZ** 82
Waterloo Street . . . . **JZ** 84

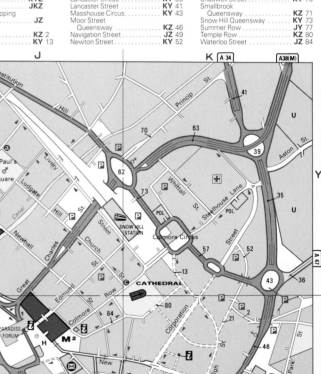

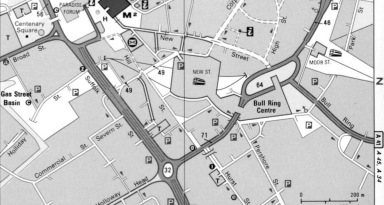

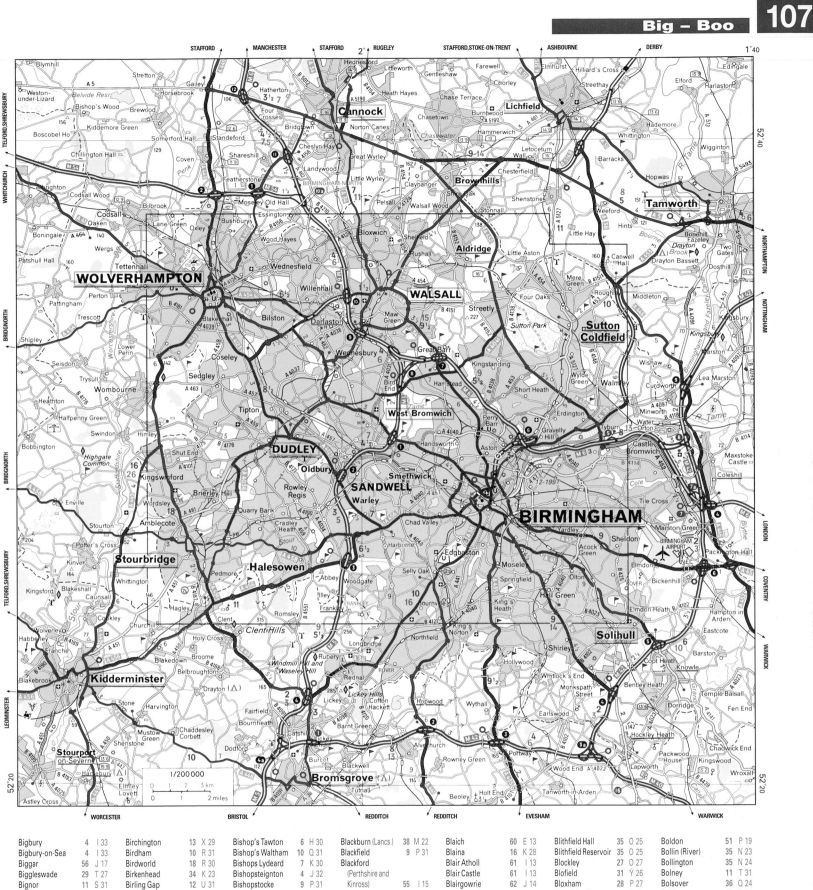

Bigbury	4 I 33	Birchington	13 X 29	Bishop's Tawton	6 H 30	Blackburn (Lancs.)	38 M 22	Blaich	60 E 13	Blithfield Hall	35 O 25	Boldon	51 P 19
Bigbury-on-Sea	4 I 33	Birdham	10 R 31	Bishop's Waltham	10 Q 31	Blackfield	9 P 31	Blaina	16 K 28	Blithfield Reservoir	35 O 25	Bollin (River)	35 N 23
Biggar	56 J 17	Birdworld	18 R 30	Bishops Lydeard	7 K 30	Blackford		Blair Atholl	61 I 13	Blockley	27 O 27	Bollington	35 N 24
Biggleswade	29 T 27	Birkenhead	34 K 23	Bishopsteignton	4 J 32	(Perthshire and		Blair Castle	61 I 13	Blofield	31 Y 26	Bolney	11 T 31
Bignor	11 S 31	Birling Gap	12 U 31	Bishopstoke	9 P 31	Kinross)	55 I 15	Blairgowrie	62 J 14	Bloxham	28 P 27	Bolsover	36 Q 24
Bildeston	23 W 27	Birmingham	27 O 26	Bishopston	15 I 28	Blackford (Cumbria)	50 L 19	Blakeney (Glos.)	17 M 28	Blue John Cavern	35 O 23	Boltby	46 Q 21
Bill of Portland	8 M 32	Birnam	62 J 14	Bishopstone	17 P 29	Blacklunans	62 J 13	Blakeney (Norfolk)	30 X 25	Bluemull Sound	75 Q 1	Bolton	39 M 23
Billericay	22 V 29	Birsay	74 K 6	Bishopthorpe	40 Q 22	Blackmoor Gate	6 I 30	Blakesley	28 Q 27	Blyth (Northumb.)	51 P 18	Bolton Abbey	39 O 22
Billesdon	35 R 26	Birsemore	62 L 12	Bishopton	55 G 16	Blackness Castle	56 J 15	Blandford Forum	8 N 31	Blyth (Notts.)	36 Q 23	Bolton-le-Sands	38 L 21
Billingborough	37 S 25	Birstall	28 Q 25	Bix	18 R 29	Blackpool	38 K 22	Blarnalearoch	66 E 10	Blythburgh	31 Y 27	Bolton-upon-
Billinge	38 L 23	Birtley	46 P 19	Blaby	28 Q 26	Blackridge	55 I 16	Blawith	44 K 21	Blyton	41 R 23	Dearne	40 Q 23
Billingham	46 Q 20	Birtsmorton Court	26 N 27	Black Bay	53 D 17	Blackthorn	18 Q 28	Blaydon	51 O 19	Bo' Ness	55 J 15	Bonar Bridge	67 G 10
Billinghay	37 T 24	Bishop Auckland	46 P 20	Black Down Hills	7 K 31	Blackwater (River)	23 W 28	Bleaklow Hill	39 O 23	Boarhills	57 L 15	Bonawe Quarries	60 E 14
Billingshurst	11 S 30	Bishop Monkton	40 P 21	Black Isle	67 G 11	Blackwater		Blean	13 X 30	Boat of Garten	67 I 12	Boncath	24 G 27
Bilsington	12 W 30	Bishop's Castle	26 L 26	Black Mount	60 F 14	Reservoir	60 F 13	Blenheim Palace	18 P 28	Bocking	22 V 28	Bonhill	55 G 16
Bilsthorpe	36 Q 24	Bishop's Caundle	8 M 31	Black Mountain	15 I 28	Blackwaterfoot	53 D 17	Bletchley	28 R 27	Boddam	69 O 11	Bonnybridge	55 I 16
Bilston	27 N 26	Bishop's Cleeve	27 N 28	Black Mountains	16 K 28	Blackwood	16 K 29	Blewbury	18 Q 29	Bodenham	26 L 27	Bonnyrigg	56 K 16
Binbrook	41 T 23	Bishop's Nympton	6 I 31	Black Water		Bladnoch	48 G 19	Blickling Hall	31 X 25	Bodiam Castle	12 V 30	Bont-faen/
Binfield	19 R 29	Bishop's Palace		Valley	66 F 11	Bladon	18 P 28	Blidworth	36 Q 24	Bodmin	3 F 32	Cowbridge	16 J 29
Bingham	36 R 25	(near St. David's)	14 E 28	Blackburn		Blaenau Ffestiniog	32 I 25	Blindley Heath	19 T 30	Bodmin Moor	3 G 32	Boosbeck	47 R 20
Bingley	39 O 22	Bishop's Palace		(Aberdeenshire)	69 N 12	Blaenavon	16 K 28	Blisland	3 F 32	Bodnant Garden	33 I 24	Bootle (Cumbria)	43 J 21
Binham	30 W 25	(near Tenby)	14 F 28	Blackburn (West		Blaengarw	15 J 29	Blisworth	28 R 27	Bognor Regis	11 R 31	Bootle
Binns (The)	56 J 16	Bishop's Stortford	22 U 28	Lothian)	56 J 16	Blagdon	16 L 30	Blithe	35 O 25	Boisdale (Loch)	64 Y 12	(Merseyside)	38 K 23

BLACKPOOL
CENTRE

Church Street

Abingdon Street	2
Adelaide Street	3
Caunce Street	7
Clifton Street	12
Cookson Street	14
Deansgate	15
George Street	17
Grosvenor Street	21
High Street	22
King Street	23
Lark Hill Street	24
New Bonny Street	25
Pleasant Street	27
South King St	35
Talbot Square	39
Topping Street	40

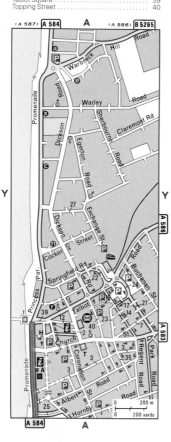

Border Forest Park (The)	57	M 18
Bordon Camp	10	R 30
Boreham	22	V 28
Boreham Street	12	V 31
Borehamwood	20	T 29
Borgue	43	H 19

BOURNEMOUTH
CENTRE

Commercial Road	**CY**	13
Old Christchurch Road	**DY**	
Square (The)	**CY**	63
Westover Road	**DZ**	75
Branksome Wood Road	**CY**	9
Durley Road	**CZ**	17
Exeter Road	**CDZ**	20
Fir Vale Road	**DY**	23
Gervis Place	**DY**	24
Hinton Road	**DZ**	27
Lansdowne (The)	**DY**	28
Lansdowne Road	**DY**	30
Madeira Road	**DY**	34
Manor Road	**EY**	35
Meyrick Road	**EYZ**	36
Post Office Road	**CY**	43
Priory Road	**CZ**	45
Richmond Hill	**CY**	47
Russell Cotes Road	**DZ**	49
St. Michael's Road	**CZ**	51
St. Paul's Road	**EY**	52
St. Peter's Road	**DY**	53
St. Stephen's Road	**CY**	55
St. Swithuns Road South	**EY**	56
Suffolk Road	**CY**	64
Triangle (The)	**CY**	67
Upper Hinton Road	**DZ**	68
West Cliff Promenade	**CZ**	71

Borness	43	H 19
Borough Green	21	U 30
Boroughbridge	40	P 21
Borrobol Forest	73	H 9
Borrowash	35	P 25
Borth	24	H 26
Borve (Barra Isle)	64	X 13
Borve (Isle of Lewis)	70	A 8
Bosbury	26	M 27
Boscastle	3	F 31
Boscombe	9	O 31
Bosham	10	R 31
Bosherston	14	F 29
Boston	37	T 25
Boston Spa	40	P 22
Botesdale	30	W 26
Bothel	44	K 19
Bothwell	55	H 16
Botley	10	Q 31
Bottesford	36	R 25
Bottisham	29	U 27
Boughton	36	Q 24
Boughton House	28	R 26
Boughton Street	12	W 30
Boultham	36	S 24
Bourne	37	S 25
Bournemouth	9	O 31
Bourton	8	N 30
Bourton-on-the-Water	17	O 28
Bovey Tracey	4	I 32
Bovingdon	19	S 28
Bowerchalke	9	O 30
Bowes	45	N 20
Bowhill	50	L 17
Bowland (Forest of)	38	M 22
Bowmore	52	B 16
Bowness-on-Windermere	44	L 20
Bowness-on-Solway	44	K 19
Bowood House	17	N 29
Box	17	N 29
Box Hill	20	T 30
Boxford	23	W 27
Boxworth	29	T 27
Brabourne Lees	12	W 30
Bracadale (Loch)	65	A 12
Bracebridge Heath	36	S 24
Brackley	28	Q 27
Bracknell	19	R 29
Braco	55	I 15
Bradan Resr (Loch)	48	G 18
Bradfield	18	Q 29
Bradford	39	O 22
Bradford Abbas	8	M 31
Bradford-on-Avon	17	N 29
Brading	10	Q 31

Bradwell	35	O 24
Bradwell-on-Sea	23	W 28
Bradworthy	6	G 31
Brae	75	P 2
Brae Roy Lodge	60	F 13
Braemar	62	J 12
Braeriach	61	I 12
Braich y Pwll	32	F 25
Bràigh Mór	70	Y 9
Brailes	27	P 27
Brailsford	35	P 25
Braintree	22	V 28
Braishfield	9	P 30
Braithwell	40	Q 23
Bramcote	36	Q 25
Bramfield	31	Y 27
Bramford	23	X 27
Bramhall	35	N 23
Bramham	40	P 22
Bramhope	39	P 22
Bramley (South Yorks.)	36	Q 23
Bramley (Surrey)	19	S 30
Brampton (Cambs.)	29	T 27
Brampton (Cumbria)	50	L 19
Brampton (South Yorks.)	40	P 23
Brampton (Suffolk)	31	Y 26
Brancaster	30	V 25
Branderburgh	68	K 10
Brandesburton	41	T 22
Brandon (Durham)	46	P 19
Brandon (Suffolk)	30	V 26
Branscombe	5	K 31
Bransgore	9	O 31
Branston	37	S 24
Bratton Fleming	6	I 30
Braughing	22	U 28
Braunston	28	R 26
Braunstone	28	Q 26
Braunton	6	H 30
Bray-on-Thames	18	R 29
Bray Shop	3	G 32
Brayton	40	Q 22
Breadalbane	61	G 14
Bream	17	M 28
Breamore House	9	O 31
Breasclete	70	Z 9
Breaston	36	Q 25
Brechin	63	M 13
Breckland	30	V 26
Brecon/Aberhonddu	25	J 28
Brecon Beacons National Park	15	J 28
Bredbury	39	N 23
Brede	12	V 31
Bredenbury	26	M 27
Bredon	27	N 27
Bredwardine	26	L 27

BRADFORD
CENTRE

Bank Street	**AZ**	
Broadway	**BZ**	8
Charles Street	**BZ**	13
Kirkgate Centre	**AZ**	26
Market Street	**BZ**	28
Canal Road	**BZ**	10
Cheapside	**BZ**	14
Darley Street	**AZ**	18
Drewton Road	**AZ**	19
East Parade	**BZ**	22
Harris Street	**BZ**	23
Ivegate	**AZ**	25
Otley Road	**BZ**	31
Peckover Street	**BZ**	32
Prince's Way	**AZ**	33
School Street	**BZ**	35
Stott Hill	**BZ**	39

Brenchley	12	V 30	
Brendon Hills	7	J 30	
Brenig Reservoir	33	J 24	
Brent (London Borough)	20	T 29	
Brent Knoll	16	L 30	
Brent Pelham	22	U 28	
Brentwood	21	U 29	
Brenzett	12	W 30	
Bressay	75	Q 3	
Bretherton	38	L 22	
Brewlands Bridge	62	K 13	
Brewood	27	N 25	
Bride	42	G 20	
Bridestowe	3	H 31	
Bridge	13	X 30	
Bridge of Allan	55	I 15	
Bridge of Avon	68	J 11	
Bridge of Craigisla	62	K 13	
Bridge of Don	69	N 12	
Bridge of Earn	56	J 14	
Bridge of Forss	73	J 8	
Bridge of Gairn	62	K 12	
Bridge of Orchy	60	F 14	
Bridgemary	10	Q 31	
Bridgend/Pen-y-bont (Bridgend)	15	J 29	
Bridgend (Perthshire and Kinross)	62	J 14	
Bridgend (Islay)	52	B 16	
Bridgend of Lintrathen	62	K 13	
Bridgnorth	26	M 26	
Bridgwater	7	L 30	
Bridlington	41	T 21	
Bridport	8	L 31	
Brierfield	39	N 22	
Brierley Hill	27	N 26	
Brigg	41	S 23	
Brighouse	39	O 22	
Brighstone	9	P 32	
Brightlingsea	23	X 28	
Brighton	11	T 31	
Brightwell	18	Q 29	
Brigstock	29	S 26	
Brill	18	Q 28	
Brimfield	26	L 27	
Brimham Rocks	39	O 21	
Brimington	35	P 24	
Brinkburn Priory	51	O 18	
Brinklow	28	P 26	
Brinkworth	17	O 29	
Brinyan	74	L 6	
Brisley	30	W 25	
Bristol	17	M 29	
Briston	30	X 25	
Briton Ferry	15	I 29	
Brittle (Loch)	65	B 12	
Brixham	4	J 32	
Brixworth	28	R 27	
Brize Norton	18	P 28	
Broad Bay	71	B 9	
Broad Blunsdon	17	O 29	
Broad Chalke	9	O 30	
Broad Law	49	J 17	

Broadclyst	4	J 31
Broadford	65	C 12
Broadlands	9	P 31
Broadmayne	8	M 31
Broadstairs	13	Y 29
Broadstone	9	O 31
Broadwas	26	M 27
Broadway	27	O 27
Broadwey	8	M 32
Broadwindsor	8	L 31
Broch of Gurness	49	J 17
Brockenhurst	9	P 31
Brockley	16	L 29
Brockworth	17	N 28
Brodick	53	E 17
Brodick Castle	53	E 17
Brodick Bay	53	E 17
Brodie Castle	67	I 11
Brolass	59	B 14
Bromborough	34	L 24
Brome	31	X 26
Bromfield	26	L 26
Bromham	17	N 29
Bromley (London Borough)	21	U 29
Brompton (near Northallerton)	46	P 20
Brompton-by-Sawdon	47	S 21
Brompton (Kent)	12	V 29
Brompton on Swale	45	O 20
Brompton Regis	7	J 30
Bromsgrove	27	N 26
Bromyard	26	M 27
Bronllys	25	K 27
Brooke	31	Y 26
Brookland	12	W 30
Brookmans Park	19	T 28
Broom (Loch)	66	E 10
Broomfield	7	K 30
Broomhaugh	51	O 19
Brora	73	H 9
Brotherton	40	Q 22
Brotton	47	R 20
Brough	45	N 20
Brough Head	74	J 6
Brough Lodge	75	R 2
Brough of Birsay	74	J 6
Broughton (Cumbria)	43	J 19
Broughton (North Lincs.)	40	S 23
Broughton (Hants.)	9	P 30
Broughton (Lancs.)	38	L 22
Broughton (Northants.)	28	R 26
Broughton (Oxon.)	28	P 27
Broughton-in-Furness	38	K 21
Broughty Ferry	62	L 14
Brownhills	27	O 26
Brownsea Island	9	O 31
Broxbourne	19	T 28
Broxburn	56	J 16
Bruichladdich	52	A 16
Brundall	31	Y 26

Brushford	7	J 30
Bruton	8	M 30
Brymbo	33	K 24
Brympton d'Evercy	8	L 31
Brynamman	15	I 28
Brynbuga/Usk	16	L 28
Bryncethin	15	J 29
Bryn-Henllan	14	F 27
Brynmawr	16	K 28
Bubwith	41	R 22
Buchlyvie	55	H 15
Buckden (Cambs.)	29	T 27
Buckden (North Yorks.)	45	N 21
Buckfast Abbey	4	I 32
Buckfastleigh	4	I 32
Buckhaven	56	K 15
Buckie	68	L 10
Buckingham	28	Q 27
Buckinghamshire (County)	18	R 28
Buckland (Herts.)	29	T 28
Buckland (Oxon.)	18	P 28
Buckland Abbey	3	H 32
Buckland Newton	8	M 31
Buckland St. Mary	7	K 31
Bucklers Hard	9	P 31
Buckley/Bwcle	33	K 24
Buckminster	36	R 25
Bucknell	26	L 26
Bucksburn	69	N 12
Bude	6	G 31
Budleigh Salterton	4	K 32
Bugle	3	F 32
Bugthorpe	40	R 21
Buildwas Abbey	26	M 26
Builth Wells/Llanfair-ym-Muallt	25	J 27
Bulford	17	O 30
Bulkington	27	P 26
Bulwell	36	Q 24
Bunarkaig	60	F 13
Bunessan	59	B 15
Bungay	31	Y 26
Buntingford	29	T 28
Burbage (Leics.)	28	P 26
Burbage (Wilts.)	17	O 29
Bures	23	W 28
Burford	18	P 28
Burgess Hill	11	T 31
Burgh-by-Sands	44	K 19
Burgh-le-Marsh	37	U 24
Burghead	68	J 10
Burghley House	29	S 26
Burley-in-Wharfedale	39	O 22
Burneside	44	L 20
Burnham	20	S 29
Burnham Market	30	W 25
Burnham-on-Crouch	23	W 29
Burnham-on-Sea	7	L 30
Burnhaven	69	O 11
Burniston	47	S 21
Burnley	39	N 22

BRIGHTON AND HOVE

Churchill Square		
Shopping Centre	**BYZ**	
London Road	**CX**	
North Street	**CZ**	

Western Road	**ABY**	
Adelaide Crescent	**AY**	2
Brunswick Place	**AY**	3
Brunswick Square	**AYZ**	4
Chatham Place	**BX**	6
Denmark Road	**BY**	7
East Street	**CZ**	8
Gladstone Terrace	**CX**	12

Gloucester Place	**CY**	13
Gloucester Road	**CY**	14
Goldsmid Road	**BX**	15
Grand Junction Road	**CZ**	16
Market Place	**CX**	20
Marlborough Place	**CY**	21
Montpelier Place	**BY**	22
Old Steine	**CZ**	23
Pavillon Parade	**CZ**	26

Richmond Place	**CY**	27
Richmond Terrace	**CX**	28
St. George's Place	**CY**	30
St. Peter's Place	**CX**	31
Terminus Road	**BCX**	32
Upper Lewes		
Road	**CX**	33
Waterloo Place	**CX**	39
York Place	**CY**	42

BRISTOL CENTRE

Broadmead	**DY**	
Fairfax Street	**CDY**	35
Galleries'		
Shopping Centre (The)	**DY**	
Horse Fair (The)	**DY**	
Merchant Street	**DY**	47
Nelson Street	**CY**	51
Park Street	**CY**	

Bedminster Parade	**CZ**	5
Bridgehead	**CZ**	9
Broad Quay	**CYZ**	13
Broad Street	**CY**	14
College Green	**CZ**	30
College Street	**CYZ**	32
Colston Avenue	**CY**	33
Frog Lane	**CY**	37
Haymarket	**DY**	38
High Street	**CDY**	39
Lower Castle Street	**DY**	43
Marlborough Street	**DY**	46

Narrow Plain	**DY**	50
North Street	**DY**	52
Old Market Street	**DY**	54
Passage Street	**DY**	55
Quay Street	**CY**	58
Queen Charlotte Street	**CZ**	60
Redcliffe Mead Lane	**DZ**	61
Rupert Street	**CY**	65
St. Augustine's Parade	**CY**	66
Temple Gate	**DZ**	75
Trenchard Street	**CY**	77
Wine Street	**DY**	80

Burntisland	56	K 15				Calne	17	N 29
Burpham	20	S 31	**C**			Calow	35	P 24
Burravoe	75	Q 2	Cabrach	68	K 12	Calstock	3	H 32
Burray	74	L 7	Cadair Idris	32	I 25	Calvay	64	Y 12
Burrelton	62	K 14	Cadhay	4	K 31	Calvine	61	I 13
Burrington	6	I 31	Cadishead	34	M 23	Cam	29	U 27
Burrow Head	42	G 19	Cadnam	9	P 31	Cam Loch	72	E 9
Burry Port/			Caerdydd/Cardiff	16	K 29	Camas Chil		
Porth Tywyn	15	H 28	Caerffili/Caerphilly	16	K 29	Mhalieu	60	D 14
Burscough	38	L 23	Caerfyrddin/			Camber	12	W 31
Burscough Bridge	38	L 23	Carmarthen	15	H 28	Camberley	18	R 30
Bursledon	10	Q 31	Caergwrle	33	K 24	Camborne	2	E 33
Burslem	35	N 24	Caergybi/Holyhead	32	G 24	Cambrian		
Burton	44	L 21	Caerlaverock Castle	49	J 19	Mountains	25	I 27
Burton Agnes	41	T 21	Caerleon	16	L 29	Cambridge	29	U 27
Burton Bradstock	8	L 31	Caernarfon	32	H 24	Cambridgeshire		
Burton Constable			Caernarfon Bay	32	G 24	(County)	29	T 26
Hall	41	T 22	Caerphilly/Caerffili	16	K 29	Cambusbarron	55	I 15
Burton in Lonsdale	38	M 21	Caersws	25	J 26	Camden (London		
Burton Joyce	36	Q 25	Caerwent	16	L 29	Borough)	20	T 29
Burton Latimer	28	R 26	Cailliness Point	42	F 19	Camelford	3	F 32
Burton Leonard	40	P 21	Cairn Edward			Cammachmore	63	N 12
Burton Pidsea	41	T 22	Forest	49	H 18	Campbeltown	53	D 17
Burton-upon-			Cairn Gorm	62	J 12	Campsie Fells	55	H 15
Stather	41	R 23	Cairn Table	49	H 17	Canewdon	23	W 29
Burton-upon-Trent	35	P 25	Cairn Toul	61	I 12	Canisbay	74	K 8
Burwarton	26	M 26	Cairnborrow	68	L 11	Canna	65	A 12
Burwell (Cambs.)	29	U 27	Cairndow	54	F 15	Cannich	66	F 11
Burwell (Lincs.)	37	U 24	Cairnpapple Hill	56	J 16	Cannich (Glen)	66	F 11
Bury	39	N 23	Cairnryan	48	E 19	Cannington	7	K 30
Bury St. Edmunds	22	W 27	Cairnsmore			Cannock	27	N 25
Busby	55	H 16	of Carsphairn	49	H 18	Canonbie	50	L 18
Buscot	17	P 28	Cairnsmore of Fleet	48	G 19	Canterbury	13	X 30
Bushey	20	S 29	Cairraig Fhada	52	B 17	Canvey Island	22	V 29
Bute (Kyles of)	54	E 16	Caister-on-Sea	31	Z 26	Caol	60	E 13
Bute (Island of)	54	E 16	Caistor	41	T 23	Caolas a' Mhòrain	64	Y 10
Bute (Sound of)	54	E 16	Calbourne	9	P 31	Caolis	58	X 13
Butt of Lewis	71	B 8	Caldbeck	44	K 19	Caolisport (Loch)	53	D 16
Buttermere	44	K 20	Caldecott	28	R 26	Cape Cornwall	2	C 33
Buxted	12	U 31	Calder (Loch)	73	J 8	Cape Wrath	72	E 8
Buxton (Derbs.)	35	O 24	Calder Bridge	43	J 20	Capel	11	T 30
Buxton (Norfolk)	31	X 25	Caldercruix	55	I 16	Capel Curig	33	I 24
Bwcle/Buckley	33	K 24	Caldey Island	14	F 29	Capel Garmon	33	I 24
Bwlch	16	K 28	Calf of Man	42	F 21	Capel Le Ferne	13	X 30
Bwlch Oerddrws	33	I 25	Calfsound	74	L 6	Capel St. Mary	23	X 27
Bwlch-y-Groes	15	I 28	Calgary Bay	59	B 14	Capesthorne Hall	34	N 24
Bwlch-y-Sarnau	25	J 26	Caliach Point	59	B 14	Caputh	62	J 14
Byfield	28	Q 27	Callander	55	H 15	Cara Island	53	C 17
Byfleet	20	S 30	Callater (Glen)	62	J 13	Carbis Bay	2	D 33
Byland Abbey	46	Q 21	Callington	3	H 32	Carbost	65	A 12

CAMBRIDGE CENTRE

Grafton Centre .... Y
Lion Yard Centre .... Z
Market Hill .... Z 18
Market Street .... Y 19
Petty Cury .... Z 27
Rose Crescent .... Z 28
St. Andrew's St. .... Z 30
Sidney Street .... Y 34
Trinity Street .... Y 36

Bridge Street .... Y 2
Corn Exchange
  Street. .... Z 6
Downing Street .... Z 7
Free School Lane .... Z 12

Hobson Street .... Y 14
King's Parade .... Y 15
Madingley Rd .... Y 16
Magdalene St. .... Y 17
Milton Road .... Y 20
Newmarket Road .... Y 21
Northampton
  Street .... Y 22
Parker Street .... Y 23
Peas Hill .... Y 25
Pembroke Street .... Y 26
St John's Street .... Y 31
Short Street .... Y 32
Trumpington Road ...... Z 37
Wheeler Street .... Z 39

COLLEGES

CHRIST'S .... Y A
CLARE .... Z B
CORPUS
  CHRISTI .... Z C
DARWIN .... Z D
DOWNING .... Z E
EMMANUEL .... Z F
GONVILLE
  AND CAIUS .... Y G
HARVEY COURT .... Z K
HUGUES HALL .... Z J
JESUS .... Y K
KING'S .... Z

LUCY
  CAVENDISH. .... Y O
MAGDALENE .... Y N
PEMBROKE .... Z N
PETERHOUSE .... Z
QUEENS' .... Z
RIDSLEY HALL .... Z Q
ST CATHARINE'S ...... Z R
ST EDMUNDS
  HOUSE. .... Y U
ST JOHN'S. .... Y
SIDNEY SUSSEX. ...... Y P
TRINITY .... Y V
TRINITY HALL .... Y V
WESTMINSTER .... Y W

CARDIFF
CAERDYDD

Duke Street .... BZ 26
High Street. .... BZ
Queen Street .... BZ
Queens Arcade
  Shopping Centre ...... BZ 54
St. David's Shopping Centre ... BZ
St. Mary Street .... BZ

Working Street .... BZ 67
Castle Street .... BZ 9
Cathays Terrace .... BY 10
Central Square .... BZ 12
Church Street .... BZ 14
City Hall Road .... BY 15
College Road .... BY 20
Corbett Road .... BY 21
Customhouse Street .... BZ 23
David Street .... BZ 25
Dumfries Place .... BY 28

Greyfriars Road .... BY 29
Guilford Street .... BZ 30
Hayes (The). .... BZ 32
King Edward VII Avenue . BY 36
Mary Ann Street .... BZ 39
Moira Terrace .... BZ 42
Nantes (Boulevard de) .. BZ 44
Penarth Road .... BZ 49
St. Andrews Place ...... BY 56
St. John Street .... BZ 58
Station Terrace .... BY 61
Stuttgart Street .... BY 62

CANTERBURY

Burgate .... Y
Butchery Lane .... Y 5
Guildhall Street .... Y 6
High Street .... Y 8
Mercery Lane .... Y 12

Palace Street .... Y
St. George's Street ..... Z 17
St. Margaret's Street ... YZ 18
St. Peter's Street ...... Y 20

Beercart Lane .... YZ 2
Borough (The) .... Y 4
Lower Bridge Street .... Z 9

Lower Chantry Lane ..... Z 10
Rhodaus Town .... Z 13
Rosemary Lane .... Z 14
St. George's Place ...... Z 16
St. Mary's Street .... Z 19
St. Radigund's Street ... Y 21
Upper Bridge Street .... Z 23
Watling Street. .... Z 25

Cardiff/Caerdydd	16 K 29	Carhampton	7 J 30	Carlton (Notts.)	36 Q 25
Cardigan/Aberteifi	24 G 27	Carinish	64 Y 11	Carlton (South.
Cardigan Bay	24 G 26	Carisbrooke	10 Q 31	Yorks.)	40 Q 22
Cardinham	3 G 32	Cark	44 L 21	Carlton Colville	31 Z 26
Cardross	54 G 16	Carlisle	44 L 19	Carlton in Lindrick	36 Q 23
Carew	14 F 28	Carloway	70 Z 9	Carlton-on-Trent	36 R 24

CARLISLE

Botchergate .... BZ
Castle Street .... BY 6
English Street .... BY 13
Scotch Street .... BY 19

Annetwell Street .... AY 2

Bridge Street .... AY 3
Brunswick Street .... BZ 4
Cecil Street .... BZ 5
Charlotte Street .... AZ 7
Chiswick Street .... BY 8
Church Street .... AY 10
Eden Bridge .... BY 12
Lonsdale Street .... BY 14
Lowther Street .... BY 15

Port Road .... AY 16
St. Marys Gate .... BY 17
St. Nicholas Street ..... BZ 18
Spencer Street .... BY 20
Tait Street .... BZ 22
Victoria Viaduct .... ABZ 24
West Tower Street ..... BY 26
West Walls .... ABY 27
Wigton Road .... AZ 29

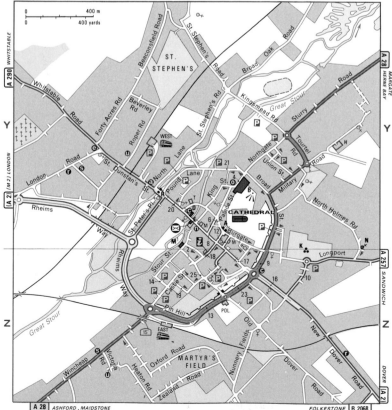

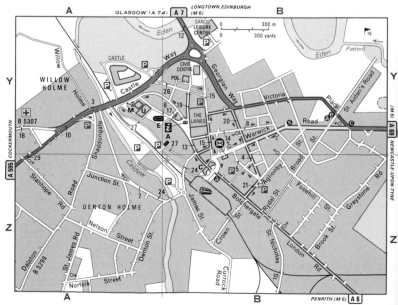

CHESTER

Bridge Street 3	Boughton 2
Eastgate Street 5	Frodsham Street 6
Northgate Street 18	Grosvenor Park Road 7
Watergate Street	Grosvenor Street 8
	Handbridge 10
	Little St. John Street 12
	Liverpool Road 13

Lower Bridge Street 15	
Nicholas Street 17	
Parkgate Road 20	
Pepper Street 21	
St. John Street 23	
St. Martins Way 24	
Vicar's Lane 25	

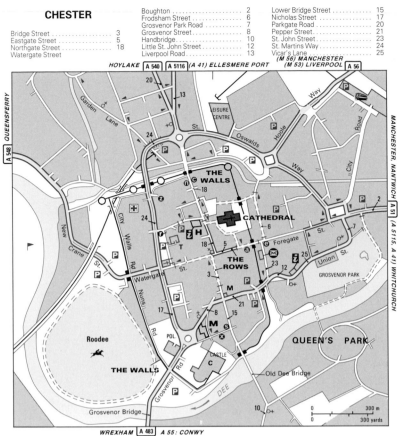

HOYLAKE A 540   (A 5116) (A 41) ELLESMERE PORT   (M 56) MANCHESTER
(M 53) LIVERPOOL   A 56
QUEENSFERRY A 548
LEISURE CENTRE
THE WALLS
CATHEDRAL
THE ROWS
GROSVENOR PARK
Roodee
QUEEN'S PARK
THE WALLS
Old Dee Bridge
DEE
Grosvenor Bridge
WREXHAM A 483   A 55: CONWY
MANCHESTER, NANTWICH A 51 (A 5115, A 41) WHITCHURCH

Carluke	55 I 16	Castle Rising	30 V 25
Carmarthen/		Castlebay	64 X 13
Caerfyrddin	15 H 28	Castleford	40 P 22
Carmel Head	32 G 23	Castlemartin	14 E 29
Carmunnock	55 H 16	Castlerigg	44 K 20
Carn Ban	61 H 12	Castleton (North	
Carn Coire		Yorks.)	46 R 20
na h-Easgainn	67 H 12	Castleton (Derbs.)	35 O 23
Carn Eige	66 E 12	Castletown	42 G 21
Carn Glas-choire	67 I 11	Castletown	73 J 8
Carn Mairg	61 H 14	Catacol Bay	53 D 16
Carnedd Llewelyn	32 I 24	Caterham	20 T 30
Carnforth	38 L 21	Catfield	31 Y 25
Carnoustie	63 L 14	Catlodge	61 H 12
Carnwath	56 J 16	Caton	38 L 21
Carradale	53 D 17	Catrine	48 H 17
Carradale Bay	53 D 17	Catteral	38 L 22
Carrbridge	67 I 12	Catterick	46 P 20
Carrick	54 F 15	Catterick Garrison	45 O 20
Carrick Roads	2 E 33	Catworth	29 S 26
Carron (Loch)	66 C 11	Cauldcleuch Head	50 L 18
Carse of Gowrie	62 K 14	Cava	74 K 7
Carsluith	42 G 19	Cavendish	22 V 27
Carsphairn	48 H 18	Cawdor	67 I 11
Carstairs	55 I 16	Cawood	40 Q 22
Carterton	18 P 28	Caythorpe	36 S 24
Carterway Heads	45 O 19	Ceall (Loch nan)	59 C 13
Cartmel	44 L 21	Cefn-Coed-y-	
Cas-Gwent/		cymmer	16 J 28
Chepstow	16 M 29	Cefn Bryn	15 H 29
Casnewydd/		Cefn-mawr	33 K 25
Newport	16 L 29	Ceinewydd/	
Cassley (Glen)	72 F 9	New Quay	24 G 27
Castell-Nedd/Neath	15 I 29	Ceiriog (Vale of)	33 K 25
Castell Newydd		Cemaes	32 G 23
Emlyn/		Cemaes Head	24 F 27
Newcastle		Cemmaes	25 I 26
Emlyn	24 G 27	Cenarth	24 G 27
Castle Acre	30 W 25	Cerne Abbas	8 M 31
Castle Ashby	28 R 27	Cerrigydrudion	33 J 24
Castle Bolton	45 O 21	Chadderton	39 N 23
Castle Campbell	55 I 15	Chaddesden	35 P 25
Castle Cary	8 M 30	Chadlington	18 P 28
Castle Combe	17 N 29	Chadwell	
Castle Donington	35 P 25	St. Mary	21 V 29
Castle Douglas	49 I 19	Chagford	4 I 31
Castle Drogo	4 I 31	Chàirn Bhain	
Castle Fraser	69 M 12	(Loch a')	72 E 9
Castle Hedingham	22 V 28	Chalfont	
Castle Howard	40 R 21	St. Giles	20 S 29
Castle Kennedy	42 F 19	Chalfont	
Castle Lachlan	54 E 15	St. Peter	20 S 29
Castle Loch	42 F 19	Chalford	17 N 28

Chalgrove	18 Q 29	Chesham	20 S 28
Challock	12 W 30	Chesham Bois	20 S 28
Chambercombe		Cheshire (County)	34 M 24
Manor	6 H 30	Cheshunt	21 T 28
Chandler's Ford	9 P 31	Chesil Beach	8 M 32
Channel Islands	5	Cheslyn Hay	27 N 26
Chapel-en-le-Frith	35 O 24	Chester	34 L 24
Chapel St.		Chester-le-Street	46 P 19
Leonards	37 V 24	Chesterfield	35 P 24
Chapelhall	55 I 16	Chesters Fort	51 N 18
Chapeltown	40 P 23	Chesterton	18 Q 28
Chapmanslade	17 N 30	Cheviot (The)	51 N 17
Chard	7 L 31	Cheviot Hills (The)	50 M 17
Chardstock	7 L 31	Chew Magna	16 M 29
Charing	12 W 30	Chewton Mendip	17 M 30
Charlbury	18 P 28	Chichester	10 R 31
Charlecote Park	27 P 27	Chickerell	8 M 32
Charleston Manor	12 U 31	Chicklade	8 N 30
Charlestown	3 F 33	Chiddingfold	11 S 30
Charlton Kings	17 N 28	Chiddingstone	12 U 30
Charlton Marshall	8 N 31	Chideock	8 L 31
Charlwood	11 T 30	Chigwell	21 U 29
Charminster	8 M 31	Chilcompton	17 M 30
Charmouth	7 L 31	Chilham	12 W 30
Charsfield	23 X 27	Chillingham	51 O 17
Chartham	13 X 30	Chilmark	8 N 30
Chartwell	21 U 30	Chiltern Hills	18 R 29
Chastleton	27 P 28	Chilton	18 Q 29
Chatburn	39 M 22	Chippenham	17 N 29
Chatham	12 V 29	Chipping	38 M 22
Chatsworth House	35 P 24	Chipping Campden	27 O 27
Chatteris	29 U 26	Chipping Norton	18 P 28
Chatton	51 O 17	Chipping	
Chawleigh	6 I 31	Ongar	21 U 28
Cheadle		Chipping Sodbury	17 M 29
(Gtr. Mches.)	35 N 23	Chipping Warden	28 Q 27
Cheadle (Staffs.)	35 O 25	Chirbury	25 K 26
Cheddar Gorge	16 L 30	Chirk	33 K 25
Cheddington	19 S 28	Chirk Castle	33 K 25
Cheddleton	35 N 24	Chirnside	57 N 16
Chedworth	17 O 28	Chiseldon	17 O 29
Chelford	34 N 24	Chislet	13 X 30
Chellaston	35 P 25	Chitterne	8 N 30
Chelmsford	22 V 28	Chittlehamholt	6 I 31
Cheltenham	17 N 28	Chittlehampton	6 I 30
Chelveston	29 S 27	Chobham	20 S 29
Chepstow/		Choire (Loch)	73 H 9
Cas-Gwent	16 L 29	Cholderton	
Cheriton Bishop	4 I 31	Cholesbury	19 S 28
Chertsey	20 S 29	Cholsey	18 Q 29
Cherwell (River)	18 Q 28	Chon (Loch)	55 G 15
Cheselbourne	8 M 31	Chopwell	51 O 19
		Chorley	38 M 23
		Chorleywood	20 S 29

Christchurch	9 O 31	Cleethorpes	41 T 23
Chroisg (Loch a')	66 E 11	Cleeve Abbey	7 J 30
Chudleigh	4 J 32	Clehonger	26 L 27
Chulmleigh	6 I 31	Cleigh	60 D 14
Church	39 M 22	Clent	27 N 26
Church Eaton	35 N 25	Cleobury Mortimer	26 M 26
Church Fenton	40 Q 22	Cleobury North	26 M 26
Church Stoke	25 K 26	Clephanton	67 I 11
Church Stretton	26 L 26	Clevedon	16 L 29
Churchill (North		Cleveland Hills	46 Q 20
Somerset)	16 L 29	Cleveleys	38 K 22
Churchill (Oxon.)	18 P 28	Cley Next the Sea	30 X 25
Churnet	35 N 24	Cliffe	22 V 29
Churt	10 R 30	Clifton Hampden	18 Q 29
Cilcain	33 K 24	Clisham	70 Z 10
Cilgerran	24 G 27	Clitheroe	39 M 22
Cilmery	25 J 27	Cliveden House	19 R 29
Cinderford	17 M 28	Clocaenog Forest	33 J 24
Cirencester	17 O 28	Clola	69 O 11
City of London		Clophill	29 S 27
(London Borough)	20 T 29	Clouds Hill	8 N 31
Clach Leathad	60 F 14	Cloughton	47 S 20
Clachan	53 D 16	Clova (Glen)	62 K 13
Clachan Mór	58 Z 14	Clovelly	6 G 31
Clachan		Clovulin	60 E 13
of Glendaruel	54 E 15	Clowne	36 Q 24
Clackavoid	62 J 13	Cluanie Loch	66 E 12
Clackmannan	55 I 15	Clumber Park	36 Q 24
Clacton-on-Sea	23 X 28	Clun	25 K 26
Claggain Bay	52 B 16	Clunbury	26 L 26
Claidh (Loch)	70 A 10	Clunes Forest	60 F 13
Clandon Park	20 S 30	Clunie	62 J 14
Clapham (Beds.)	29 S 27	Clutton	17 M 30
Clapham (North		Clwydian Range	33 K 24
Yorks.)	39 M 21	Clydach	15 I 28
Clàr (Loch nan)	73 H 9	Clyde (Firth of)	48 F 17
Clare	22 V 27	Clyde (River)	55 I 16
Clashmore	67 H 10	Clydebank	55 G 16
Clashnessie	72 E 9	Clydesdale	55 I 16
Clatteringshaws		Clywedog Resr.	25 J 26
(Loch)	49 H 18	Coalville	35 P 25
Clauchlands Point	53 E 17	Coatbridge	55 H 16
Claverley	26 N 26	Cobham	20 S 30
Claverton Manor	17 N 29	Cock Bridge	68 K 12
Clawdd-newydd	33 J 24	Cockburnspath	57 M 16
Clawton	6 G 31	Cockenzie	
Claxton	40 R 21	and Port Seton	56 L 16
Clay Cross	35 P 24	Cockermouth	43 J 20
Claydon	23 X 27	Cocking	10 R 31
Claydon House	18 R 28	Codford St. Mary	8 N 30
Clayton	11 T 31	Codicote	19 T 28
Clayton-le-Moors	39 M 22	Codnor	35 P 24
Clayton West	39 P 23	Codsall	27 N 26
Cleadale	59 B 13	Coe (Glen)	60 F 14
Cleadon	51 P 19	Coed y Brenin	
Cleator Moor	43 J 20	Forest	33 I 25
Cleckheaton	39 O 22	Coedpoeth	33 K 24
Cleehill	26 M 26	Coggeshall	22 W 28
		Coigach	72 E 10

Coignafearn Forest	67 H 12	
Colby	42 F 21	
Colchester	23 W 28	
Cold Fell	45 M 19	
Coldbackie	72 G 8	
Colden Common	10 Q 31	
Coldingham	57 N 16	
Coldstream	57 N 17	
Coleford (Glos.)	16 M 28	
Coleford (Somerset)	17 M 30	
Coleshill	27 O 26	
Colgrave Sound	75 R 2	
Coll	59 A 14	
Collieston	69 O 11	
Collin	49 J 18	
Collingham (Notts.)	36 R 24	
Collingham (West		
Yorks.)	40 P 22	
Collyweston	29 S 26	
Colmonell	48 F 18	
Coln (River)	17 O 28	
Colnabaichin	68 K 12	
Colne	39 N 22	
Colne (River)	23 X 28	
Colonsay	52 B 15	
Colpy	69 M 11	
Colquhon Castle	69 N 11	
Colsterworth	36 S 25	
Coltishall	31 Y 25	
Colwall Stone	26 M 27	
Colwyn Bay/		
Bae Colwyn	33 I 24	
Colyton	5 K 31	
Combe Florey	7 K 30	
Combe Martin	6 H 30	
Combwich	7 K 30	
Compton (Berks.)	18 Q 29	
Compton (West		
Sussex)	10 R 31	
Compton Castle	4 J 32	
Compton Wynyates	27 P 27	
Comrie	61 I 14	
Cona Glen	60 D 13	
Condover	26 L 26	
Congleton	35 N 24	
Congresbury	16 L 29	
Coningsby	37 T 24	
Conisbrough	40 Q 23	
Coniston	44 K 20	
Connah's Quay	33 K 24	
Connel	60 D 14	
Conon Bridge	67 G 11	
Consett	45 O 19	
Constantine Bay	2 E 32	
Contin	67 G 11	
Convinth (Glen)	67 G 11	
Conway Falls	33 I 24	
Conwy	33 I 24	
Conwy (River)	33 I 24	

COVENTRY

Broadgate 6	
Corporation Street	
Shopping Precincts	
Bayley Lane 3	
Bishop Street 5	
Burges 7	
Earl Street 10	
Fairfax Street 12	

Far Gosford Street 13	
Gosford Street 15	
Greyfriars Lane 16	
Hales Street 17	
High Street 22	
Ironmonger Row 24	
Jordan Well 26	
Leicester Row 29	
Light Lane 30	
Little Park Street 31	
Primrose Hill	
Street 34	

Queen Victoria Road 35	
St. Johns (Ringway) 38	
St. Nicholas (Ringway) . . . 39	
Swanswell (Ringway) 40	
Trinity Street 41	
Upper Well Street 43	
Vecqueray Street 45	
Victoria Street 46	
Warwick Row 49	
White Street 51	
Windsor Street 52	
White Friars (Ringway) . . 54	

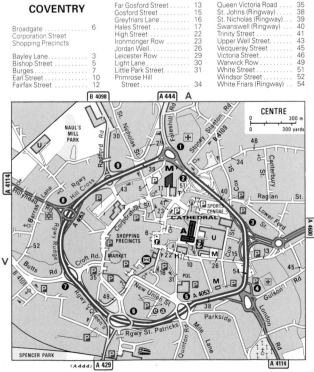

CENTRE
NAUL'S MILL PARK
CATHEDRAL
SHOPPING PRECINCTS
MARKET
SPENCER PARK
(A 444) A 429

Conwy (Vale of) 33 I 24
Cooden Beach 12 V 31
Cookham 19 R 29
Coolham 11 S 31
Coombe Bissett 9 O 30
Copdock 23 X 27
Copmanthorpe 40 Q 22
Copplestone 7 I 31
Copthorne 11 T 30
Coquet (River) 51 N 17
Corbridge 51 N 19
Corby 28 R 26
Corby Glen 36 S 26
Corfe Castle 8 N 32
Corhampton 10 Q 31
Cornhill 69 L 11
Cornhill-on-Tweed 57 N 17
Cornwall (County) 3 F 32
Cornwood 4 I 32
Corpach 60 E 13
Corpusty 31 X 25
Corran 60 E 13
Corrie 53 E 17
Corrieshalloch Gorge 66 E 10
Corrimony 67 F 11
Corringham 22 V 29
Corryvreckan (Gulf of) 52 C 15
Corscombe 8 L 31
Corsham 17 N 29
Corsham Court 17 N 29
Corstopitum 51 N 19
Corwen 33 J 25
Cosby 28 Q 26
Cosham 10 Q 31
Costessey 31 X 26
Cotehele 3 H 32
Cotherstone 45 O 20
Cothi (River) 15 H 28
Cotswold Hills 17 N 29
Cotswold Wildlife Park 17 O 28
Cottenham 29 U 27
Cottered 29 T 28
Cottingham (East Riding of Yorks.) 41 S 22
Cottingham (Northants.) 28 R 26
Countesthorpe 28 Q 26
Coupar Angus 62 K 14
Cove Bay 69 N 12
Coventry 28 P 26
Coverack 2 E 33
Cowal 54 E 15
Cowan Bridge 45 M 21
Cowbridge/ Bont-faen 16 J 29
Cowdenbeath 56 K 15
Cowdray House 10 R 31
Cowes 10 Q 31
Cowfold 11 T 31
Cowplain 10 Q 31
Coxheath 12 V 30
Coylton 48 G 17
Crackington Haven 6 G 31
Cragside Gardens 51 O 18
Craig 66 E 11
Craig-y-nos 15 I 28
Craigellachie 68 K 11
Craighead 57 M 15
Craighouse 53 C 16
Craigievar Castle 69 L 12
Craignish (Loch) 54 D 15
Craignure 59 C 14
Craigrothie 56 L 15
Craik 50 K 17
Crail 57 M 15
Cramlington 51 P 18
Cramond 56 K 16
Cranborne 9 O 31
Cranbrook 12 V 30
Cranfield 29 S 27
Cranleigh 11 S 30
Crathes Castle 63 M 12
Crathie 62 K 12
Crathorne 46 Q 20
Craven Arms 26 L 26
Crawford 49 J 17
Crawley (Hants.) 9 P 30
Crawley (West Sussex) 11 T 30
Crawley Down 11 T 30
Creag Meagaidh 61 G 13
Creagorry 64 Y 11
Crediton 7 J 31

Creetown 48 G 19
Creran (Loch) 60 D 14
Cressage 26 M 26
Creswell 36 Q 24
Crewe 34 M 24
Crewkerne 8 L 31
Crianlarich 60 G 14
Criccieth 32 H 25
Crich 35 P 24
Crichton 56 L 16
Crick 28 Q 26
Cricket St. Thomas 8 L 31
Crickhowell 16 K 28
Cricklade 17 O 29
Crickley Hill 17 N 28
Crieff 61 I 14
Crimond 69 O 11
Crinan 54 D 15
Crinan (Loch) 54 D 15
Cringleford 31 X 26
Crocketford 4 I 18
Crockham Hill 21 U 30
Croft 26 L 27
Croft-on-Tees 46 P 20
Croggan 59 C 14
Cromalt Hills 72 E 9
Cromar 68 L 12
Cromarty 67 H 10
Cromarty Firth 67 H 11
Cromdale 68 J 11
Cromdale (Hills of) 68 J 12
Cromer 31 X 25
Cromford 35 P 24
Crondall 18 R 30
Crook 45 O 19
Crook of Devon 56 J 15
Crookham Village 18 R 30
Cropwell Bishop 36 R 25
Crosby 38 K 23
Crosby Ravensworth 45 M 20
Croscombe 8 M 30
Cross 71 B 8
Cross Fell 45 M 19
Cross Hands 15 H 28
Cross Inn 24 H 27
Crossapol 58 Z 14
Crosshill (South Ayrshire) 48 G 18
Crosshill (Fife) 56 K 15
Crosshouse 54 G 17
Crosskeys 16 K 29
Crosskirk 73 J 8
Crossmichael 49 I 19
Crouch (River) 23 W 29
Crowborough 12 U 30
Crowcombe 7 K 30
Crow Hill 17 M 28
Crowhurst 12 V 31
Crowland 29 T 25
Crowle 41 R 23
Crowlin Island 66 C 11
Crowthorne 19 R 29
Croxley Green 20 S 29
Croy 67 H 11
Croyde 6 H 30
Croydon (London Borough) 20 T 29
Cruden Bay 69 O 11
Crudgington 34 M 25
Crudwell 17 N 29
Crug-y-bar 24 I 27
Crulivig 70 Z 9
Crymmych 24 G 28
Crynant 15 I 28
Cuckfield 11 T 30
Cuckney 36 Q 24
Cuddington 34 M 24
Cudworth 40 P 23
Cuffley 20 T 28
Cuillin Sound 65 B 12
Cuillins (The) 65 B 12
Culdrose 2 E 33
Cullen 68 L 10
Cullen Bay 68 L 10
Cullipool 54 D 15
Cullompton 7 J 31
Culmington 26 L 26
Culmstock 7 K 31
Culrain 72 G 10
Culross 56 J 15
Culter Fell 49 J 17
Cults 69 N 12
Culzean Castle 48 F 17
Cumbernauld 55 I 16
Cumbria (County) 44 K 19

Cumbrian Moutains 44 K 20
Cuminestown 69 N 11
Cummersdale 44 L 19
Cummertrees 49 J 19
Cumnock 49 H 17
Cumnor 18 P 28
Cunninghame 54 G 17
Cunninghamhead 54 G 17
Cupar 56 K 15
Curdridge 10 Q 31
Currie 56 K 16
Curry Rivel 8 L 30
Cwm 16 K 28
Cwm Bychan 32 H 25
Cwmbrân 16 K 29
Cwmllynfell 15 I 28
Cwmystwyth 25 I 26
Cydweli/Kidwelly 15 H 28
Cymmer 16 J 29
Cymyran Bay 32 G 24

D

Dailly 48 F 18
Daimh (Loch an) 61 G 14
Dairsie or Osnaburgh 56 L 14
Dalavich 54 E 15
Dalbeattie 49 I 19
Dalby 42 F 21
Dale 14 E 28
Daliburgh 64 X 12
Dalkeith 56 K 16
Dallas 68 J 11
Dallington 12 V 31
Dalmally 60 F 14
Dalmellington 48 G 18
Dalmeny 56 J 16
Dalnabreck 59 C 13
Dalry (North Ayrshire) 54 F 16
Dalry (Dumfries and Galloway) 49 H 18
Dalrymple 48 G 17
Dalston 44 L 19
Dalton (Dumfries and Galloway) 49 J 18
Dalton (North Yorks.) 46 P 21
Dalton in Furness 44 K 21
Damh (Loch) 66 D 11
Dan-yr-Ogof 15 I 28
Danbury 22 V 28
Dane 35 N 24
Darenth 21 U 29
Darfield 40 P 23
Darlington 46 P 20
Darowen 25 I 26
Dartford 21 U 29
Dartford Tunnel 21 U 29
Dartington 4 I 32
Dartmeet 4 I 32
Dartmoor National Park 4 I 32
Dartmouth 4 J 32
Darton 39 P 23
Darvel 55 H 17
Darwen 39 M 22
Datchet 20 S 29
Dava 68 J 11
Daventry 28 Q 27
Davidstow 3 G 32
Daviot 67 H 11
Dawley 26 M 26
Dawlish 4 J 32
Deal 13 Y 30
Dean Forest Park 17 M 28
Deanich Lodge 67 F 10
Deanston 55 H 15
Dearham 44 J 19
Deben (River) 23 X 27
Debenham 23 X 27
Deddington 28 Q 28
Dedham 23 X 28
Dee (River) (Scotland) 69 N 12
Dee/Afon Dyfrdwy (River) (Wales) 33 K 24
Deene 29 S 26
Deeping St. Nicholas 37 T 25
Deeps (The) 75 P 3
Defford 27 N 27

Delabole 3 F 32
Delamere Forest 34 L 24
Delph 39 N 23
Denbigh/Dinbych 33 J 24
Denby Dale 39 P 23
Denham 20 S 29
Denholm 50 L 17
Denmead 10 Q 31
Dennington 31 Y 27
Denny 55 I 15
Denton 39 N 23
Derby 35 P 25
Derbyshire (County) 35 O 24
Dersingham 30 V 25
Dervaig 59 B 14
Derwent (River) (R. Ouse) 40 R 22
Derwent (River) (R. Trent) 35 P 24
Derwent (River) (R. Tyne) 45 O 19
Derwent Dale 39 O 23
Derwent Reservoir (Derbs.) 35 O 23
Derwent Reservoir (Northumb.) 45 N 19
Derwent Water 44 K 20
Desborough 28 R 26
Desford 28 Q 26
Detling 12 V 30
Deveron (River) 69 M 11
Devil's Beef Tub 49 J 17
Devil's Bridge/ Pontarfynach 25 I 26
Devil's Elbow 62 J 13
Devil's Punch Bowl 11 R 30
Devizes 17 O 29
Devon (County) 6 I 31
Devonport 3 H 32
Dewsbury 39 P 22
Dherue (Loch an) 72 G 8
Didcot 18 Q 29
Diddlebury 26 L 26
Dighty Water 62 K 14
Dilwyn 26 L 27
Dinas Dinlle 32 G 24
Dinas Head 14 F 27
Dinbych/Denbigh 33 J 24
Dinbych-y-pysgod/ Tenby 14 F 28
Dingwall 67 G 11
Dinnet 62 L 12
Dinnington 36 Q 23
Dinton 9 O 30
Dirleton 57 L 15
Dishforth 40 P 21
Diss 31 X 26
Distington 43 J 20
Ditcheat 8 M 30
Ditchley Park 18 P 28
Ditchling 11 T 31
Ditton Priors 26 M 26
Doc Penfro/ Pembroke Dock 14 F 28
Docherty (Glen) 66 E 11
Dochgarroch 67 H 11
Docking 30 V 25
Doddington (Cambs.) 29 U 26
Doddington (Kent) 12 W 30
Doddington (Lincs.) 36 S 24
Doddington (Northumb.) 51 O 17
Dodman Point 3 F 33
Dodworth 39 P 23
Dolfor 25 K 26
Dolgellau 32 I 25
Dolgoch Falls 24 I 26
Dollar 55 I 15
Dolton 6 H 31
Don (River) 40 Q 23
Don (River) 68 K 12
Doncaster 40 Q 23
Donington 37 T 25
Donington Park Circuit 35 P 25
Donington-on-Bain 37 T 24
Donisthorpe 35 P 25
Donnington (Berks.) 18 Q 29
Donnington (Salop) 34 M 25
Donyatt 7 L 31
Doon (Loch) 48 G 18
Dorchester (Dorset) 8 M 31
Dorchester (Oxon.) 18 Q 29

DERBY

East Street — Z 18
Full Street — Y 19
Jury Street — Y 23
King Street — Y 25
Leopold Street — Z 26
Market Place — YZ 27
Midland Road — Z 28
Mount Street — Z 29
Normanton Road — Z 31
Queen Street — Y 32
St. Mary's Gate — Y 33
St. Peter's Street — Z 34
Sacheverel Street — Z 36
Stafford Street — Z 37
Wardwick — Z 43

Corn Market — Z 13
Iron Gate — Y 22
Eagle Shopping Centre — Z
Victoria Street — Z 41

Albert Street — Z 2
Babington Lane — Z 3
Bold Lane — Y 4
Bradshaw Way — Z 5
Cathedral Road — Y 7
Charnwood Street — Z 9
Corporation Street — YZ 12
Duffield Road — Y 17

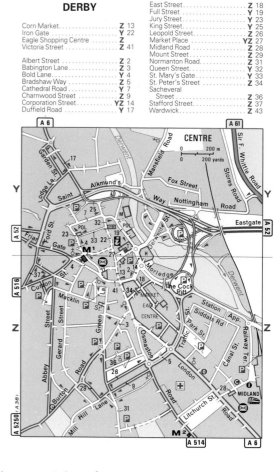

Dordon 27 P 26
Dorking 19 T 30
Dormans Land 11 U 30
Dormanstown 46 Q 20
Dornie 66 D 12
Dornoch 67 H 10
Dornoch Firth 67 H 10
Dorrington 26 L 26
Dorset (County) 8 M 31
Dorstone 25 K 27
Douchary (Glen) 66 F 10
Douglas (South Lanarkshire) 49 I 17
Douglas (Isle of Man) 42 G 21
Douglastown 62 L 14
Dounby 74 K 6

Doune 55 H 15
Dove (River) 35 O 24
Dove Cottage 44 K 20
Dovedale 35 O 24
Dover 13 X 30
Doveridge 35 O 25
Dovey/Dyfi (River) 24 I 26
Downderry 3 G 32
Downham 29 U 26
Downham Market 30 V 26
Downies 63 N 12
Downton 9 O 31
Draycott 35 O 25
Draycott-in-the-Moors 35 N 25
Drayton (Norfolk) 31 X 25
Drayton (Oxon.) 18 Q 29

Dreghorn 54 G 17
Drenewydd/ Newtown 25 K 26
Dreswick Point 42 G 21
Drigg 43 J 20
Drimnin 59 C 14
Droitwich 27 N 27
Dronfield 35 P 24
Drongan 48 G 17
Droylsden 39 N 23
Druidibeg (Loch) 64 Y 12
Druim a' Chliabhain (Loch) 73 H 8
Drum Castle 69 M 12
Drumbeg 72 E 9
Drumclog 55 H 17
Drumlanrig Castle 49 I 18

DOVER

Bench Street — 3
Biggin Street — 4
Cannon Street — 5
High Street
King Street — 13
Pencester Road

Castle Street — 6
Charlton Green — 7
Ladywell, Park Street — 15
London Road — 17
Priory Road — 18
Priory Street — 19
Queen St. — 20
Worthington Street — 25

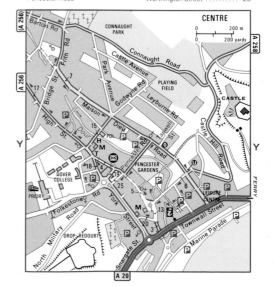

DUNDEE

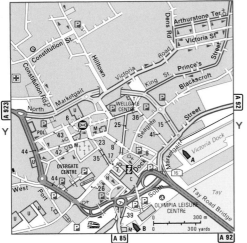

Commercial Street 8
High Street 17
Murraygate 25
Nethergate 26
Overgate Centre
Reform Street 35
Wellgate Centre

Bell Street 6
City Square 7
East Marketgait ...... Y 15
Meadowside 23
St. Andrews Street 36
South Union Street 39
Trades Lane 41
Ward Road 42
West Bell Street 43
West Marketgait ...... Y 44

DURHAM

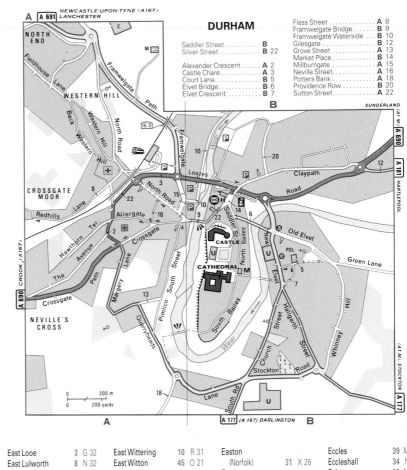

Saddler Street .... B
Silver Street .... B 22

Alexander Crescent ..... A 2
Castle Chare .... A 5
Court Lane .... A
Elvet Bridge .... B 6
Elvet Crescent .... B 7

Flass Street .... A 8
Framwelgate Bridge ..... B 9
Framwelgate Waterside .. B 10
Gilesgate .... B 12
Grove Street .... A 13
Market Place .... B 14
Millburngate .... A 15
Neville Street .... A 16
Potters Bank .... A 18
Providence Row .... B 20
Sutton Street .... A 22

Drumlithie   63 M 13
Drummond Castle   55 I 14
Drummore   42 F 19
Drummossie Muir   67 H 11
Drumnadrochit   67 G 11
Drumtochty Forest   63 M 13
Druridge Bay   51 P 18
Drybrook   17 M 28
Dryburgh Abbey   50 M 17
Drygarn Fawr   25 J 27
Drymen   55 G 15
Ducklington   18 P 28
Duddington   29 S 26
Dudley   27 N 26
Duff House   69 M 11
Duffield   35 P 25
Dufftown   68 K 11
Duffus   68 J 10
Duich (Loch)   66 D 12
Duirinish   65 C 12
Duke's Pass   55 G 15
Dukinfield   39 N 23
Dulnain Bridge   68 J 12
Duloe   3 G 32
Dulverton   7 J 30
Dumbarton   55 G 16
Dumfries   49 J 18
Dun Carloway
  Broch   70 Z 9
Dunbar   57 M 15
Dunbeath   73 J 9
Dunblane   55 I 15
Duncansby Head   74 K 8
Dunchurch   28 Q 26
Duncton   11 S 31
Dundee   62 L 14
Dundonald   48 G 17
Dundrennan   43 I 19
Dunecht   69 M 12
Dunfermline   56 J 15
Dungeness   12 W 31
Dunholme   37 S 24
Dunkeld   56 J 14
Dunkery Beacon   7 J 30
Dunlop   55 G 16
Dunnet   73 J 8
Dunnet Bay   73 J 8
Dunnet Head   74 J 7
Dunning   56 J 15
Dunnottar Castle   63 N 13
Dunoon   54 F 16
Dunrobin Castle   73 I 10
Duns   57 M 16
Dunscore   49 I 18
Dunsfold   11 S 30
Dunsford   4 I 31
Dunsop Bridge   38 M 22
Dunstable   19 S 28
Dunstaffnage
  Castel   60 D 14
Dunstanburgh
  Castle   51 P 17

Dunster   7 J 30
Duntelchaig (Loch)   67 H 11
Dunure   48 F 17
Dunvegan   65 A 11
Dunvegan (Loch)   65 A 11
Dunvegan Castle   65 A 11
Dunvegan Head   64 Z 11
Dunwich   31 Y 27
Durdle Door   8 N 32
Durham   46 P 19
Durham (County)   45 N 19
Durlston Head   9 O 32
Durness   72 F 8
Durrington   17 O 30
Dursley   17 M 28
Dury Voe   75 Q 2
Duston   28 R 27
Duxford   29 U 27
Dyce   69 N 12
Dyfi/Dovey (River)   24 I 26
Dykehead   62 K 13
Dykends   62 K 13
Dymchurch   13 W 30
Dymock   26 M 28
Dyrham   17 M 29
Dyrham Park   17 M 29
Dyserth   33 J 24

E

Eaglescliffe   46 P 20
Eaglesham   55 H 16
Eakring   36 R 24
Ealing (London
  Borough)   20 T 29
Earba (Lochan na
  h-)   61 G 13
Earby   39 N 22
Eardisley   25 K 27
Earl Shilton   28 Q 26
Earl Soham   23 X 27
Earl Stonham   23 X 27
Earley Winnersh   18 R 29
Earls Barton   28 R 27
Earls Colne   22 W 28
Earl's Colne   23 W 28
Earlsferry   56 L 15
Earlston   57 L 17
Earn (Loch)   61 H 14
Earn (River)   61 H 14
Earn (River)   56 J 14
Easdale   54 D 15
Easebourne   10 R 31
Easington   46 P 19
Easington Lane   46 P 19
Easingwold   40 Q 21
East Barkwith   37 T 24
East Bergholt   23 X 28
East Brent   16 L 30
East Budleigh   4 K 32
East Cowes   10 Q 31

East Dereham   30 W 25
East Glen (River)   37 S 25
East Grinstead   11 T 30
East Hagbourne   18 Q 29
East Hanney   18 P 29
East Harling   30 W 26
East Hendred   18 P 29
East Hoathly   12 U 31
East Horsley   20 S 30
East Huntspill   8 L 30
East Ilsley   18 Q 29
East Kilbride   55 H 16
East Knoyle   8 N 30
East Lambrook   8 L 31
East Leake   36 Q 25
East Linton   57 M 16
East Loch Roag   70 Z 9
East Loch Tarbet   70 Z 10

East Looe   3 G 32
East Lulworth   8 N 32
East Markham   36 R 24
East Meon   10 Q 31
East Midlands
  Airport   36 Q 25
Easter Ross   67 G 10
East Moor   35 P 24
East Rhidorroch
  Lodge   72 F 10
East Sussex
  (County)   12 U 30
East Wemyss   56 K 15

East Wittering   10 R 31
East Witton   45 O 21
Eastbourne   12 U 31
Eastchurch   12 W 29
Eastdean   12 U 31
Easter Ross   67 G 10
Eastergate   11 S 31
Eastham   34 L 24
Eastington   17 N 28
Eastleigh   9 P 31
Easton
  (Dorset)   8 M 32

Easton
  (Norfolk)   31 X 26
Easton-
  in-Gordano   16 L 29
Eastriggs   50 K 19
Eastry   13 X 30
Eastville   37 U 24
Eastwood   36 Q 24
Ebbw Vale/
  Glyn Ebwy   16 K 28
Ebchester   45 O 19
Ecclefechan   50 K 18

Eccles   39 M 23
Eccleshall   34 N 25
Echt   69 M 12
Eckington
  (Derbs.)   35 P 24
Eckington (Heref.
  and Worc.)   27 N 27
Edale   35 O 23
Eday   74 L 6
Edderton   67 H 10
Eddrachillis Bay   72 E 9
Edenbridge   12 U 30

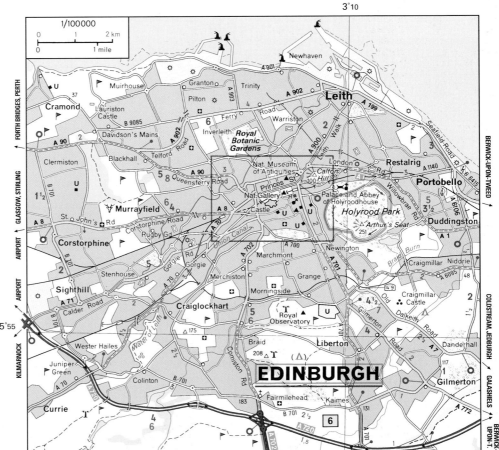

EDINBURGH

EDINBURGH
CENTRE

Castle Street	DY
Frederick Street	DY
George Street	DY
Hanover Street	DY
High Street	EYZ 37
Lawnmarket	EYZ 46
Princes Street	DY
St. James Centre	EY
Waverley Market	EY
Bernard Terrace	EZ 3
Bread Street	DZ 6
Bristo Place	EZ 7
Candlemaker Row	EZ 9
Castlehill	DZ 10
Chambers Street	EZ 12
Chapel Street	EZ 13
Charlotte Square	CY 14
Deanhaugh Street	CY 23
Douglas Gardens	CY 25
Drummond Street	EZ 27
Forrest Road	EZ 31
Gardner's Crescent	CZ 32
George IV Bridge	EZ 33
Grassmarket	DZ 35
Home Street	DZ 38
Hope Street	CY 39
Johnston Terrace	DZ 42
King's Bridge	DZ 44
King's Stables Road	DZ 45
Leith Street	EY 47
Leven Street	DZ 48
Lothian Street	EZ 51
Mound (The)	DY 55
North Bridge	EY 61
North St. Andrew Street	EY 66
Raeburn Place	CY 69
Randolph Crescent	CY 71
St. Andrew Square	EY 73
St. Mary's Street	EY 75
Shandwick Place	CYZ 77
South Charlotte Street	DY 78
South St. David Street	DEY 79
Spittal Street	DZ 83
Victoria Street	EZ 84
Waterloo Place	EY 87
Waverley Bridge	EY 89
West Maitland Street	CZ 92

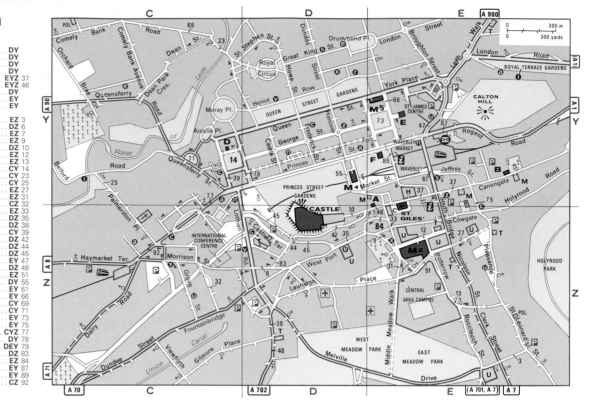

Eden (River)	44 K 19	Egham	20 S 29	Eil (Loch)	60 E 13	Eilean Mullagrach	72 D 9	Elham	13 X 30	Enville	27 N 26	Ettrick	50 K 17
Edgmond	34 M 25	Egilsay	74 L 6	Eilde Mór		Eilean nan Each	59 B 13	Elie	56 L 15	Eoropie	71 B 8	Ettrick Forest	50 K 17
Edinburgh	56 K 16	Eglingham	51 O 17	(Loch)	60 F 13	Eilean Trodday	65 B 10	Elkesley	36 R 24	Eorsa	59 B 14	Ettrick Pen	50 K 17
Edington	17 N 30	Egremont	43 J 20	Eilean a' Chalmain	59 A 15	Eilt (Loch)	60 D 13	Elkstone	17 N 28	Eport (Loch)	64 Y 11	Euxton	38 L 22
Edlesborough	19 S 28	Egton	47 R 20	Eilean Beag	66 C 11	Eishort (Loch)	65 C 12	Elland	39 O 22	Epping	21 U 28	Evanton	67 G 11
Edwinstowe	36 Q 24	Eigg	59 B 13	Eilean Chathastail	59 B 13	Elan Valley	25 J 27	Ellastone	35 O 25	Epping Forest	21 U 29	Evercreech	8 M 30
Edzell	63 M 13	Eigheach		Eilean Donan		Elan Village	25 J 27	Ellesmere	34 L 25	Epsom	20 T 30	Everleigh	17 O 30
Eggerness Point	42 G 19	(Loch)	61 G 13	Castle	66 D 12	Elgin	68 K 11	Ellesmere Port	34 L 24	Epworth	41 R 23	Evershot	8 M 31
Eggleston	45 N 20	Eight Ash Green	23 W 28	Eilean Flodigarry	65 B 10	Elgol	65 B 12	Ellon	69 N 11	Eredine Forest	54 D 15	Everton	36 R 23
								Elmdon	29 U 27	Eriboll (Loch)	72 F 8	Evesham	27 O 27
								Elmswell	30 W 27	Ericht (Loch)	61 G 13	Evesham	
								Elphin	72 E 9	Eriska	60 D 14	(Vale of)	27 O 27
								Elsenham	22 U 28	Eriskay	64 Y 12	Ewe (Isle of)	66 D 10
								Elstead	10 R 30	Erisort (Loch)	70 A 9	Ewell	20 T 29
								Elstree	20 T 29	Ermington	4 I 32	Ewelme	18 Q 29
								Elswick	38 L 22	Erpingham	31 X 25	Ewhurst	11 S 30
								Eltisley	29 T 27	Erraid	59 A 15	Exbourne	6 I 31
								Elton	29 S 26	Errochty		Exe (River)	7 J 31
								Elvington	41 R 22	(Loch)	61 H 13	Exebridge	7 J 30
								Ely	29 U 26	Errol	62 K 14	Exeter	4 J 31
								Emberton	28 R 27	Ersary	64 X 13	Exford	7 J 30
								Embleton	51 P 17	Erskine Bridge	55 G 16	Exminster	4 J 31
								Embo	73 I 10	Esha Ness	75 P 2	Exmoor National	
								Embsay	39 O 22	Esher	20 S 29	Park	7 I 30
								Emneth	29 U 26	Esk (Glen)	62 L 13	Exmouth	4 J 32
								Empingham	29 S 26	Esk (River)	50 K 19	Exton	7 J 30
								Emsworth	10 R 31	Eskdale	50 K 18	Eyam	35 O 24
								Enard Bay	72 D 9	Eskdalemuir	50 K 18	Eye (Cambs.)	29 T 26
								Enderby	28 Q 26	Essendon	19 T 28	Eye (Suffolk)	31 X 27
								Endon	35 N 24	Essex (County)	22 V 28	Eye Peninsula	71 B 9
								Enfield (London		Essich	67 H 11	Eyemouth	57 N 16
								Borough)	20 T 29	Eston	46 Q 20	Eynort (Loch)	
								Enford	17 O 30	Etchingham	12 V 30	(Highland)	65 A 12
								Englefield		Etherow (River)	39 N 23	Eynort (Loch)	
								Green	20 S 29	Etherow Park	39 N 23	(Western Isles)	64 Y 12
								Enham Alamein	18 P 30	Etive (Glen)	60 F 14	Eynsford	21 U 29
								Enmore	7 K 30	Etive (Loch)	60 E 14	Eynsham	18 P 28
								Ensay	59 B 14	Eton	20 S 29	Eyre Point	65 B 12
								Enstone	18 P 28	Ettington	27 P 27	Eythorne	13 X 30

EXETER
CENTRE

Bedford Street	Y 6	Alphington Road	Z 2	New Bridge Street	Z 31
Fore Street	Z	Barnfield Road	Z 3	Palace Gate	Z 36
Guildhall		Bartholomew Road	Z 5	Paul Street	Y 37
Shopping Centre	Y	Castle Street	Y 13	Preston Street	Z 40
High Street	Y	Cowick Street	Z 15	Princessbay	Y 44
		Edmund Street	Z 18	Quay Hill	Z 45
		King Street	Z 22	Queen's Terrace	Y 46
		Mary Arches Street	Z 26	St. Martin's Lane	Y 49
		Mint (The)	Z 28	Summerland	Y 50

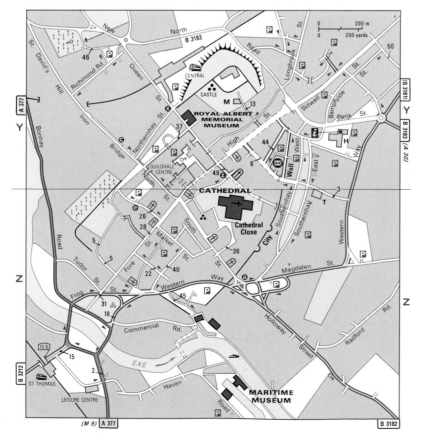

F

Fada	66 E 10	Farne Islands	51 P 17	Fenwick	57 O 17
Fada (Loch)	64 Y 11	Farnham (Dorset)	8 N 31	Feochan (Loch)	60 D 14
Failsworth	39 N 23	Farnham (Surrey)	19 R 30	Feolin Ferry	52 B 16
Fair Isle	75 P 5	Farnham Royal	20 S 29	Ferndown	9 O 31
Fair Oak	10 Q 31	Farningham	21 U 29	Ferness	67 I 11
Fairbourne	32 H 25	Farnsfield	36 Q 24	Fernhurst	10 R 30
Fairford	17 O 28	Farnworth	39 M 23	Ferryden	63 M 13
Fairlie	54 F 16	Farrington Gurney	17 M 30	Ferryhill	46 P 19
Fairlight	12 V 31	Farway	5 K 31	Feshie (Glen)	61 I 12
Fakenham	30 W 25	Fasnakyle Forest	66 F 11	Fetcham	20 S 30
Falfield	17 M 29	Fasque	63 M 13	Fetlar	75 R 2
Falkirk	55 I 16	Fauldhouse	55 I 16	Fetterangus	69 N 11
Falkland	56 K 15	Faversham	12 W 30	Fettercairn	63 M 13
Fallin	55 I 15	Fawley	9 P 31	Ffestiniog	32 I 25
Falmouth	2 E 33	Fazeley	27 O 26	Ffestiniog (Vale of)	32 H 25
Fanagmore	72 E 8	Fearnan	61 H 14	Fflint/Flint	33 K 24
Fannich (Loch)	66 E 11	Fearnmore	66 C 11	Fforest Fawr	15 J 28
Fara	74 K 7	Featherstone (Staffs.)	27 N 26	Fiaray	64 X 12
Fareham	10 Q 31	Featherstone (West Yorks.)	40 P 22	Filey	47 T 21
Faringdon	18 P 29	Feering	22 W 28	Filton	16 M 29
Farleigh-Hungerford	17 N 30	Felindre	25 K 26	Finchampstead	19 R 30
Farley Mount	9 P 30	Felixstowe	23 Y 28	Finchingfield	22 V 28
Farmborough	17 M 29	Felling	51 P 19	Findhorn	68 J 11
Farmtown	68 L 11	Felpham	11 S 31	Findhorn (River)	67 H 12
Farnborough (Hants.)	19 R 30	Felsted	22 V 28	Findhorn Bay	68 J 11
Farnborough (Warw.)	27 P 27	Feltham	20 S 29	Findochty	68 L 10
Farndon	36 R 24	Felton	51 O 18	Findon	11 S 31
		Feltwell	30 V 26	Finedon	28 S 26
		Fenstanton	29 T 27	Fingest	18 R 29
				Finningley	41 R 23
				Finsbay	70 Z 10

Finstock	18 P 28	Flodday (near Sandray)	58 X 13	Forter	62 K 13
Finstown	74 K 6	Flodden Field	51 N 17	Forth	55 I 16
Fintry	55 H 15	Flodigarry	65 B 11	Forth (Firth of)	56 K 15
Fionn Loch	66 D 10	Floors Castle	57 M 17	Forth (River)	55 G 15
Fionn Loch Mór	72 F 9	Flotta	74 K 7	Forth Bridges	56 J 15
Fionnphort	59 A 15	Flowerdale Forest	66 D 11	Fortingall	61 H 14
Fishbourne	10 Q 31	Fochabers	68 K 11	Forton	34 M 25
Fisherfield Forest	66 D 10	Foinaven	72 F 8	Fortrose	67 H 11
Fishguard/Abergwaun	14 F 28	Folkestone	13 X 30	Fortuneswell	8 M 32
Fittleworth	11 S 31	Folkingham	37 S 25	Fosdyke	37 T 25
Flackwell Heath	19 R 29	Fontmell Magna	8 N 31	Fotheringhay	29 S 26
Fladbury	27 N 27	Ford	54 D 15	Foulness Point	23 W 29
Fladda-Chùain	65 A 10	Forde Abbey	7 L 31	Foulridge	39 N 22
Flamborough	41 T 21	Fordham	30 V 27	Foulsham	30 X 25
Flamborough Head	41 T 21	Fordingbridge	9 O 31	Fountains Abbey	39 P 21
Flamingo Park	47 R 21	Fordoun	63 M 13	Four Crosses	33 K 25
Flamstead	19 S 28	Fordyce	68 L 11	Four Elms	21 U 30
Flash	35 O 24	Foreland	10 Q 31	Four Marks	10 Q 30
Flatford Mill	23 X 28	Foreland Point	6 I 30	Foveran	69 N 12
Fleckney	28 Q 26	Foremark Reservoir	35 P 25	Fowey	3 G 32
Fleet	18 R 30	Forest Row	11 U 30	Fowlmere	29 U 27
Fleet (Islands of)	43 H 19	Forfar	62 L 14	Fownhope	26 M 27
Fleet (Loch)	73 H 10	Formby	38 K 23	Foxdale	42 G 21
Fleetwood	38 K 22	Formby Point	38 K 23	Foxholes	41 S 21
Flimby	44 J 19	Fornham All Saints	23 W 27	Foyers	67 G 12
Flint/Fflint	33 K 24	Forres	68 J 11	Fraddon	2 F 32
Flitton	29 S 27	Forsinard	73 I 8	Framfield	12 U 31
Flitwick	29 S 27	Fort Augustus	67 F 12	Framlingham	23 Y 27
Flodday (near Hellisay)	64 X 13	Fort George	67 H 11	Frampton-on-Severn	17 M 28
		Fort Victoria	9 P 31	Framwellgate Moor	46 P 19
		Fort William	60 E 13	Frant	12 U 30

Fraserburgh	69 O 10
Fraserburgh Bay	69 O 10
Freckenham	30 V 27
Freckleton	38 L 22
Freethorpe	31 Y 26
Freevater Forest	67 F 10
Fremington	6 H 30
Frensham	10 R 30
Freshwater	9 P 31
Freshwater Bay	9 P 31
Freshwater East	14 F 29
Freshwater West	14 E 29
Fressingfield	31 X 26
Frettenham	31 X 25
Freuchie (Loch)	61 I 14
Friday Bridge	29 U 26
Fridaythorpe	40 S 21
Frimley	19 R 30
Frinton-on-Sea	23 X 28
Friockheim	63 M 14
Frisa (Loch)	59 B 14
Friskney	37 U 24
Frittenden	12 V 30
Frizington	43 J 20
Frodsham	34 L 24
Froggatt	35 P 24
Frome	17 N 30
Fuday	64 X 12
Fuiay	58 X 13
Fulbourn	29 U 27
Fulwood	38 M 22
Funzie	75 R 2

Folkestone Terminal

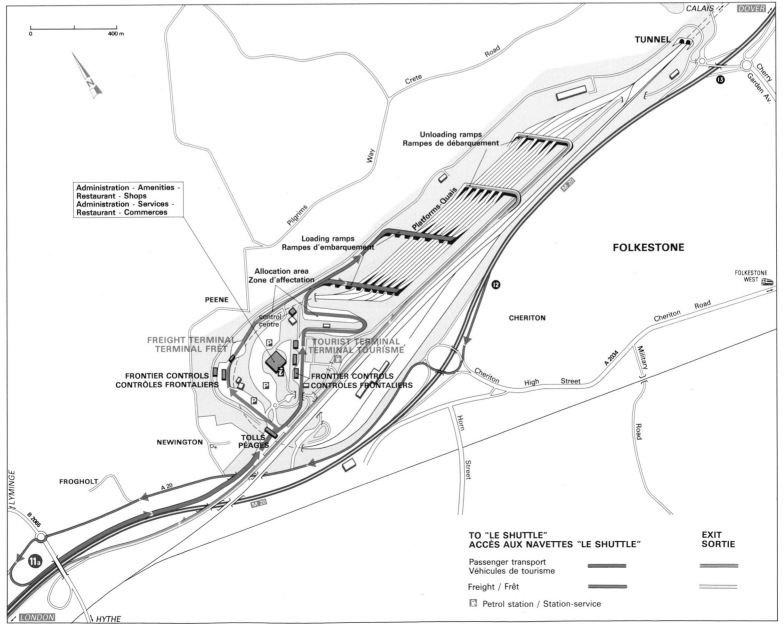

Calais Terminal

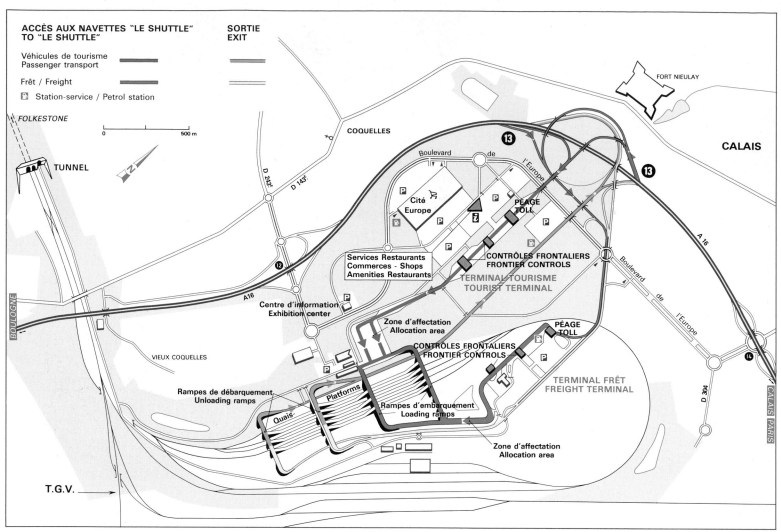

Furness Abbey	38 K 21	Garry (Glen)	
Furness Fells	44 K 20	(Highland)	60 E 12
Fyfield (Essex)	22 U 28	Garry (Loch)	60 F 12
Fyfield (Hants.)	9 P 30	Garsdale Head	39 N 21
Fyvie	69 M 11	Garsington	18 Q 28
		Garten (Loch)	68 I 12
		Garth	25 J 27
G		Gartmore	55 G 15
		Garton-on-The-	
Gainford	45 O 20	Wolds	41 S 21
Gainsborough	36 R 23	Garve	66 F 11
Gairloch	66 C 10	Garvellachs	52 C 15
Gairlochy	60 F 13	Garvock	54 F 16
Gairsay	74 L 6	Garynahine	70 Z 9
Galashiels	50 L 17	Gatehouse of Fleet	43 H 19
Galgate	38 L 22	Gateshead	51 P 19
Gallan Head	70 Y 9	Gateside	56 K 15
Galloway Forest Park	48 G 18	Gatley	35 N 23
Galmisdale	59 B 13	Gatwick Airport	11 T 30
Galmpton	4 J 32	Gaulden Manor	7 K 30
Galson	70 A 8	Gayton	30 V 25
Galston	48 G 17	Geddington	28 R 26
Galtrigill	64 Z 11	Gedney Drove End	37 U 25
Gamlingay	29 T 27	Gedney Hill	29 T 25
Gamston	36 R 24	Georgeham	6 H 30
Ganton	47 S 21	Georth	74 K 6
Garboldisham	30 W 26	Gerrards	
Gardenstown	69 N 10	Cross	20 S 29
Garelochhead	54 F 15	Gifford	57 L 16
Garenin	70 Z 9	Gigha (Sound of)	53 C 17
Garforth	40 P 22	Gigha Island	52 C 16
Gargrave	39 N 22	Gighay	64 Y 12
Gargunnock	55 H 15	Gildersome	39 P 22
Garioch	69 M 12	Gillingham (Dorset)	8 N 30
Garlieston	42 G 19	Gillingham (Kent)	12 V 29
Garmouth	68 K 11	Gilmerton	61 I 14
Garrabost	71 B 9	Girvan	48 F 18
Garrisdale Point	65 A 12	Gisburn	39 N 22
Garry (Glen)		Gittisham	7 K 31
(Perthshire and		Glaisdale	47 R 20
Kinross)	61 H 13	Glamis	62 K 14

Glamis Castle	62 K 14	Glentress	56 K 17
Glanaman	15 I 28	Glentworth	36 S 23
Glas Maol	62 J 13	Glinton	29 T 26
Glasbury	25 K 27	Glossop	39 O 23
Glascarnoch (Loch)	66 F 10	Gloucester	17 N 28
Glasgow	55 H 16	Gloucestershire	
Glass (Loch)	67 G 10	(County)	17 N 28
Glasson	38 L 22	Glusburn	39 O 22
Glastonbury	8 L 30	Glyn Ceiriog	33 K 25
Gleann Beag	66 F 10	Glyn-Ebwy/	
Gleann Mór	67 G 10	Ebbw Vale	16 K 28
Glemfield	28 Q 26	Glyn-neath	15 J 28
Glemsford	22 V 27	Glyncorrwg	15 J 28
Glen Brittle Forest	65 B 12	Glynde	12 U 31
Glen Finglas		Gnosall	35 N 25
Reservoir	55 G 15	Goat Fell	53 E 17
Glen More		Goathland	47 R 20
Forest Park	67 I 12	Gobowen	33 K 25
Glen Shee	62 J 13	Godalming	11 S 30
Glenbarr	53 C 17	Godmanchester	29 T 27
Glenborrodale	59 C 13	Godmanstone	8 M 31
Glenbuck	49 I 17	Godshill	10 Q 32
Glencarse	56 K 14	Godstone	20 T 30
Glencoe	60 E 13	Goil (Loch)	54 F 15
Glencoul (Loch)	72 F 9	Golborne	38 M 23
Glendurgan		Goldthorpe	40 Q 23
Garden	2 E 33	Golspie	73 I 10
Glenelg	66 D 12	Gomersal	39 O 22
Glenelg Bay	66 D 12	Gometra	59 B 14
Glenfarg	56 J 15	Gomshall	20 S 30
Glenfield	28 Q 26	Goodrich	16 M 28
Glenfinnan	60 D 13	Goodrington	4 J 32
Glenforsa Airport	59 C 14	Goodwick	14 F 27
Glengorm	59 B 14	Goodwood House	10 R 31
Glengrasco	65 B 11	Goole	41 R 22
Glenkens (The)	49 H 18	Gordon	57 M 16
Glenlivet	68 J 11	Gorebridge	56 K 16
Glenluce	42 F 19	Goring	18 Q 29
Glenmore	59 C 13	Gorm Loch Mór	72 F 9
Glenrothes	56 K 15	Gorran Haven	3 F 33
Glentham	36 S 23	Gorseinon	15 H 29

Gorsleston-on-Sea	31 Z 26	Great	
Gosberton	37 T 25	Bookham	20 S 30
Gosforth (Cumbria)	43 J 20	Great Bridon	46 P 20
Gosforth (Tyne and		Great Broughton	46 Q 20
Wear)	51 P 18	Great Chalfield	
Gosport	10 Q 31	Manor	8 N 30
Gotham	36 Q 25	Great Chesterford	29 U 27
Gott Bay	58 Z 14	Great Chishill	29 U 27
Goudhurst	12 V 30	Great Clifton	43 J 20
Gourdon	63 N 13	Great Coates	41 T 23
Gourock	54 F 16	Great Cumbrae	
Gowerton	15 H 29	Island	54 F 16
Goxhill	41 T 22	Great Driffield	41 S 21
Graemsay	74 K 7	Great Dunmow	22 V 28
Grain	12 W 29	Great Easton	
Grampian		(Essex)	22 U 28
Mountains	61 G 14	Great Easton	
Grandtully	61 I 14	(Leics.)	28 R 26
Grange-over-Sands	44 L 21	Great Eccleston	38 L 22
Grangemouth	55 I 15	Great Ellingham	30 W 26
Grantham	36 S 25	Great Gonerby	36 S 25
Grantown-on-Spey	68 J 12	Great Grimsby	41 T 23
Grantshouse	57 N 16	Great Harwood	39 M 22
Grasmere	44 K 20	Great Hockham	30 W 26
Grassington	39 O 21	Great Horwood	28 R 28
Gravesend	21 V 29	Great Houghton	40 Q 23
Grayrigg	45 M 20	Great Livermere	30 W 27
Grays		Great Malvern	26 N 27
Thurrock	21 V 29	Great Massingham	30 W 25
Grayshott	10 R 30	Great Milton	18 Q 28
Grayswood	10 R 30	Great Missenden	19 R 28
Great Ayton	46 Q 20	Great Musgrave	45 M 20
Great Baddow	22 V 28	Great Oakley	23 X 28
Great Badminton	17 N 29	Great Ormes Head	33 I 23
Great Bardfield	22 V 28	Great Ouse (River)	30 V 25
Great Barford	29 S 27	Great Ouseburn	40 Q 21
Great Barr	27 O 26	Great Ponton	36 S 25
Great Bedwyn	17 P 29	Great Ryburgh	30 W 25
Great Bentley	23 X 28	Great Sampford	22 V 28
Great Bernera	70 Z 9	Great Shefford	18 P 29
Great Bircham	30 V 25	Great Shelford	29 U 27

Great Somerford	17 N 29		
Great Torrington	6 H 31		
Great Wakering	23 W 29		
Great Waltham	22 V 28		
Great Whernside	39 O 21		
Great Witley	26 M 27		
Great Wolford	27 P 27		
Great Wyrley	27 N 26		
Great Yarmouth	31 Z 26		
Great Yeldham	22 V 27		
Greater			
Manchester			
(Metropolitan			
County)	39 N 23		
Greatham			
(Cleveland)	46 Q 20		
Greatham (Hants.)	10 R 30		
Greatstone-on-Sea	12 W 31		
Greenhead	50 M 19		
Greenholm	55 H 17		
Greenlaw	57 M 16		
Greenock	54 F 16		
Greenodd	44 K 21		
Greens Norton	28 Q 27		
Greenwich (London			
Borough)	21 U 29		
Grendon			
Underwood	18 Q 28		
Gresford	34 L 24		
Greshornish (Loch)	65 A 11		
Gretna	50 K 19		
Gretton	28 R 26		
Greys Court	18 R 29		
Greystoke	44 L 19		
Grimoldby	37 U 23		
Grimsay	64 Y 11		
Gringley on the Hill	36 R 23		
Groby	28 Q 26		
Groombridge	12 U 30		
Grosmont	47 R 20		
Grove	18 P 29		

Place	Page	Grid
Gruinard Bay	66	D 10
Gruinard Island	66	D 10
Gruinart (Loch)	52	B 16
Grunavat (Loch)	70	Z 9
Grundisburgh	23	X 27
Guardbridge	56	L 14
Guernsey (Channel I.)	5	
Guildtown	62	J 14
Guildford	20	S 30
Guisborough	46	Q 20
Guiseley	39	O 22
Guist	30	W 25
Gullane	56	L 15
Gunna	58	Z 14
Gunnislake	3	H 32
Gunthorpe	36	R 25
Gurnard	10	Q 31
Gutcher	75	Q 1
Guyhirn	29	U 26
Gwalchmai	32	G 24
Gwaun-Cae-Gurwen	15	I 28
Gwbert-on-Sea	24	F 27
Gweek	2	E 33
Gwyddgrug	15	H 28
Gwydir Castle	33	I 24

H

Place	Page	Grid
Habost	71	B 8
Hackney (London Borough)	21	T 29
Haddenham (Bucks.)	18	R 28
Haddenham (Cambs.)	29	U 26
Haddington	57	L 16
Haddiscoe	31	Y 26
Haddo House	69	N 11
Haddon Hall	35	P 24
Hadleigh (Essex)	22	V 29
Hadleigh (Suffolk)	23	W 27
Hadlow	12	V 30
Hadnall	34	L 25

Place	Page	Grid
Hadrian's Wall	50	M 18
Hagley	27	N 26
Hagworthingham	37	U 24
Hailsham	12	U 31
Hainton	37	T 23
Halberton	7	J 31
Hale	34	M 23
Halesowen	27	N 26
Halesworth	31	Y 26
Halford	27	P 27
Halifax	39	O 22
Halkirk	73	J 8
Hall	55	G 16
Halland	12	U 31
Halling	12	V 29
Hallow	27	N 27
Halstead	22	V 28
Haltham	37	T 24
Haltwhistle	50	M 19
Halwell	4	I 32
Halwill Junction	6	H 31
Hamble	10	Q 31
Hambleden	18	R 29
Hambledon (Hants.)	10	Q 31
Hambledon (Surrey)	11	S 30
Hambleton (Lancs.)	38	L 22
Hambleton (North Yorks.)	40	Q 22
Hambleton Hills (The)	46	Q 21
Hambridge	8	L 31
Hamilton	55	H 16
Hammersmith and Fulham (London Borough)	20	T 29
Hamnavoe	75	P 3
Hampshire (County)	9	P 30
Hampstead Norris	18	Q 29
Hampton	27	O 26
Hampton Court	20	S 29
Hamstead Marshall	18	P 29
Hamsterley	45	O 19
Hamstreet	12	W 30
Hamworthy	9	N 31
Handa Island	72	E 8

Place	Page	Grid
Handcross	11	T 30
Handforth	35	N 23
Handsworth	35	P 23
Hanley	35	N 24
Hanley Swan	27	N 27
Hanslope	28	R 27
Happisburgh	31	Y 25
Hapton	39	N 22
Harbertonford	4	I 32
Harbottle	51	N 17
Harbury	27	P 27
Harby	36	R 25
Hardham	11	S 31
Hardwick Hall	36	Q 24
Hardy Monument	8	M 31
Hare Street	22	U 28
Harewood House	39	P 22
Hargrave Green	22	V 27
Haringey (London Borough)	20	T 29
Harlech	32	H 25
Harleston	31	X 26
Harley	26	M 26
Harlington	29	S 28
Harlow	22	U 28
Harmston	36	S 24
Haroldswick	75	R 1
Harpenden	19	S 28
Harpley	30	V 25
Harport (Loch)	65	A 12
Harray (Loch of)	74	K 6
Harrietsham	12	V 30
Harringworth	28	S 26
Harris (Highland)	59	A 13
Harris (Western Isles)	70	Y 10
Harris (Sound of)	64	Y 10
Harrogate	40	P 22
Harrow (London Borough)	20	S 29
Harston	29	U 27
Hartest	22	W 27
Hartfield	12	U 30
Harthill	55	I 16
Harting	10	R 31
Hartington	35	O 24

Place	Page	Grid
Hartland	6	G 31
Hartlebury	27	N 26
Hartlepool	46	Q 19
Hartley	21	U 29
Hartley Wintney	18	R 30
Hartpury	17	N 28
Hartshill	27	P 26
Hartwell	18	R 28
Harvington	27	O 27
Harwell	18	Q 29
Harwich	23	X 28
Harworth	36	Q 23
Hascosay	75	R 2
Haselbury Plucknett	8	L 31
Hasland	35	P 24
Haslemere	10	R 30
Haslingden	39	N 22
Haslingfield	29	U 27
Hastings	12	V 31
Hatch Court	7	L 31
Hatfield (Herts.)	19	T 28
Hatfield (South Yorks.)	40	Q 23
Hatfield Broad Oak	22	U 28
Hatfield Heath	22	U 28
Hatfield Peverel	22	V 28
Hatherleigh	6	H 31
Hathern	36	Q 25
Hathersage	35	P 24
Hatton (Aberdeenshire)	69	O 11
Hatton (Derbs.)	35	O 25
Haugh of Urr	49	I 19
Haughton	35	N 25
Havant	10	R 31
Haverfordwest/Hwlffordd	14	F 28
Haverhill	22	V 27
Haverigg	44	K 21
Havering (London Borough)	21	U 29
Haverthwaite	44	K 21
Hawarden	33	K 24
Hawes	45	N 21
Hawick	50	L 17

Place	Page	Grid
Hawkedon	22	V 27
Hawkhurst	12	V 30
Hawkridge	7	J 30
Hawkshead	44	L 20
Hawkwell	22	V 29
Hawley	19	R 30
Haworth	39	O 22
Haxby	40	Q 21
Haxey	41	R 23
Hay-on-Wye	25	K 27
Haydock	38	M 23
Haydon Bridge	51	N 19
Hayfield	35	O 23
Hayle	2	D 33
Hayling Island	10	R 31
Haywards Heath	11	T 31
Hazelbank	55	I 16
Hazel Grove	35	N 23
Hazlemere	19	R 29
Heacham	30	V 25
Headcorn	12	V 30
Headington	18	Q 28
Headless Cross	27	O 27
Headley	10	R 30
Heads of Ayr	48	F 17
Heanor	35	P 24
Heath End	18	Q 29
Heath Hayes	27	O 25
Heathfield	12	U 31
Heathrow Airport	20	S 29
Hebburn	51	P 19
Hebden Bridge	39	N 22
Hebrides (Sea of the)	64	Z 12
Heckfield	18	R 29
Heckington	37	T 25
Hednesford	27	O 25
Hedon	41	T 22
Heighington (Durham)	46	P 20
Heighington (Lincs.)	37	S 24
Helensburgh	54	F 15
Helford	2	E 33
Hell's Mouth or Porth Neigwl	32	G 25

Place	Page	Grid
Hellifield	39	N 22
Hellisay	64	X 12
Helmdon	28	Q 27
Helmsdale	73	J 9
Helmsley	46	Q 21
Helperby	40	Q 21
Helpringham	37	T 25
Helsby	34	L 24
Helston	2	E 33
Helton	44	L 20
Helvellyn	44	K 20
Hemel Hempstead	19	S 28
Hemingbrough	41	R 22
Hempnall	31	X 26
Hemsby	31	Z 25
Hemsworth	40	P 23
Hemyock	7	K 31
Hendy	15	H 28
Henfield	11	T 31
Hengoed	16	K 29
Henham	22	U 28
Henley	27	O 27
Henley-on-Thames	18	R 29
Henlow	29	T 27
Hennock	4	J 32
Henstridge	8	M 31
Heptonstall	39	N 22
Hereford	26	L 27
Hereford and Worcester (County)	26	M 27
Herm (Channel I.)	5	
Herma Ness	75	R 1
Hermitage	18	Q 29
Hermitage Castle	50	L 18
Herne Bay	13	X 29
Herstmonceux	12	U 31
Hertford	19	T 28
Hertfordshire (County)	19	T 28
Hessle	41	S 22
Hest Bank	38	L 21
Heswall	33	K 24
Hetton-le-Hole	46	P 19
Heveningham	31	Y 27

Place	Page	Grid
Hever	12	U 30
Heversham	44	L 21
Hevingham	30	X 25
Hexham	51	N 19
Heybridge	22	W 28
Heysham	38	L 21
Heyshott	10	R 31
Heytesbury	8	N 30
Heywood	39	N 23
Hibaldstow	41	S 23
Hidcote Manor Garden	27	O 27
High Bentham	38	M 21
High Bickington	6	I 31
High Easter	22	V 28
High Ercall	34	M 25
High Force (The)	45	N 20
High Halstow	12	V 29
High Ham	8	L 30
High Holden	12	W 30
High Ongar	22	U 28
High Peak	35	O 23
High Willhays	4	I 31
High Wycombe	19	R 29
Higham (Kent)	12	V 29
Higham (Lancs.)	39	N 22
Higham (Suffolk)	30	V 27
Higham Ferrers	29	S 27
Highbridge	7	L 30
Highclere	18	P 29
Highcliffe	9	O 31
Higher Penwortham	38	L 22
Highland Wildlife Park	61	I 12
Highley	26	M 26
Highnam	17	N 28
Hightae	49	J 18
Hightown	38	K 23
Highworth	17	O 29
Hildenborough	12	U 30
Hilderstone	35	N 25
Hilgay	30	V 26
Hill	17	M 29
Hill of Fearn	67	I 10
Hill of Tarvit	56	L 15

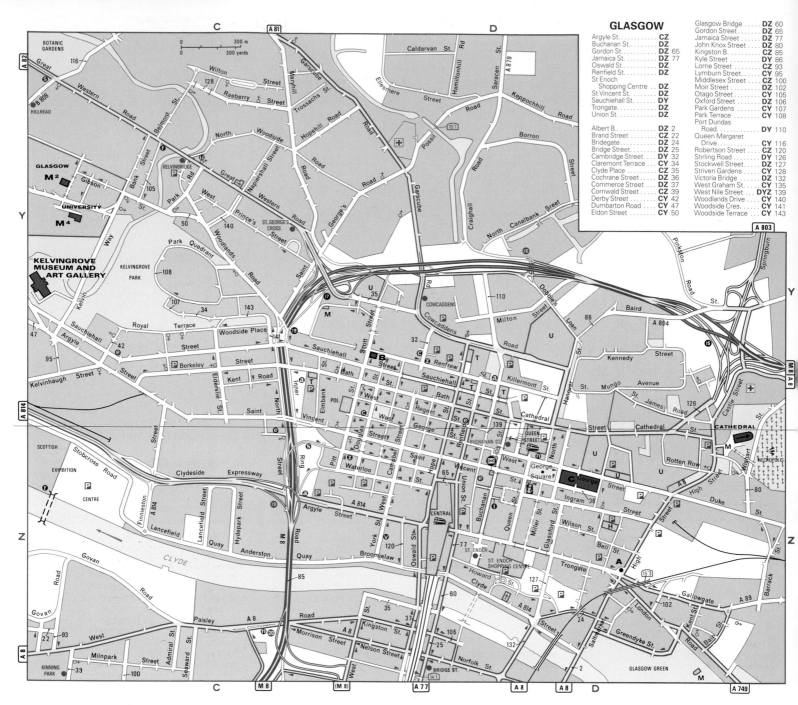

GLASGOW

Argyle St.	CZ	
Buchanan St.	DZ	
Gordon St.	DZ	65
Jamaica St.	DZ	77
Oswald St.	DZ	
Renfield St.	DZ	
St Enoch		
Shopping Centre	DZ	
St Vincent St.	DZ	
Sauchiehall St.	DY	
Trongate	DZ	
Union St.	DZ	
Albert B.	DZ	2
Brand Street	CZ	22
Bridgate	DZ	24
Bridge Street	DZ	25
Cambridge Street	DY	32
Claremont Terrace	CY	34
Clyde Place	CZ	35
Cochrane Street	DZ	36
Commerce Street	DZ	37
Cornwald Street	CZ	39
Derby Street	CY	42
Dumbarton Road	CY	47
Eldon Street	CY	50

Glasgow Bridge	DZ	60
Gordon Street	DZ	65
Jamaica Street	DZ	77
John Knox Street	DZ	80
Kingston B.	CZ	85
Kyle Street	DY	86
Lorne Street	CZ	93
Lymburn Street	CY	95
Middlesex Street	CZ	100
Moir Street	DZ	102
Otago Street	CY	105
Oxford Street	DZ	106
Park Gardens	CY	107
Park Terrace	CY	108
Port Dundas		
Road	DY	110
Queen Margaret		
Drive	CY	116
Robertson Street	CZ	120
Stirling Road	DY	126
Stockwell Street	DZ	127
Striven Gardens	CY	128
Victoria Bridge	DZ	132
West Graham St.	CY	135
West Nile Street	DYZ	139
Woodlands Drive	CY	140
Woodside Cres.	CY	141
Woodside Terrace	CY	143

Hillingdon (London			Holbury	9	P 31	Holywell/			Horsham	11	T 30	Hoyland Nether	40	P 23	Huthwaite	36	Q 24	Ilminster	7	L 31
Borough)	20	S 29	Holcombe	17	M 30	Treffynnon	33	K 24	Horsham St. Faith	31	X 25	Hucknall	36	Q 24	Huttoft	37	U 24	Ilsington	4	I 32
Hillside	63	M 13	Holdenby	28	Q 27	Holywell Bay	2	E 32	Horsmonden	12	V 30	Huddersfield	39	O 23	Hutton Cranswick	41	S 22	Ilsley	18	Q 29
Hillswick	75	P 2	Holford	7	K 30	Honiton	5	K 31	Horsted Keynes	11	T 30	Hugh Town (I. of			Hutton Rudby	46	Q 20	Immingham	41	T 23
Hilperton	17	N 30	Holkam Hall	30	W 25	Hoo St. Werburgh	12	V 29	Horton	9	O 31	Scilly)	2		Huyton	34	L 23	Immingham		
Hilpsford Point	38	K 21	Hollesley Bay	23	Y 27	Hook	18	R 30	Horton Court	17	M 29	Hughenden	19	R 29	Hwlffordd/			Dock	41	T 23
Hilton	35	P 25	Hollingworth	39	O 23	Hooke	8	M 31	Horton-			Huish Episcopi	8	L 30	Haverfordwest	14	F 28	Ince-in-Makerfield	38	M 23
Hinchingbrooke			Hollybush	48	G 17	Hook Norton	27	P 28	in-Ribblesdale	39	N 21	Hull (River)	41	S 22	Hyde	39	N 23	Inch Kenneth	59	B 14
House	29	T 27	Holme	44	L 21	Hope (Flintshire)	33	K 24	Horwich	38	M 23	Hullbridge	22	V 29	Hynish Bay	58	Z 14	Inchard		
Hinckley	28	P 26	Holme upon			Hope (Derbs.)	35	O 23	Houghton Hall	30	V 25	Humber (River)	41	T 23	Hythe (Hants.)	9	P 31	(Loch)	72	E 8
Hinderwell	47	R 20	Spalding-Moor	41	R 22	Hope (Loch)	72	G 8	Houghton House	29	S 27	Humber Bridge	41	S 22	Hythe (Kent)	13	X 30	Inchkeith	56	K 15
Hindhead	10	R 30	Holmes Chapel	34	M 24	Hope			Houghton-le-			Humberston	41	T 23				Inchlaggan	60	E 12
Hindley	38	M 23	Holmesfield	35	P 24	under Dinmore	26	L 27	Spring	46	P 19	Hungerford	18	P 29				Inchmarnock	54	E 16
Hindon	8	N 30	Holmfirth	39	O 23	Hopeman	68	J 10	Hounslow (London			Hunmanby	47	T 21	I			Inchnadamph	72	F 9
Hingham	30	W 26	Holmhead	48	H 17	Hopetoun House	56	J 16	Borough)	20	S 29	Hunstanton	30	V 25				Inchture	62	K 14
Hinstock	34	M 25	Holsworthy	6	G 31	Hopton	31	Z 26	Hourn (Loch)	66	D 12	Huntingdon	29	T 26	Ibstock	27	P 25	Indaal (Loch)	52	A 16
Hintlesham	23	X 27	Holt (Wrexham)	34	L 24	Horam	12	U 31	House of The			Huntingtower			Ickleford	29	T 28	Ingatestone	21	V 28
Hirwaun	16	J 28	Holt (Dorset)	9	O 31	Horbury	39	P 23	Binns (The)	56	J 16	Castle	62	J 14	Icklingham	30	V 27	Ingham	30	W 27
Histon	29	U 27	Holt (Norfolk)	30	X 25	Horden	46	Q 19	Housesteads			Huntly	68	L 11	Ickworth House	22	V 27	Ingleton		
Hitcham	23	W 27	Holt (Wilts.)	17	N 30	Horeb	24	G 27	Fort	50	N 18	Huntspill	7	L 30	Iden	12	W 31	(Durham)	45	O 20
Hitchin	29	T 28	Holton (Lincs.)	37	T 24	Horley	11	T 30	Hove	11	T 31	Hurlford	48	G 17	Iden Green	12	V 30	Ingleton (North		
Hockering	30	X 25	Holton (Norfolk)	31	Y 26	Hornby	38	M 21	Hoveton	31	Y 25	Hursley	9	P 30	Idrigill Point	65	A 12	Yorks.)	39	M 21
Hockley	22	V 29	Holy Island			Horncastle	37	T 24	Hovingham	46	R 21	Hurst Green	12	V 30	Ightham	21	U 30	Inglewood		
Hockley Heath	27	O 26	(Anglesey)	32	F 24	Horning	31	Y 25	How Caple	26	M 28	Hurstbourne			Ightham Mote	21	U 30	Forest	44	L 19
Hockliffe	19	S 28	Holy Island (North			Horninglow	35	P 25	Howden	41	R 22	Priors	18	P 30	Ilchester	8	L 30	Ingliston	56	J 16
Hoddesdon	19	T 28	Ayrshire)	53	E 17	Horn's Cross	6	H 31	Howe of the			Hurstbourne			Ilderton	51	O 17	Ingoldmells	37	V 24
Hodnet	34	M 25	Holy Island			Hornsea	41	T 22	Mearns	63	M 13	Tarrant	18	P 30	Ilfracombe	6	H 30	Ingoldsby	36	S 25
Hogsthorpe	37	U 24	(Northumb.)	57	O 16	Horrabridge	3	H 32	Howmore	64	X 12	Hurstpierpoint	11	T 31	Ilkeston	36	Q 25	Ings	44	L 20
Holbeach	37	U 25	Holybourne	10	R 30	Horseheath	22	V 27	Hoxa (Sound of)	74	K 7	Hurworth-on-Tees	46	P 20	Ilkley	39	O 22	Innellan	54	F 16
Holbeton	4	H 32	Holyhead/Caergybi	32	G 24	Horsell	20	S 30	Hoy	74	J 7	Husbands			Illogan	2	E 33	Inner Hebrides	58	Y 14
Holbrook	23	X 28	Holystone	51	N 18	Horsforth	39	P 22	Hoylake	33	K 23	Bosworth	28	Q 26	Ilmington	27	O 27	Inner Sound	65	C 11

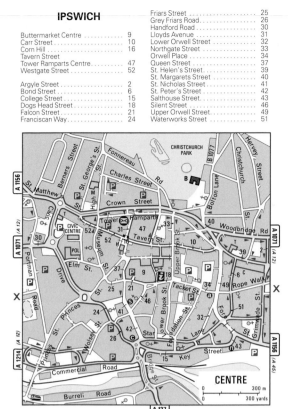

IPSWICH

Buttermarket Centre 9
Carr Street 10
Corn Hill 16
Tavern Street
Tower Ramparts Centre 47
Westgate Street 52

Argyle Street 2
Bond Street 6
College Street 15
Dogs Head Street 18
Falcon Street 21
Franciscan Way 24
Friars Street 25
Grey Friars Road 26
Handford Road 30
Lloyds Avenue 31
Lower Orwell Street 32
Northgate Street 33
Orwell Place 34
Queen Street 37
St. Helen's Street 39
St. Margarets Street 40
St. Nicholas Street 41
St. Peter's Street 42
Salthouse Street 43
Silent Street 46
Upper Orwell Street 49
Waterworks Street 51

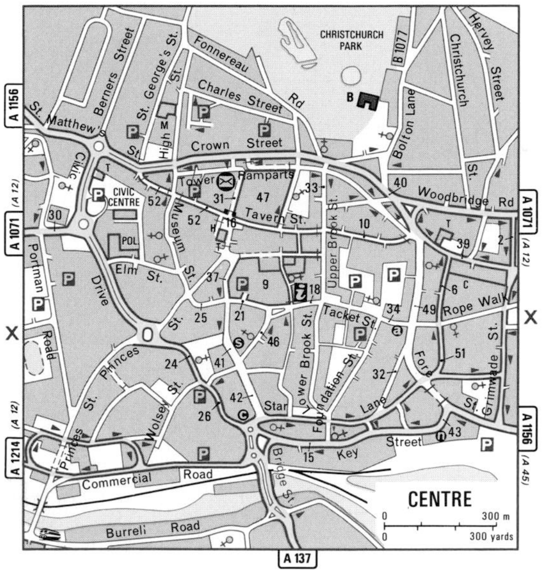

KINGSTON-UPON-HULL

Carr Lane Y
George Street X
Jameson Street Y 17
King Edward Street Y 19
Paragon Street Y 29
Princes Quay Shopping Centre Y
Prospect Shopping Centre X
Prospect Street X
Whitefriargate Y 49

Bond Street X 3
Commercial Road Y 8
Dock Office Row X 10
Dock Street X 12
Ferensway XY 14
Grimston Street X 15
Humber Dock Street Y 16
Jarratt Street X 18
Lowgate Y 23
Market Place Y 24
Prince's Dock Street Y 32
Queen Street Y 35
Queen's Dock Avenue X 36
Reform Street X 37
Sculcoates Bridge X 42
Waterhouse Lane Y 47
Wilberforce Drive X 50
Worship Street X 52

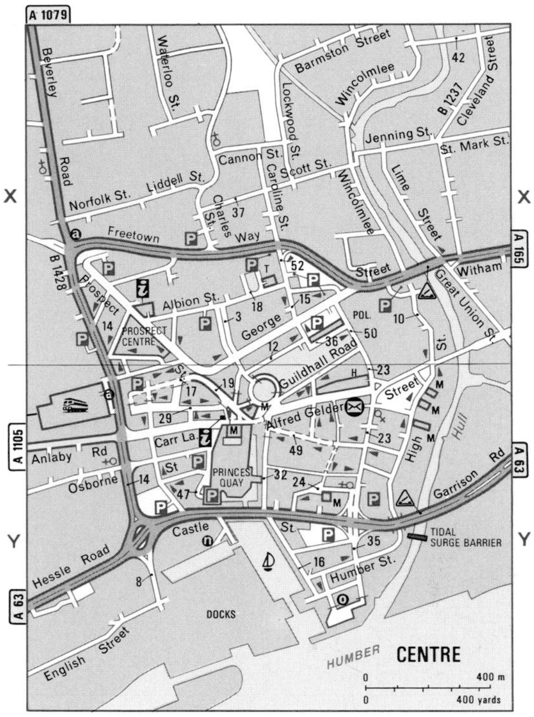

Innerleithen 50 K 17
Insch 69 M 11
Instow 6 H 30
Inver (Loch) 72 E 9
Inver Bay 67 I 10
Inver Valley 72 E 9
Inverallochy 69 O 10
Inveraray 54 E 15
Inverbeg 55 G 15
Inverbervie 63 N 13
Invercreran 60 E 14
Inverewe Gardens 66 C 10
Inverey 62 J 13
Invergarry 60 F 12
Invergordon 67 H 10
Invergowrie 62 K 14
Inverkeithing 56 J 15
Inverkeithny 69 M 11
Inverkip 54 F 16
Inverkirkaig 72 E 9
Inverliever Forest 54 D 15
Invermoriston 67 G 12
Inverness 67 H 11
Inversanda 60 D 13
Inverurie 69 M 12
Iona 59 A 15
Ipplepen 4 J 32
Ipstones 35 O 24
Ipswich 23 X 27
Ireby 44 K 19
Irfon (River) 25 I 27
Irlam 39 M 23
Iron Acton 17 M 29
Iron-Bridge 26 M 26
Irthlingborough 29 S 27
Irvine 54 F 17
Irwell (River) 38 N 23
Isla (Glen) 62 K 13
Isla (River) 62 L 14
Islay (Sound of) 52 B 16
Isleham 30 V 26
Isle of Whithorn 42 G 19
Isleornsay 65 C 12
Islington (London Borough) 20 T 29
Islip 18 Q 28
Ithon (River) 25 K 27
Iver 20 S 29
Iver Heath 20 S 29
Ivinghoe 19 S 28
Ivybridge 4 I 32
Ivychurch 12 W 30
Iwerne Minster 8 N 31
Ixworth 30 W 27

J

Jacobstowe 6 H 31
Janetstown 73 J 9
Jarrow 51 P 19
Jaywick 23 X 28
Jedburgh 50 M 17
Jedburgh Abbey 50 M 17
Jersey (Channel I.) 5
Jevington 12 U 31
John o' Groats 74 K 8
Johnshaven 63 N 13
Johnston 14 F 28
Johnstone 55 G 16
Jura (Isle of) 52 B 16
Jura (Sound of) 53 C 16
Jura Forest 52 B 16
Jurby West 42 G 20

K

Kames 54 E 16
Katrine (Loch) 55 G 15
Keal 37 U 24
Keal (Loch na) 59 B 14
Kearsley 39 M 23
Kebock Head 70 A 9
Kedleston Hall 35 P 25
Kegworth 36 Q 25
Keighley 39 O 22
Keinton Mandeville 8 M 30
Keir Mill 49 I 18
Keiss 74 K 8
Keith 68 L 11
Kellas 62 L 14
Kellie Castle 57 L 15
Kelly Bray 3 H 32
Kelsall 34 L 24
Kelso 50 M 17
Keltneyburn 61 H 14
Kelty 56 J 15
Kelvedon 22 W 28
Kelvedon Hatch 21 U 29
Kemble 17 N 28
Kemnay 69 M 12
Kempsey 27 N 27
Kempston 29 S 27
Kemsing 21 U 30
Kendal 44 L 21
Kenilworth 27 P 26
Kenmore (Perthshire and Kinross) 61 I 14
Kenmore (Highland) 66 C 11
Kennet (River) 17 O 29
Kennethmont 68 L 11
Kenninghall 30 X 26
Kennington (Kent) 12 W 30
Kennington (Oxon.) 18 Q 28
Kennoway 56 K 15
Kenovay 58 Z 14
Kensaleyre 65 B 11
Kensington and Chelsea (London Borough) 20 T 29
Kent (County) 12 V 30
Kentallen 60 E 13
Kentford 30 V 27
Kentisbeare 7 K 31
Kenton 4 J 32
Keoldale 72 F 8
Kerrera 59 D 14
Kerry 25 K 26
Kershader 70 A 9
Kesgrave 23 X 27
Kessingland 31 Z 26
Keswick 44 K 20
Kettering 28 R 26
Kettleshulme 35 N 24
Kettletoft 75 M 6
Kettlewell 39 N 21
Ketton 29 S 26
Kew 20 T 29
Kexby 36 R 23
Keyingham 41 T 22
Keymer 11 T 31
Keynsham 17 M 29
Keyworth 36 Q 25
Kibworth Harcourt 28 R 26
Kidderminster 27 N 26
Kidlington 18 Q 28
Kidsgrove 34 N 24
Kidwelly/Cydweli 15 H 28
Kielder 50 M 18
Kielder Forest 50 M 18
Kielder Reservoir 50 M 18
Kilbarchan 55 G 16
Kilbirnie 54 F 16
Kilbrannan Sound 53 D 17
Kilbride 60 D 14
Kilcadzow 55 I 16
Kilchattan 54 E 16
Kilchenzie 53 C 17
Kilchoan 59 B 13
Kilchrenan 60 E 14
Kilconquhar 56 L 15
Kilcreggan 54 F 16
Kildonan 53 E 17
Kildrummy 68 L 12
Kildrummy Castle 68 L 12
Kilham 41 S 21
Kilkhampton 6 G 31
Killearn 55 G 15
Killerton 7 J 31
Killichronan 59 C 14
Killin 61 H 14
Killinghall 39 P 21
Kilmacolm 55 G 16
Kilmaluag 65 B 10
Kilmany 62 L 14
Kilmarnock 54 G 17
Kilmartin 54 D 15
Kilmaurs 54 G 17
Kilmelford 54 D 15
Kilmorack 67 G 11
Kilmun 54 F 16
Kilninver 60 D 14
Kilnkadzow 55 I 16
Kilnsey 39 N 21
Kiloran 52 B 15
Kilpeck 26 L 28
Kilrenny 57 L 15
Kilsyth 55 H 16
Kilt Rock 65 B 11
Kilwinning 54 F 17
Kimberley 30 X 26
Kimble 18 R 28
Kimbolton 29 S 27
Kimmeridge 8 N 32
Kimpton 19 T 28
Kinbrace 73 I 9
Kincardine 55 I 15
Kincardine O' Neil 63 L 12
Kinclaven 62 J 14
Kincraig 61 I 12
Kineton 27 P 27
Kinfauns 62 J 14
King's Bromley 35 O 25
King's Cliffe 29 S 26
King's Lynn 30 V 25
King's Somborne 9 P 30
King's Sutton 28 Q 27
Kingairloch 60 D 14
Kingarth 54 E 16
Kinghorn 56 K 15
Kingie (Loch) 66 E 12
Kinglassie 56 K 15
Kings Langley 20 S 28
Kings Worthy 10 Q 30
Kingsbarns 57 M 15
Kingsbridge 4 I 33
Kingsclere 18 Q 30
Kingsdown 13 Y 30
Kingskerswell 4 J 32
Kingskettle 56 K 15
Kingsland 26 L 27
Kingsley 35 O 24
Kingsmuir 62 L 14
Kingsnorth 12 W 30
Kingsteignton 4 J 32
Kingston (Moray) 68 K 10
Kingston (Devon) 4 I 33
Kingston Bagpuize 18 P 28
Kingston Lacy 8 N 31
Kingston-upon-Hull 41 S 22
Kingston-upon-Thames (London Borough) 20 T 29
Kingstone 26 L 27
Kingswear 4 J 32
Kingswinford 27 N 26
Kingswood (South Glos.) 17 M 29
Kingswood (Glos.) 17 M 29
Kington 25 K 27
Kington Langley 17 N 29
Kingussie 61 H 12
Kinloch 65 B 12
Kinloch Rannoch 61 H 13
Kinlochard 55 G 15
Kinlochbervie 72 E 8
Kinlocheil 60 E 13
Kinlochewe 66 E 11
Kinlochleven 60 F 13
Kinlochmoidart 59 C 13
Kinloss 68 J 11
Kinneff 63 N 13
Kinnersley 26 L 27
Kinross 56 J 15
Kintbury 18 P 29
Kintore 69 M 12
Kintyre (Peninsula) 53 D 17
Kinver 27 N 26
Kippax 40 P 22
Kippen 55 H 15
Kippford 43 I 19
Kirby 38 L 23
Kirby Cross 23 X 28
Kirby Hall 28 S 26
Kirby Muxloe 28 Q 26
Kirdford 11 S 30
Kirk Ella 41 S 22
Kirk Ireton 35 P 24
Kirk Michael 42 G 21
Kirkbean 43 J 19
Kirkbride 44 K 19
Kirkburton 39 O 23
Kirkby Fleetham 46 P 20
Kirkby-in-Ashfield 36 Q 24
Kirkby Lonsdale 45 M 21
Kirkby Malham 39 N 21
Kirkby Malzeard 39 P 21
Kirkby Stephen 45 M 20
Kirkby Thore 45 M 20
Kirkbymoorside 46 R 21
Kirkcaldy 56 K 15
Kirkcolm 48 E 19
Kirkconnel 49 I 17
Kirkcowan 48 G 19
Kirkcudbright 43 H 19
Kirkcudbright Bay 43 H 19
Kirkfieldbank 55 I 16
Kirkham 38 L 22
Kirkhill 67 G 11
Kirkinner 42 G 19
Kirkintilloch 55 H 16
Kirklevington 46 P 20
Kirklington 36 R 24
Kirkmichael (Perthshire and Kinross) 62 J 13
Kirkmichael (South Ayrshire) 48 G 17
Kirkmuirhill 55 I 17
Kirknewton 56 J 16
Kirkoswald 48 F 18
Kirkpatrick Durham 49 I 18
Kirkpatrick-Fleming 50 K 18
Kirkstone Pass 44 L 20
Kirkton of Culsalmond 69 M 11
Kirkton of Durris 63 M 12
Kirkton of Glenisla 62 K 13
Kirkton of Kingoldrum 62 K 13
Kirkton of Largo 56 L 15
Kirkton of Skene 69 N 12
Kirkton of Strathmartine 62 K 14
Kirktown of Auchterless 69 M 11
Kirkwall 74 L 7
Kirkwhelpington 51 N 18
Kirriemuir 62 K 13
Kirtlebridge 50 K 18
Kirtlington 18 Q 28
Kirtomy 73 H 8
Kirton 37 T 25
Kirton-in-Lindsey 40 S 23
Kishorn (Loch) 66 D 11
Kitchener Memorial 74 J 6
Knapdale 53 D 16
Knaresborough 40 P 21
Knarsdale 45 M 19
Knebworth 19 T 28
Kneesworth 29 T 27
Knighton/Trefyclawdd 25 K 26
Knightshayes Court 7 J 31
Kniveton 35 O 24
Knock (Moray) 68 L 11
Knock (Western Isles) 71 B 9
Knockie Lodge 67 G 12
Knockin 34 L 25
Knole 21 U 30
Knossington 28 R 25
Knottingley 40 Q 22
Knowle 27 O 26
Knowsley 34 L 23
Knoydart 65 D 12
Knutsford 34 M 24
Kyle Forest 48 G 17
Kyle of Durness 72 F 8
Kyle of Lochalsh 65 C 12
Kyle of Sutherland 67 G 10
Kyle of Tongue 72 G 8
Kyleakin 65 C 12
Kylerhea 65 C 12
Kyles Scalpay 70 Z 10
Kylestrome 72 E 9
Kynance Cove 2 E 34

L

Laceby 41 T 23
Lacey Green 18 R 28
Lacock 17 N 29
Ladder Hills 68 K 12
Ladock 2 F 33
Ladybank 56 K 15
Ladybower Reservoir 35 O 23
Lagg 53 C 16
Laggan (near Invergarry) 60 F 12
Laggan (near Newtonmore) 61 H 12
Laggan (Loch) 61 G 13
Laggan Point 52 B 16
Laide 66 D 10
Laindon 22 V 29
Lair 66 E 11
Lairg 73 G 9
Lake District National Park 44 K 20
Lakenheath 30 V 26
Lamberhurst 12 V 30
Lambeth (London Borough) 20 T 29
Lambourn 18 P 29
Lamerton 3 H 32
Lamlash 53 E 17
Lamlash Bay 53 E 17
Lammermuir Hills 57 L 16
Lampeter/Llanbedr Pont Steffan 24 H 27
Lanark 55 I 16
Lancashire (County) 38 M 22
Lancaster 38 L 21
Lanchester 45 O 19
Land's End 2 C 33
Landrake 3 H 32
Lanercost 50 L 19
Langavat (Loch) (Lewis) 70 Z 9
Langavat (Loch) (South Harris) 70 Z 10
Langbank 55 G 16
Langdale Valley 44 K 20

LONDON

Brompton Road.............. HY
Camden Passage .... NS 70
Kensington High Street ...... EY
King's Road .... GHZ
Knightsbridge............... HY
Middlesex Street .... PU
Oxford Street .... KU
Piccadilly.................. JX
Portobello Road............ EV
Regent Street .... KV
Sloane Street............... HY

Westbourne Ter. Rd. .... FU 452
West Smithfield........... NU 454
Wharfdale Rd............. LS 455
Whitechapel High St. ...... PU 456
Whitehall Court............ LX 460
Whitehall Pl............... LX 462
Whitmore Rd.............. PS 464
Wormwood St............ PU 472

Abingdon Rd .... EY 2
Allsop Pl. .... HU 4
Appold Street .... PU 5
Atterbury St................ LZ 9
Battersea Park Rd.......... JZ 19
Belvedere Rd............... MX 23
Bernard St. .... LT 25
Bessborough St............ KZ 30
Bethnal Green Rd.......... PT 32
Bevis Marks .... PU 34
Bishopsgate................ PU 36
Blackfriars Bridge.......... NV 38
Bloomsbury St............. LU 39
Bowling Green La. .... NT 43
Bridgefoot .... LZ 49
Broad Sanctuary........... LY 52
Byward St. .... PV 62
Calthorpe St............... MT 65
Camomile St............... PU 71
Carriage Drive North .... IZ 75
Chapel Market .... NS 78
Charlbert St................ HT 79
Charterhouse Sq........... OU 81
Charterhouse St........... NU 83
Cornwall Rd............... MX 108
Corporation Row........... NT 110
Cowcross St............... NU 113
Crawford Pl............... HU 116
Cromwell Cres. .... EZ 119
Crucifix Lane .... PX 125
Curtain Rd................ PT 126
Dante Rd.................. NZ 129
Dufferin St................ OT 141
Duke's Pl. .... PV 145
Durham St. .... MZ 150
Eardley Cres. .... EZ 151
Eastcheap................. PV 154
Ebury Bridge .... IZ 156
Edwardes St............... EY 158
Elephant Rd............... OZ 163
Fann St. .... OU 166
Farringdon St.............. NU 168
Fetter Lane .... NU 169
Garden Row .... NY 173
Giltspur St................ OU 178
Goodge St................. KU 184
Gracechurch St............ PV 187
Great Eastern St........... PT 192
Great George St. .... LY 193
Great Smith St. .... LY 196
Great Tower St............ PV 197
Greycoat Pl............... KY 200
Gunter Grove .... FZ 202
Harleyford St.............. MZ 211
Herbrand St................ LT 218
Hercules Rd............... MY 219
Holland Walk .... EY 225
Horseguards Av. .... LX 228
Hornton St................ FY 229
Howland St................ KU 232
Hunter St. .... LT 233
Hyde Rd.................. PS 235
Kenway Rd................ FZ 245
King Edward St............ OU 247
King William St............ PV 250
Leadenhall St.............. PV 260
Little Britain.............. OU 264
Lloyd Baker St............. MT 265
Lombard St................ PV 268
Long Lane City............ OU 270
Lothbury.................. PU 273
Lower Marsh .... MY 277
Lower Thames St........... PV 278
Mansell St................ PV 282
Miles St.................. LZ 290
Montague St............... OU 291
Moreland St............... OT 293
Myddelton St.............. NT 296
Nevern Place .... EZ 298
Nevern Sq................ EZ 299
New Bridge St............. NV 301
New Change .... OV 304
Newington Butts .... OZ 306
Newington Causeway ...... OY 307
Northumberland Av. .... LX 317
Old Bailey .... NV 318
Old Broad St.............. PU 319
Old Marylebone Rd........ HU 324
Paddington St............. IU 333
Park Cres................. IU 337
Parliament St.............. LY 340
Parry St.................. LZ 341
Pembroke Gdns .... EY 342
Penn St.................. PS 343
Penton Rise .... MT 344
Penton St................. MT 345
Penywern Rd.............. FZ 347
Philbeach Gdns .... EZ 348
Pilgrimage St.............. PY 349
Poole St.................. PS 350
Porchester Rd............. FU 351
Poultry................... OV 352
Princes St................. PV 357
Queen's Circus .... IZ 361
Queen St................. OV 365
Rossmore Rd.............. HT 369
St. Andrews St............ NU 372
St. Bride St............... NV 376
St. John's Wood
  High St. .... GT 378
St. John's Wood Park ..... GS 379
St. Martin's-le-Grand...... OU 380
Shoreditch High St. .... PT 384
Sidmouth St.............. LT 385
Snows Fields .... PX 386
Southampton Row .... LU 387
South Pl.................. PU 391
Southwark Bridge .... OV 395
Spencer St................ NT 398
Spital Sq................. PU 399
Storeys Gate .... LY 402
Tabard St................. OY 408
Tavistock Sq.............. LT 409
Templeton St.............. EZ 410
Threadneedle St........... PV 417
Throgmorton St........... PU 418
Tower Hill .... PV 425
Trebovir Rd............... FZ 426
Upper Ground .... NX 428
Upper Thames St.......... OV 431
Upper Woburn Pl.......... LT 432
Vincent St................ LZ 436
Warwick Av............... FU 441
Westbourne Park Villas .... FU 449

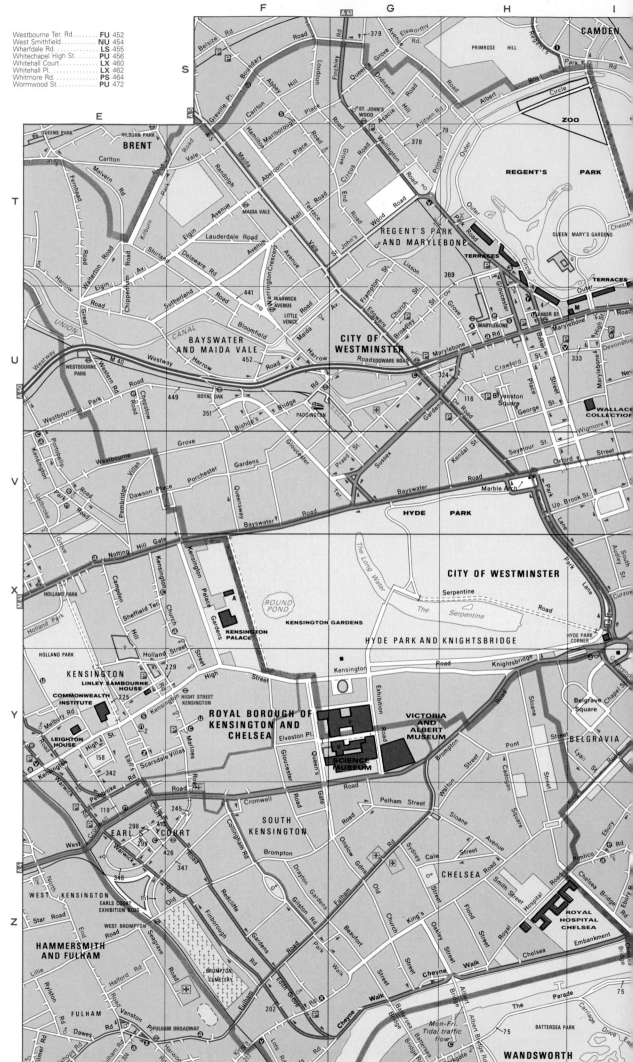

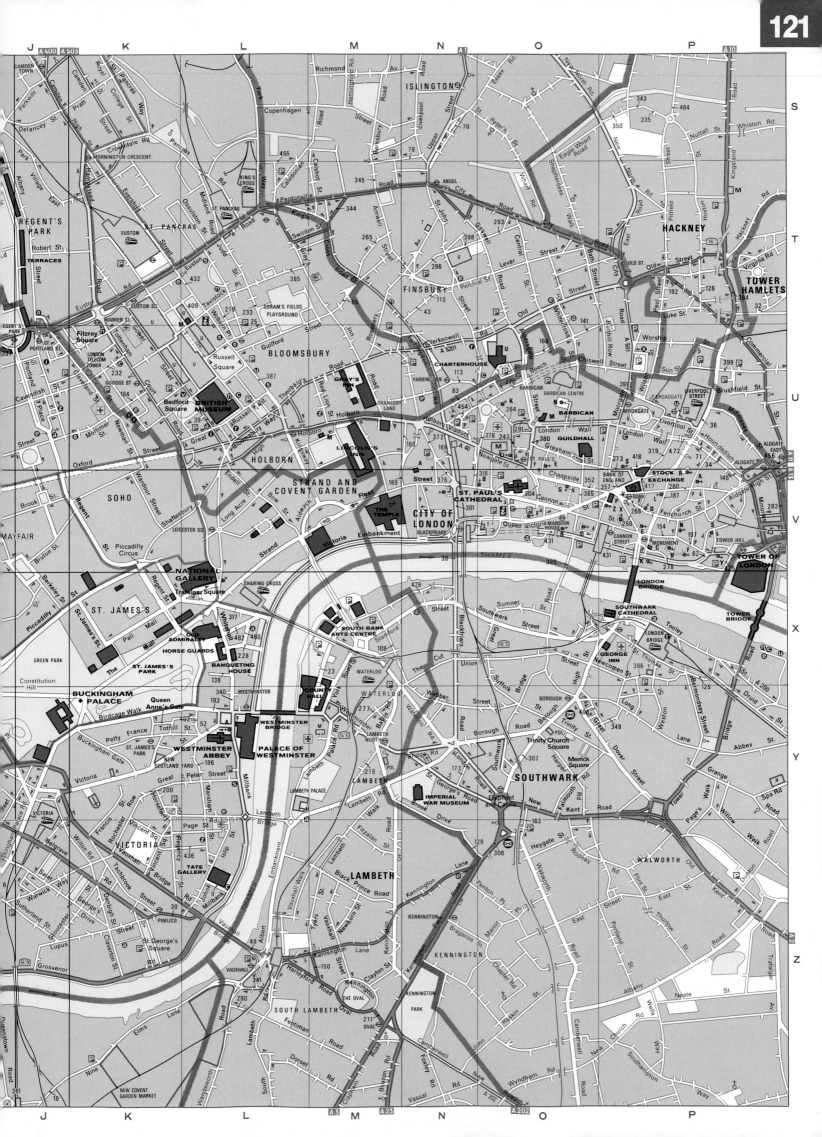

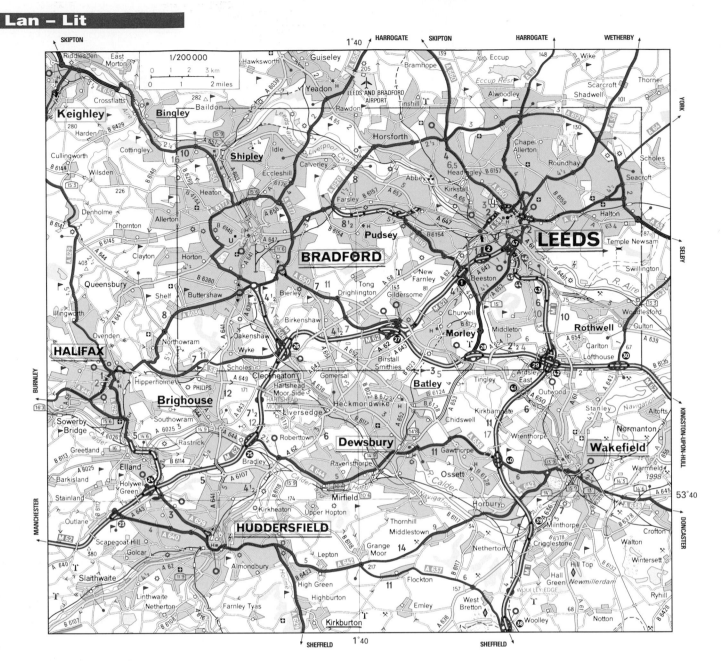

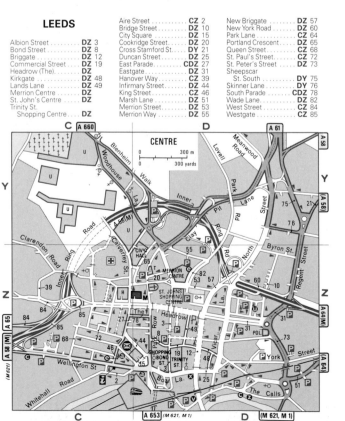

LEEDS

Albion Street	DZ 3	
Bond Street	DZ 8	
Briggate	DZ 12	
Commercial Street	DZ 19	
Headrow (The)	DZ	
Kirkgate	DZ 48	
Lands Lane	DZ 49	
Merrion Centre	DZ	
St. John's Centre	DZ	
Trinity St. Shopping Centre	DZ	

Aire Street	CZ 2	
Bridge Street	DZ 10	
City Square	DZ 15	
Cookridge Street	DZ 20	
Cross Stamford St.	DY 21	
Duncan Street	DZ 25	
East Parade	CDZ 27	
Eastgate	DZ 31	
Hanover Way	CZ 39	
Infirmary Street	DZ 44	
King Street	CZ 46	
Marsh Lane	DZ 51	
Merrion Street	DZ 53	
Merrion Way	DZ 55	

New Briggate	DZ 57	
New York Road	DZ 60	
Park Lane	CZ 64	
Portland Crescent	DZ 65	
Queen Street	CZ 68	
St. Paul's Street	CZ 72	
St. Peter's Street	DZ 73	
Sheepscar St. South	DY 75	
Skinner Lane	DY 76	
South Parade	CDZ 78	
Wade Lane	DZ 82	
West Street	CZ 84	
Westgate	CZ 85	

Langenhoe	23 W 28
Langford	29 T 27
Langholm	50 L 18
Langley	20 S 29
Langold	36 Q 23
Langport	8 L 30
Langsett	39 O 23
Langstrothdale Chase	45 N 21
Langtoft	41 S 21
Langton Matravers	9 O 32
Langwathby	45 L 19
Lanhydrock	3 F 32
Lanivet	3 F 32
Lanreath	3 G 32
Lansallos	3 G 32
Lapford	6 I 31
Larbert	55 I 15
Largs	54 F 16
Larkhall	55 I 16
Larkhill	17 O 30
Lasswade	56 K 16
Lastingham	46 R 21
Latchingdon	22 W 28
Lauder	57 L 16
Lauderdale	57 L 16
Laugharne	14 G 28
Laughton	12 U 31
Launceston	3 G 32
Laurencekirk	63 M 13
Lauriston Castle	56 K 16
Lavant	10 R 31
Lavenham	22 W 27
Laverstoke	9 P 30
Lawford	23 X 28
Laxey	42 G 21
Laxey Bay	42 G 21
Laxfield	31 Y 27

Laxford (Loch)	72 E 8
Laxford Bridge	72 E 8
Laxo	75 Q 2
Layer-de-la-Haye	23 W 28
Layer Marney	23 W 28
Lazonby	44 L 19
Leaden Roding	22 U 28
Leadenham	36 S 24
Leadgate	45 M 19
Leadhills	49 I 17
Lealholm	47 R 20
Leasingham	37 S 24
Leathaid Bhuain (Loch an)	72 F 9
Leatherhead	20 T 30
Leathley	39 P 22
Lecale Peninsula	99 O 5
Lechlade	17 O 28
Lecht Road	68 K 12
Ledbury	26 M 27
Ledmore	72 F 9
Lee	6 H 30
Lee-on-the-Solent	10 Q 31
Leebotwood	26 L 26
Leeds (Kent)	12 V 30
Leeds (West Yorks.)	39 P 22
Leedstown	2 D 33
Leek	35 N 24
Leeming Bar	46 P 21
Leicester	28 Q 26
Leicestershire (County)	27 P 26
Leigh	38 M 23
Leigh-on-Sea	22 V 29
Leighton Buzzard	19 S 28
Leintwardine	26 L 26
Leiston	23 Y 27
Leith	56 K 16

Lemreway	70 A 9
Lenham	12 W 30
Lennoxlove	56 L 16
Lennoxtown	55 H 16
Leominster	26 L 27
Lerwick	75 Q 3
Lesbury	51 P 17
Leslie	56 K 15
Lesmahagow	55 I 17
Leswalt	48 E 19
Letchworth	29 T 28
Letham (Angus)	62 L 14
Letham (Fife)	56 K 15
Letheringsett	30 X 25
Letterewe Forest	66 D 10
Letterston	14 F 28
Leuchars	62 L 14
Leven (East Riding of Yorks.)	41 T 22
Leven (Fife)	56 K 15
Leven (Highland)	60 F 13
Leven (Loch)	60 E 13
Levens	44 L 21
Levens Hall	44 L 21
Levenwick	75 Q 4
Leverington	29 U 25
Leverton with Habblesthorpe	36 R 24
Lewdown	3 H 32
Lewes	11 U 31
Lewis and Harris (Isle of)	70 Z 8
Lewisham (London Borough)	21 T 29
Leyburn	45 O 21
Leyland	38 L 22
Leysdown-on-Sea	12 W 29
Lezant	3 G 32

Lhanbryde	68 K 11
Liathach	66 D 11
Lichfield	27 O 25
Liddesdale	50 L 18
Lidgate	22 V 27
Lifton	3 H 32
Ligger or Perran Bay	2 E 32
Lilleshall	34 M 25
Limpsfield	21 U 30
Lincoln	36 S 24
Lincolnshire (County)	36 S 24
Lincolnshire Wolds	37 T 23
Lindfield	11 T 30
Lindores	56 K 14
Lingay (near Eriskay)	64 X 12
Lingay (near Pabbay)	58 X 13
Lingfield	21 T 30
Liniclate	64 X 11
Linlithgow	56 J 16
Linn of Dee	62 J 13
Linn of Tummel	61 I 13
Linney Head	14 E 29
Linnhe (Loch)	60 D 14
Linslade	19 R 28
Linton	29 U 27
Linton-on-Ouse	40 Q 21
Lintrathen (Loch of)	62 K 13
Linwood	55 G 16
Liphook	10 R 30
Liskeard	3 G 32
Lismore	60 D 14
Liss	10 R 30
Litcham	30 W 25
Litherland	38 L 23

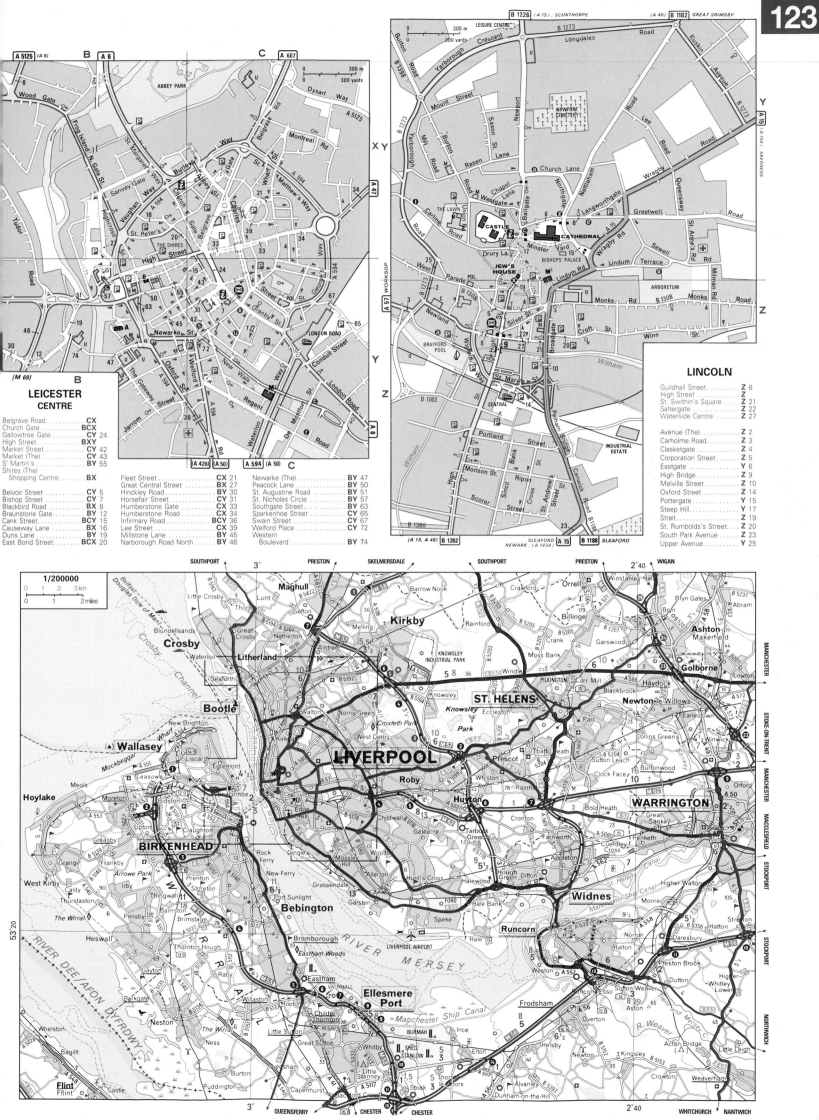

LEICESTER
CENTRE

Belgrave Road............ **CX**
Church Gate............. **BCX**
Gallowtree Gate......... **CY** 24
High Street.............. **BXY**
Market Street........... **CY** 42
Market (The)............ **CY** 43
S¹ Martin's.............. **BY** 55
Shires (The)
Shopping Centre...... **BX**

Belvoir Street........... **CY** 5
Bishop Street........... **CY** 7
Blackbird Road.......... **BX** 8
Braunstone Gate........ **BY** 12
Cank Street............. **BCY** 15
Causeway Lane.......... **BX** 16
Duns Lane.............. **BY** 19
East Bond Street....... **BCX** 20

Fleet Street............ **CX** 21
Great Central Street..... **BX** 27
Hinckley Road........... **BY** 30
Horsefair Street......... **CY** 31
Humberstone Gate....... **CY** 33
Humberstone Road....... **CX** 34
Infirmary Road.......... **BCY** 36
Lee Street.............. **CX** 39
Millstone Lane.......... **BY** 45
Narborough Road North... **BY** 46

Newarke (The).......... **BY** 47
Peacock Lane........... **BY** 50
St. Augustine Road...... **BY** 51
St. Nicholas Circle...... **BY** 57
Southgate Street........ **BY** 63
Sparkenhoe Street....... **CY** 65
Swain Street........... **CY** 67
Welford Place.......... **BY** 72
Western
Boulevard.......... **BY** 74

LINCOLN

Guildhall Street.......... **Z** 8
High Street.............. **Z**
St. Swithin's Square...... **Z** 21
Saltergate.............. **Z** 22
Waterside Centre........ **Z** 27

Avenue (The)............ **Z** 2
Carholme Road.......... **Z** 3
Clasketgate............ **Z** 4
Corporation Street....... **Z** 5
Eastgate............... **Y** 6
High Bridge............. **Z** 9
Melville Street.......... **Z** 10
Oxford Street........... **Z** 14
Pottergate............. **Y** 15
Steep Hill.............. **Z** 17
Strait.................. **Z** 19
St. Rumbolds's Street.... **Z** 20
South Park Avenue....... **Z** 23
Upper Avenue........... **Y** 25

LIVERPOOL CENTRE

Bold Street	DZ
Church Street	DY
Lime Street	DEY
London Road	DEY
Lord Street	CDY
Parker Street	DY 103
Ranelagh Street	DY 108
Renshaw Street	DEZ
St. Johns Centre	DY
Argyle Street	DZ 6
Blackburne Place	EZ 11
Brunswick Road	EY 19
Canning Place	CZ 23
Churchill Way	DY 25
Clarence Street	EYZ 26
College Lane	DZ 28
Commutation Row	DY 30
Cook Street	CY 32
Crosshall Street	DY 36
Daulby Street	EY 40
Erskine Street	EY 45
Fontenoy Street	DY 48
Forrest Street	DZ 49
George's Dock Gate	CY 51
Grafton Street	DZ 53
Great Charlotte Street	DY 54
Great Howard Street	CY 56
Hatton Garden	DY 57
Haymarket	DY 58
Hood Street	DY 62
Houghton Street	DY 65
Huskisson Street	EZ 66
James Street	CY 68
King Edward Street	CY 69
Knight Street	EZ 72
Leece Street	EZ 73
Liver Street	CZ 76
Mansfield Street	DEY 80
Mathew Street	CDY 81
Moss Street	EY 86
Mount Street	EZ 88
Myrtle Street	EZ 89
Newington	DZ 92
New Quay	CY 93
North John Street	CY 96
Norton Street	EY 97
Parker Street	DY 103
Prescot Street	EY 105
Prince's Road	EZ 107
Ranelagh St.	DZ 108
Richmond Street	DY 109
Roe Street	DY 114
St. James Place	EZ 117
St. John's Lane	DY 118
School Lane	DYZ 122
Scotland Place	DY 123
Sefton Street	DZ 129
Seymour Street	EY 130
Skelhorne Street	DY 133
Stanley Street	CDY 135
Suffolk Street	DZ 137
Tarleton Street	DY 139
Victoria Street	DY 143
Water Street	CY 150
William Brown Street	DY 156
York Street	DZ 157

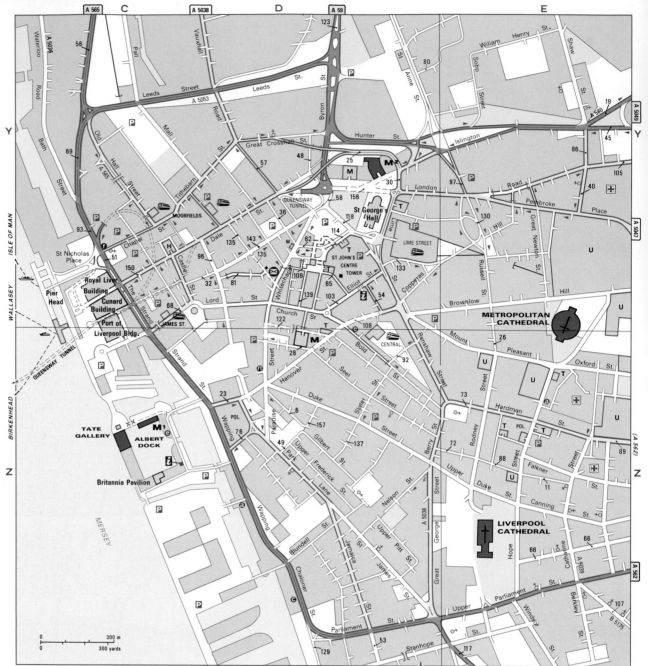

Little Berkhamsted	19 T 28	Lizard	2 E 34	Llanfair	32 H 25	Llanrhidian	15 H 29	Llyswen	25 K 27	Lodsworth	11 R 31	Longfield	21 U 29
Little Budworth	34 M 24	Lizard Peninsula	2 E 33	Llanfair-Caereinion	25 K 26	Llanrhystud	24 H 27	Loanhead	56 K 16	Loftus	46 R 20	Longford	9 O 30
Little Bytham	37 S 25	Llanarth	24 H 27	Llanfair-		Llanrwst	33 I 24	Lochaber	66 D 12	Logan Gardens	42 F 19	Longforgan	62 K 14
Little Chalfont	20 S 28	Llanbadarn Fawr	24 H 26	Pwllgwyngyll	32 H 24	Llansanffraid Glan		Lochailort	59 D 13	Logie Coldstone	68 L 12	Longhope	74 K 7
Little Clacton	23 X 28	Llanbedr	32 H 25	Llanfair-ym-Muallt/		Conwy	33 I 24	Lochaline	59 C 14	Logiealmond	61 I 14	Longhorsley	51 O 18
Little Colonsay	59 B 14	Llanbedr Pont		Builth	25 J 27	Llansantffraid	24 H 27	Lochans	42 E 19	Lomond (Loch)	55 G 15	Longhoughton	51 P 17
Little Cumbrae		Steffan/		Llanfairfechan	33 I 24	Llansantffraid-		Locharbriggs	49 J 18	London	20 T 29	Longleat House	8 N 30
Island	54 F 16	Lampeter	24 H 27	Llanfyllin	33 K 25	ym-Mechain	33 K 25	Lochawe	60 E 14	London Colney	19 T 28	Longniddry	56 L 16
Little Glenshee	62 J 14	Llanbedrog	32 G 25	Llangadog	15 I 28	Llansawel	24 H 27	Lochay (Glen)	61 G 14	Long Bennington	36 R 25	Longnor	35 O 24
Little Hadham	22 U 28	Llanberis	32 H 24	Llangammarch		Llansilin	33 K 25	Lochboisdale	64 Y 12	Long Buckby	28 Q 27	Longridge	38 M 22
Little Hallingbury	22 U 28	Llanbister	25 K 26	Wells	25 J 27	Llansoy	16 L 28	Lochbuie	59 C 14	Long Crendon	18 R 28	Longside	69 O 11
Little Loch Broom	66 D 10	Llanbrynmair	25 J 26	Llangefni	32 H 24	Llanthony	16 K 28	Lochcarron	66 D 11	Long Eaton	36 Q 25	Longton	35 N 25
Little Loch Roag	70 Z 9	Llanddewi Brefi	24 I 27	Llangeinor	15 J 29	Llantwit Major	15 J 29	Lochearnhead	61 H 14	Long Hanborough	18 P 28	Longtown	50 L 18
Little Minch (The)	64 Z 11	Llandegai	32 H 24	Llangeitho	24 H 27	Llanuwchllyn	33 I 25	Lochgarthside	67 G 12	Long (Loch)		Lonmore	65 A 11
Little Moreton Hall	35 N 24	Llandegla	33 K 24	Llangollen	33 K 25	Llanwddyn	33 J 25	Lochgelly	56 K 15	(Angus)	62 K 14	Looe	3 G 32
Little Ouse (River)	30 V 26	Llandeilo Ferwallt	15 H 29	Llangorse	16 K 28	Llanwenog	24 H 27	Lochgilphead	54 D 15	Long (Loch) (Argyll		Lorn	60 E 14
Little Ouseburn	40 Q 21	Llandenny	16 L 28	Llangranog	24 G 27	Llanwrda	15 I 28	Lochgoilhead	54 F 15	and Bute)	54 F 15	Lorn (Firth of)	59 D 14
Little Snoring	30 W 25	Llandissilio	14 F 28	Llangunllo	25 K 26	Llanwrtyd Wells	25 J 27	Lochinver	72 E 9	Long Man (The)	12 U 31	Lossiemouth	68 K 10
Little Walsingham	30 W 25	Llandovery/		Llangurig	25 J 26	Llanybydder	24 H 27	Lochluichart	66 F 11	Long Marston	40 Q 22	Lostwithiel	3 G 32
Little Waltham	22 V 28	Llanymddyfri	15 I 28	Llangwn	16 L 29	Llanymddyfri/		Lochmaben	49 J 18	Long Melford	22 W 27	Loudwater	19 R 29
Littleborough	39 N 23	Llandrindod Wells	25 J 27	Llangwnnadl	32 F 25	Llandovery	15 I 28	Lochmaddy	64 Y 11	Long Mountain	25 K 26	Loughborough	36 Q 25
Littlebourne	13 X 30	Llandrinio	33 K 25	Llangwyryfon	24 H 27	Llanymynech	33 K 25	Lochore	56 K 15	Long Mynd (The)	26 L 26	Loughor	
Littlebury	29 U 27	Llandudno	33 I 24	Llangybi	24 H 27	Llanystumdwy	32 H 25	Lochranza	53 E 16	Long Preston	39 N 21	(River)	15 H 29
Littlecote House	18 P 29	Llandudno		Llangynidr	16 K 28	Lledrod	24 I 27	Lochsie (Glen)	62 J 13	Long Stratton	31 X 26	Loughton	21 U 29
Littlehampton	11 S 31	Junction	33 I 24	Llangynog	33 J 25	Lleyn Peninsula	32 G 25	Lochton	63 M 12	Long Sutton (Lincs.)	37 U 25	Louth	37 U 23
Littleport	29 U 26	Llandybie	15 H 28	Llanhilleth	16 K 28	Llwyngwril	24 H 25	Lochwinnoch	55 G 16	Long Sutton		Low Street	31 Y 25
Littlestone-		Llandysul	24 H 27	Llanidloes	25 J 26	Llwynmawr	33 K 25	Lochy (Loch)	60 F 13	(Somerset)	8 L 30	Lowca	43 J 20
on-Sea	12 W 31	Llanegryn	24 H 26	Llanilar	25 I 26	Llyfnant Valley	25 I 26	Locking	16 L 30	Longay	65 C 12	Lowdham	36 Q 24
Liverpool	34 L 23	Llanelli	15 H 28	Llanmadoc	15 H 29	Llyn Brianne	25 I 27	Lockerbie	49 J 18	Longbenton	51 P 18	Lower Bentham	38 M 21
Liverton	46 R 20	Llanelltyd	32 I 25	Llannefydd	33 J 24	Llyn Celyn	33 I 25	Locking	16 L 30	Longbridge		Lower Cam	17 M 28
Livet (Glen)	68 K 12	Llanengan	32 G 25	Llanrhaeadr-		Llyn Tegid or Bala		Loddon	31 Y 26	Deverill	8 N 30	Lower Diabaig	66 C 11
Livingston	56 J 16	Llanerchymedd	32 G 24	ym-Mochnant	33 K 25	Lake	33 J 25	Lode	29 U 27	Longburton	8 M 31	Lowestoft	31 Z 26

Lowick	57 O 17	Luthrie	56 K 14	**M**		Mainland (Orkney		Mapledurham	18 Q 29	Marshchapel	41 U 23	Mayfield (Staffs.)	35 O 24
Lowick Bridge	44 K 21	Luton	19 S 28			Islands)	74 J 6	Mar (Forest of)	62 J 12	Marshfield	17 N 29	Meadie (Loch)	72 G 9
Lowther	49 I 17	Luton Hoo	19 S 28	Maaruig	70 Z 10	Mainland (Shetland		Marazion	2 D 33	Marske-by-the-Sea	46 Q 20	Mealsgate	44 K 19
Lowther Hills	49 J 18	Lutterworth	28 Q 26	Mablethorpe	37 U 23	Islands)	75 R 3	March	29 U 26	Marston Magna	8 M 31	Meare	8 L 30
Loxwood	11 S 30	Luxborough	7 J 30	Mc Arthur's Head	52 B 16	Maisemore	17 N 28	Marcham	18 P 29	Marston		Measach (Falls of)	66 E 10
Loyal (Loch)	73 G 8	Lybster	74 K 9	Macaskin (Island)	54 D 15	Malborough	4 I 33	Marchwood	9 P 31	Moretaine	29 S 27	Measham	27 P 25
Loyne (Loch)	60 E 12	Lydbury North	26 L 26	Macclesfield	35 N 24	Malden Bradley	8 N 30	Marden	12 V 30	Martham	31 Y 25	Medbourne	28 R 26
Lùb Score	65 A 10	Lydd	12 W 31	Macduff	69 M 10	Maldon	22 W 28	Maree (Loch)	66 D 10	Martin	9 O 31	Medmenham	18 R 29
Lubenham	28 R 26	Lydd-on-Sea	12 W 31	Machars (The)	42 G 19	Malham	39 N 21	Mareham-le-Fen	37 T 24	Martin (Isle)	66 E 10	Medway (River)	12 W 29
Lubnaig		Lydford	3 H 32	Machir Bay	52 A 16	Mallaig	65 C 12	Maresfield	12 U 31	Martley	26 M 27	Meidrim	14 G 28
(Loch)	55 H 15	Lydham	26 L 26	Machrihanish	53 C 17	Mallory Park Circuit	28 P 26	Margam	15 I 29	Martock	8 L 31	Meigle	62 K 14
Luccombe	7 J 30	Lydiard Park	17 O 29	Machrihanish Bay	53 C 17	Mallwyd	25 I 25	Margaretting	22 V 28	Marwell Zoological		Melbost	71 B 9
Luce Bay	42 F 19	Lydney	17 M 28	Machynlleth	61 I 14	Malmesbury	17 N 29	Margnaheglish	53 E 17	Park	10 Q 31	Melbourn	29 U 27
Ludgershall		Lyme Bay	5 L 32	Maddy (Loch)	64 Y 11	Malpas	34 L 24	Margate	13 Y 29	Mary Arden's		Melbourne	35 P 25
(Bucks.)	18 Q 28	Lyme Park	35 N 23	Madeley (Salop)	26 M 26	Maltby	36 Q 23	Market Bosworth	27 P 26	House	27 O 27	Melfort	54 D 15
Ludgershall		Lyme Regis	7 L 31	Madeley (Staffs.)	34 M 24	Maltby-le-Marsh	37 U 24	Market Deeping	29 T 25	Mary Tavy	3 H 32	Melksham	17 N 29
(Wilts.)	17 P 30	Lyminge	13 X 30	Madingley	29 U 27	Malton	40 R 21	Market Drayton	34 M 25	Maryburgh	67 G 11	Mellerstain	50 M 17
Ludgvan	2 D 33	Lymington	9 P 31	Madron	2 D 33	Malvern Wells	26 N 27	Market Harborough	28 R 26	Maryculter	69 N 12	Melling	38 M 21
Ludham	31 Y 25	Lymm	34 M 23	Maenclochog	14 F 28	Mamble	26 M 26	Market Lavington	17 O 30	Marykirk	63 M 13	Mellon Udrigle	71 D 10
Ludlow	26 L 26	Lympne	13 X 30	Maentwrog	32 I 25	Mamore Forest	60 F 13	Market Rasen	37 T 24	Marypark	68 J 11	Melmerby	45 M 19
Lugton	55 G 16	Lympstone	4 J 32	Maerdy	15 J 28	Man (Isle of)	42 G 21	Market Weighton	40 S 22	Maryport	44 J 19	Melrose	50 L 17
Luichart (Loch)	67 F 11	Lyndhurst	9 P 31	Maes Howe	74 K 7	Manaton	4 I 32	Markfield	28 Q 25	Marywell	63 M 14	Meltham	39 O 23
Luing	54 D 15	Lyneham	17 O 29	Maesteg	15 J 29	Manchester	39 N 23	Markinch	56 K 15	Masham	46 P 21	Melton Mowbray	36 R 25
Lulworth Cove	8 N 32	Lyness	74 K 7	Maghull	38 L 23	Manderston	57 O 16	Marks Tey	23 W 28	Matlock	35 P 24	Melvaig	66 C 10
Lumphanan	69 L 12	Lynmouth	6 I 30	Magor	16 L 29	Manea	29 U 26	Markyate	19 S 28	Matlock Bath	35 P 24	Melvich	73 I 8
Lunanhead	62 L 14	Lynton	6 I 30	Maiden Bradley	8 N 30	Mangotsfield	17 M 29	Marlborough	17 O 29	Mattishall	30 X 26	Menai Bridge/	
Lundie (Loch)	66 C 11	Lyon (Glen)	61 H 14	Maiden Castle	8 M 31	Manningtree	23 X 28	Marldon	4 J 32	Mauchline	48 G 17	Porthaethwy	32 H 24
Lundin Links	56 L 15	Lyon (Loch)	61 G 14	Maiden Newton	8 M 31	Manorbier	14 F 29	Marlow	19 R 29	Maud	69 N 11	Menai Strait	32 H 24
Lundy	6 G 30	Lyonshall	26 L 27	Maidenhead	19 R 29	Mansfield	36 Q 24	Marnhull	8 N 31	Maughold Head	42 H 21	Mendip Hills	16 L 30
Lune (River)	44 L 20	Lytchett Minster	8 N 31	Maidens	48 F 17	Mansfield		Marple	35 N 23	Mawbray	44 J 19	Menston	39 O 22
Lurgainn		Lytes Cary	8 L 30	Maidford	28 Q 27	Woodhouse	36 Q 24	Marsden	39 O 23	Maybole	48 F 17	Menteith Hills	55 H 15
(Loch)	72 E 9	Lytham	38 L 22	Maidstone	12 V 30	Manton	28 R 26	Marshall	8 N 31	Mayfield (East		Mentmore	19 R 28
Luss	55 G 15	Lytham St. Anne's	38 K 22	Manuden	22 U 28			Marsham	31 X 25	Sussex)	12 U 30	Meonstoke	10 Q 31

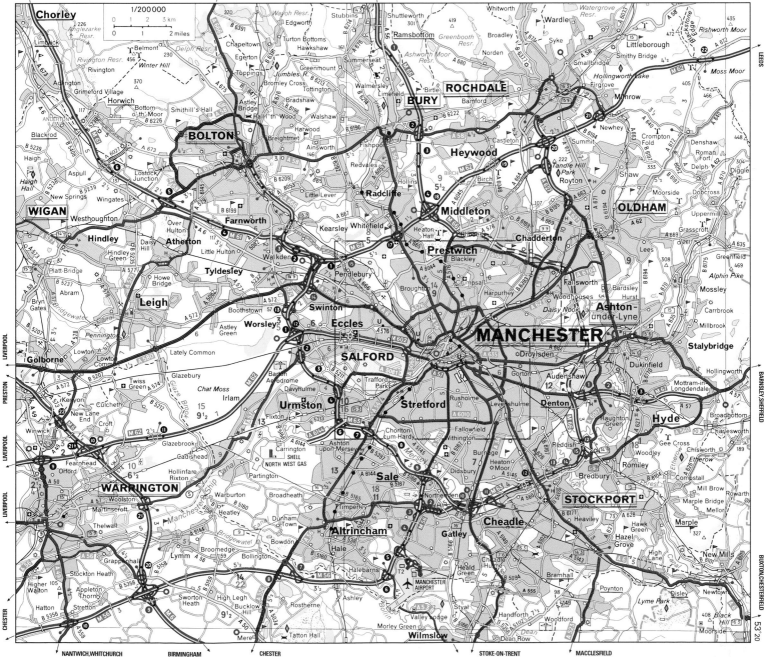

MANCHESTER
CENTRE

Arndale
  Shopping Centre .... **CY**
Deansgate .... **CYZ**
Lower Mosley Street .... **CZ**
Market Place .... **CY**
Market Street .... **CY** 75
Mosley Street .... **CZ**
Princess Street .... **CZ**

Addington Street .... **CY** 2
Albert Square .... **CZ** 6
Aytoun Street .... **CZ** 10

Blackfriars Road .... **CY** 15
Blackfriars Street .... **CY** 17
Brazennose Street .... **CZ** 18
Cannon Street .... **CY** 21
Cateaton Street .... **CY** 22
Charlotte Street .... **CZ** 25
Cheetham Hill Road .... **CY** 27
Chepstow Street .... **CZ** 28
Chorlton Street .... **CZ** 29
Church Street .... **CY** 31
Dale Street .... **CZ** 38
Ducie Street .... **CZ** 45
Fairfield Street .... **CZ** 49
Fennel Street .... **CY** 50
Great Bridgewater Street ... **CZ** 53
Great Ducie Street .... **CY** 57

High Street .... **CY** 62
John Dalton Street .... **CZ** 63
King Street .... **CY** 64
Liverpool Road .... **CZ** 68
Lloyd Street .... **CZ** 69
Lower Byrom Street .... **CZ** 70
Nicholas Street .... **CZ** 84
Parker Street .... **CZ** 91
Peter Street .... **CZ** 92
St. Ann's Street .... **CY** 101
St. Peter's Square .... **CZ** 104
Spring Gardens .... **CY** 106
Viaduct Street .... **CY** 109
Whitworth Street West ...... **CZ** 112
Withy Grove .... **CY** 113
York Street .... **CZ** 115

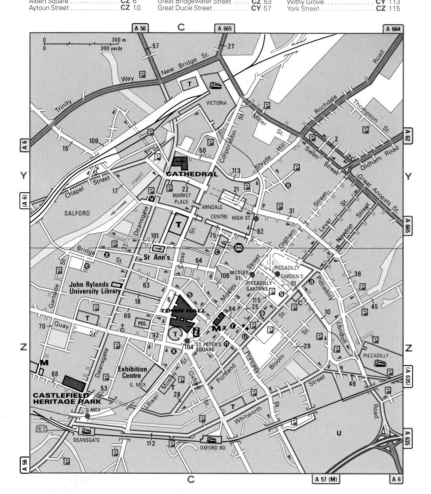

Mid Yell	75 Q 2	Minsterworth	17 N 28	Mortehoe	6 H 30
Midbea	74 L 6	Minterne Magna	8 M 31	Mortimer	18 Q 29
Middle Wallop	9 P 30	Mintlaw	69 O 11	Morton (near
Middleham	45 O 21	Minto	50 L 17	Bourne)	37 S 25
Middle Rasen	37 S 23	Mirfield	39 O 22	Morton (near
Middlesbrough	46 Q 20	Misterton (Notts.)	41 R 23	Gainsborough)	36 R 23
Middlestown	39 P 23	Misterton		Morven	73 J 9
Middleton (Argyll		(Somerset)	8 L 31	Morvern	59 C 14
and Bute)	58 Z 14	Mistley	23 X 28	Morville	26 M 26
Middleton		Mitcheldean	17 M 28	Morwelham	3 H 32
(Gtr. Mches.)	39 N 23	Mitchell	2 E 32	Morwenstow	6 G 31
Middleton Cheney	28 Q 27	Modbury	4 I 32	Moss Bank	38 L 23
Middleton-		Moelfre	32 H 23	Mossend	55 H 16
in-Teesdale	45 N 20	Moffat	49 J 17	Mossley	39 N 23
Middleton-on-Sea	11 S 31	Moidart	59 C 13	Mosstodloch	68 K 11
Middleton		Moira	35 P 25	Motherwell	55 I 16
St George	46 P 20	Mold/Yr Wyddgrug	33 K 24	Moulton (Lincs.)	37 T 25
Middletown	33 K 25	Monadhliath		Moulton
Middlewich	34 M 24	Mountains	67 H 12	(Northants.)	28 R 27
Midhurst	10 R 31	Monar (Loch)	66 E 11	Moulton Chapel	37 T 25
Midlem	50 L 17	Monaughty		Mountain Ash/
Midsomer Norton	17 M 30	Forest	68 J 11	Aberpennar	16 J 28
Migdale (Loch)	67 H 10	Moneydie	62 J 14	Mount's Bay	2 D 33
Milborne Port	8 M 31	Moniaive	49 I 18	Mountsorrel	36 Q 25
Milborne St.		Monifieth	62 L 14	Mousa	75 Q 4
Andrew	8 N 31	Monikie	62 L 14	Mousehole	2 D 33
Mildenhall	30 V 26	Monk Fryston	40 Q 22	Mouswald	49 J 18
Mile End	23 W 28	Monkokehampton	6 H 31	Mow Cop	35 N 24
Milford	11 S 30	Monks Eleigh	23 W 27	Moy	67 H 11
Milford Haven/		Monksilver	7 K 30	Much Hoole	38 L 22
Aberdaugleddau	14 E 28	Monmouth/		Much Wenlock	26 M 26
Milford-on-Sea	9 P 31	Trefynwy	16 L 28	Muchalls	63 N 12
Millom	44 K 21	Monreith	42 G 19	Muck	59 B 13
Millport	54 F 16	Montacute	8 L 31	Muckle Roe	75 P 2
Milltown (Moray)	68 L 11	Montgarrie	69 L 12	Mudford	8 M 31
Milltown (Highland)	66 F 11	Montgomery/		Muick (Loch)	62 K 13
Milnathort	56 J 15	Trefaldwyn	25 K 26	Muir of Fowlis	69 L 12
Milngavie	55 H 16	Montrose	63 M 13	Muir of Ord	67 G 11
Milnrow	39 N 23	Monymusk	69 M 12	Muirdrum	63 L 14
Milnthorpe	44 L 21	Moonen Bay	64 Z 11	Muirhead	55 H 16
Milovaig	64 Z 11	Moorfoot Hills	56 K 16	Muirkirk	49 H 17
Milton (Cambs.)	29 U 27	Moors (The)	48 F 19	Muirshearlich	60 E 13
Milton		Morar	59 C 13	Muker	45 N 20
(Dumfries and		Moray Firth	67 H 11	Muldoanich	58 X 13
Galloway)	42 F 19	Morchard Bishop	7 I 31	Mull (Isle of)	59 B 14
Milton Abbas	8 N 31	Mordiford	26 M 27	Mull (Sound of)	59 C 14
Milton Abbot	3 H 32	More (Glen)	59 C 14	Mull of Oa	52 A 17
Milton Bryan	28 S 28	More (Loch) (near		Mull of Galloway	42 F 20
Milton Ernest	29 S 27	Kinloch)	72 F 9	Mullardoch
Milton Keynes	28 R 27	More (Loch)		(Loch)	66 E 12
Milton Libourne	17 O 29	(near Westerdale)	73 J 8	Mullion	2 E 33
Milton of Campsie	55 H 16	Morebath	7 J 30	Mumbles (The)	15 I 29
Milverton	7 K 30	Morebath		Mundesley	31 Y 25
Milwich	35 N 25	Morecambe	38 L 21	Mundford	30 V 26
Minard	54 E 15	Morecambe Bay	38 L 21	Munlochy	67 H 11
Minch (The)	71 C 9	Moreton	22 U 28	Munlochy Bay	67 H 11
Minehead	7 J 30	Moreton-in-Marsh	27 O 28	Munslow	26 L 26
Minety	17 O 29	Moreton-		Murrayfield	56 K 16
Mingary	64 X 12	hampstead	4 I 32	Murton	46 P 19
Minginish	65 B 12	Morfa Nefyn	32 G 25	Musselburgh	56 K 16
Mingulay	58 X 13	Moricambe Bay	44 K 19	Muthill	55 I 15
Minnigaff	48 G 19	Morie (Loch)	67 G 10	Mwnt	24 G 27
Minster (near		Moriston (Glen)	66 F 12	Mybster	73 J 8
Ramsgate)	13 X 29	Morley	39 P 22	Mynach Falls	25 I 26
Minster (near		Morlich (Loch)	67 I 12	Mynydd Eppynt	25 J 27
Sheppey)	12 W 29	Morpeth	51 O 18	Mynydd Preseli	14 F 28
Minsterley	26 L 26	Morte Bay	6 H 30		

Meopham	21 V 29	Merseyside		Messingham	40 S 23	Mhór (Loch)	67 G 12
Mere (Cheshire)	34 M 24	(Metropolitan		Metheringham	37 S 24	Miavaig	70 Z 9
Mere (Wilts.)	8 N 30	County-Liverpool)	34 L 23	Methil	56 K 15	Michelham Priory	12 U 31
Mereworth	12 V 30	Merthyr Tydfil	16 J 28	Methlick	69 N 11	Mickleover	35 P 25
Meriden	27 P 26	Merton (Devon)	6 H 31	Methven	62 J 14	Mickleton	27 O 27
Merrick	48 G 18	Merton (London		Methwold	30 V 26	Mid Ardlaw	69 N 10
Merriott	8 L 31	Borough)	20 T 29	Mevagissey	3 F 33	Mid Calder	56 J 16
Mersey (River)	38 M 23	Meshaw	6 I 31	Mexborough	40 Q 23	Mid Sannox	53 E 17

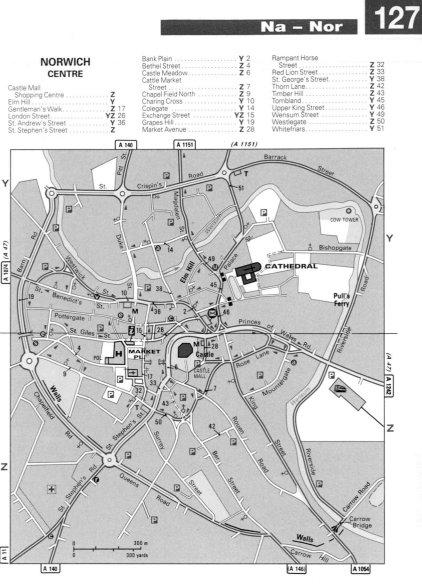

N

Na Cùiltean	53	C 16
Nafferton	41	S 21
Nailsworth	17	N 28
Nairn	67	I 11
Nant (Loch)	60	E 14
Nant-y-Moch Reservoir	25	I 26
Nantgwynant Valley	32	H 24
Nantwich	34	M 24
Nantyglo	16	K 28
Napton	28	Q 27
Narberth/Arberth	14	F 28
Narborough	30	V 25
Nash Point	15	J 29
Nateby	45	M 20
National Exhibition Centre (N.E.C.)	27	O 26
National Motor Museum	9	P 31
Navenby	36	S 24
Naver (Loch)	72	G 9
Nayland	23	W 28
Naze (The)	23	X 28
Neath (River)	15	I 28
Neath/Castell-nedd	15	I 29
Needham Market	23	X 27
Needles (The)	9	P 32

Nefyn	32	G 25
Neidpath Castle	56	K 17
Neilston	55	G 16
Neist Point	64	Z 11
Nelson	39	N 22
Nene (River)	29	T 26
Ness	71	B 8
Ness (Loch)	67	G 12
Neston	33	K 24
Nether Broughton	36	R 25
Nether Langwith	36	Q 24
Nether Stowey	7	K 30
Netheravon	17	O 30
Netherhampton	9	O 30
Nethertown	74	K 7
Nethy Bridge	68	J 12
Netley	9	P 31
Nettlebed	18	R 29
Nettleham	36	S 24
Nevern	24	F 27
Nevis (Glen)	60	E 13
Nevis (Loch)	65	C 12
New Abbey	49	J 19
New Aberdour	69	N 11
New Alresford	10	Q 30
New Buckenham	31	X 26
New Byth	69	N 11
New Cumnock	49	H 17
New Deer	69	N 11
New Forest	9	P 31

New Forest Forest Park	9	P 31
New Galloway	49	H 18
New Holland	41	S 22
New Hythe	12	V 30
New Leeds	69	N 11
New Mills	35	O 23
New Milton	9	P 31
New Pitsligo	69	N 11
New Quay/Ceinewydd	24	G 27
New Romney	12	W 31
New Rossington	40	Q 23
New Sauchie	55	I 15
New Scone	62	J 14
New Tredegar	16	K 28
Newark-on-Trent	36	R 24
Newbiggin-by-the-Sea	51	P 18
Newbigging	62	L 14
Newbold Verdon	27	P 26
Newborough	32	G 24
Newbridge-on-Wye	25	J 27
Newburgh (Lancashire)	38	L 23
Newburgh (Aberdeenshire)	69	N 12
Newburgh (Fife)	56	K 14
Newburn	51	O 19

NEWCASTLE-UPON-TYNE

Blackett Street	CYZ
Eldon Square Shopping Centre	CYZ
Grey Street	CZ
Newgate Street	CZ
Pilgrim Street	CZ 57

Bridge Street	CZ	10
Broad Chare	CZ	12
Collingwood Street	CZ	25
Forth Street	CZ	30
George Street	CZ	32
Great North Street	CY	33
Jesmond Road	CY	40
John Dobson Street	CY	41
Leazes Park Road	CY	43
Low Friar Street	CZ	46
Market Street	CZ	47

Mosley Street	CZ	50
Neville Street	CZ	52
New Bridge St. West	CY	53
Northumberland Street	CY	56
Railway Street	CZ	60
Rutherford Street	CZ	63
St. Mary's Place	CY	65
St. Nicholas Street	CZ	66
Scotswood Road	CZ	70
Thornton Street	CZ	80
Wellington Street	CY	84

NORWICH CENTRE

Castle Mall Shopping Centre	Z
Elm Hill	Y
Gentleman's Walk	Z 17
London Street	YZ 26
St. Andrew's Street	Y 36
St. Stephen's Street	Z

Bank Plain	Y 2
Bethel Street	Z 4
Castle Meadow	Z 6
Cattle Market Street	Z 7
Chapel Field North	Z 9
Charing Cross	Y 10
Colegate	Y 14
Exchange Street	YZ 15
Grapes Hill	Y 19
Market Avenue	Z 28

Rampant Horse Street	Z 32
Red Lion Street	Z 33
St. George's Street	Y 38
Thorn Lane	Z 42
Timber Hill	Z 43
Tombland	Y 45
Upper King Street	Y 46
Wensum Street	Y 49
Westlegate	Z 50
Whitefriars	Y 51

Newbury	18	Q 29
Newby Bridge	44	L 21
Newby Hall	40	P 21
Newcastle Emlyn/Castell Newydd Emlyn	24	G 27
Newcastle-under-Lyme	34	N 24
Newcastle-upon-Tyne Airport	51	O 18
Newcastle-upon-Tyne	51	P 19
Newcastleton	50	L 18
Newchurch	12	W 30
Newdigate	11	T 30
Newent	17	M 28
Newgale	14	E 28
Newhall	34	M 24
Newham (London Borough)	21	U 29
Newhaven	11	U 31
Newick	11	U 31
Newington	12	V 29
Newland	16	M 28
Newlyn	2	D 33
Newmachar	69	N 12
Newmains	55	I 16
Newmarket (Isle of Lewis)	70	A 9
Newmarket (Suffolk)	22	V 27
Newmill	68	L 11
Newmilns	48	G 17
Newnham (Glos.)	17	M 28
Newnham (Kent)	12	W 30
Newnham Bridge	26	M 27
Newport/Casnewydd (Newport)	16	L 29
Newport (Pembrokes)	14	F 27
Newport (Essex)	22	U 28
Newport (I.O.W.)	10	Q 31
Newport (Salop)	34	M 25
Newport-on-Tay	62	L 14

Newport Pagnell	28	R 27
Newquay	2	E 32
Newstead	36	Q 24
Newstead Abbey	36	Q 24
Newton	39	M 22
Newton Abbot	4	J 32
Newton-Aycliffe	46	P 20
Newton Ferrers	3	H 33
Newton-le-Willows	34	M 23
Newton Longville	28	R 28
Newton Mearns	55	H 16
Newton Poppleford	4	K 31
Newton St. Cyres	4	J 31
Newton Stewart	48	G 19
Newton Wamphray	49	J 18
Newtongrange	56	K 16
Newtonmore	61	H 12
Newtown (Cheshire)	35	N 23
Newtown (Heref. and Worc.)	26	M 27
Newtown/Drenewydd (Powys)	25	K 26
Newtown St. Boswells	50	L 17
Newtyle	62	K 14
Neyland	14	F 28
Nigg Bay	67	H 10
Ninfield	12	V 31
Nith (River)	49	J 19
Niths	49	I 18
Niton	10	Q 32
Norfolk (County)	30	W 25
Norfolk Broads	31	Y 25
Norham	57	N 16
Normandy	20	S 30
Normanton	40	P 22
North Ashton	38	L 23
North Baddesley	9	P 31
North Ballachulish	60	E 13
North Berwick	57	L 15
North Bovey	4	I 32
North Bradley	17	N 30
North Cadbury	8	M 30
North Cave	40	S 22

North Channel	53	D 18
North Creake	30	W 25
North Curry	7	L 30
North Downs	18	R 30
North Erradale	66	C 10
North Esk (Riv.)	63	L 13
North Foreland	13	Y 29
North Grimston	40	R 21
North Harris	70	Z 10
North Hinksey	18	Q 28
North Holmwood	19	T 30
North Kelsey	41	S 23
North Kessock	67	H 11
North Leigh	18	P 28
North Morar	59	C 13
North Newbald	40	S 22
North Nibley	17	M 29
North Petherton	7	K 30
North Petherwin	3	G 31
North Ronaldsay	75	M 5
North Shields	51	P 18
North Somercotes	41	U 23
North Sound (The)	74	L 6
North Sunderland	51	P 17
North Thoresby	41	T 23
North Tidworth	17	P 30
North Uist	64	X 11
North Walsham	31	Y 25
North Warnborough	18	R 30
North Weald Bassett	22	U 28
North York Moors National Park	47	R 20
North Yorkshire (County)	39	O 21
Northallerton	46	P 20
Northam	6	H 30
Northampton	28	R 27
Northamptonshire (County)	28	R 26
Northchapel	11	S 30
Northchurch	19	S 28
Northfleet	21	V 29

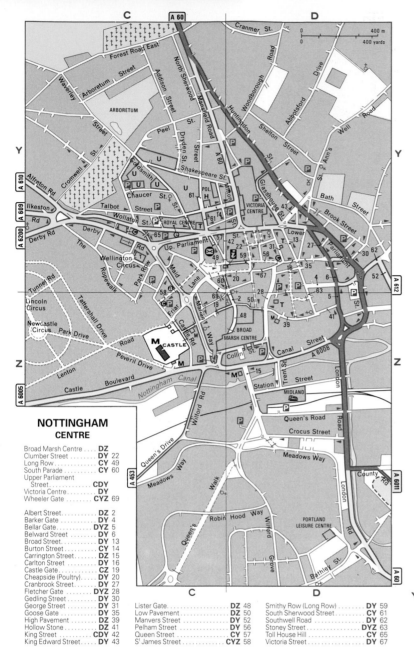

NOTTINGHAM CENTRE

Broad Marsh Centre	**DZ**
Clumber Street	**DY** 22
Long Row	**CY** 49
South Parade	**CY** 60
Upper Parliament Street	**CDY**
Victoria Centre	**DY**
Wheeler Gate	**CYZ** 69
Albert Street	**DZ** 2
Barker Gate	**DY** 4
Bellar Gate	**DYZ** 5
Belward Street	**DY** 6
Broad Street	**DY** 13
Burton Street	**CY** 14
Carrington Street	**DZ** 15
Carlton Street	**DY** 16
Castle Gate	**CZ** 19
Cheapside (Poultry)	**DY** 27
Cranbrook Street	**DY** 27
Fletcher Gate	**DYZ** 28
Gedling Street	**DY** 30
George Street	**DY** 31
Goose Gate	**DY** 35
High Pavement	**DZ** 39
Hollow Stone	**DZ** 41
King Street	**CDY** 42
King Edward Street	**DY** 43
Lister Gate	**DZ** 48
Low Pavement	**DZ** 50
Manvers Street	**DY** 52
Pelham Street	**DY** 56
Queen Street	**CY** 57
S' James Street	**CYZ** 58
Smithy Row (Long Row)	**DY** 59
South Sherwood Street	**CY** 61
Southwell Road	**DY** 62
Stoney Street	**DYZ** 63
Toll House Hill	**CY** 65
Victoria Street	**DY** 67

Northiam	12	V 31	Oathlaw	62	L 13	Old Windsor	20	S 29
Northleach	17	O 28	Oban	60	D 14	Oldany Island	72	E 9
Northop	33	K 24	Ochil Hills	55	I 15	Oldbury	27	N 26
Northton	70	Y 10	Ochiltree	48	G 17	Oldcotes	36	Q 23
Northumberland (County)	50	M 18	Ockley	11	S 30	Oldham	39	N 23
			Odiham	18	R 30	Oldmeldrum	69	N 11
Northumberland National Park	51	N 18	Offa's Dyke Path	26	K 26	Ollaberry	75	P 2
			Ogbourne St. George	17	O 29	Ollay (Loch)	64	X 12
Northwich	34	M 24				Ollerton	36	Q 24
Northwold	30	V 26	Ogmore Vale	15	J 29	Olney	28	R 27
Norton	40	R 21	Ogmore-by-Sea	15	J 29	Olveston	17	M 29
Norton Fitzwarren	7	K 30	Oich (Loch)	60	F 12	Ombersley	27	N 27
Norton St. Philip	17	N 30	Oidhche (Loch na h-)	66	D 11	Onchan	42	G 21
Norwich	31	X 26	Oigh-Sgeir	58	Z 13	Onich	60	E 13
Noss Head	74	K 8	Okeford Fitzpaine	8	N 31	Orchy (Glen)	60	F 14
Noss (Isle of)	75	Q 3	Okehampton	4	H 31	Ord	65	C 12
Nottingham	36	Q 25	Old Alresford	10	Q 30	Orford	23	Y 27
Nottinghamshire (County)	36	Q 24	Old Bolingbroke	37	U 24	Orford Ness	23	Y 27
Nuneaton	27	P 26	Old Burghclere	18	Q 29	Ormesby	46	Q 20
Nunney	17	M 30	Old Deer	69	N 11	Ormesby St. Margaret	31	Z 25
Nunthorpe	46	Q 20	Old Fletton	29	T 26	Ormskirk	38	L 23
Nunton	64	X 11	Old Harry Rocks	9	O 32	Oronsay	52	B 15
Nutley	11	U 30	Old Head	74	L 7	Orosay (near Fuday)	64	X 12
			Old Kilpatrick	55	G 16	Orosay (near Lochboisdale)	64	X 12
O			Old Knebworth	19	T 28			
			Old Leake	37	U 24	Orphir	74	K 7
Oa (The)	52	B 17	Old Man of Hoy	74	J 7	Orrin (Glen)	66	F 11
Oadby	28	Q 26	Old Man of Storr	65	B 11	Orrin Reservoir	66	F 11
Oakengates	26	M 25	Old Radnor	25	K 27	Orsay	52	A 16
Oakham	28	R 25	Old Rayne	69	M 11	Orsett	21	V 29
Oakhill	17	M 30	Old' Sarum	9	O 30	Orton	45	M 20
Oare	12	W 30	Old Sodbury	17	M 29	Orwell	29	T 27
			Old Warden	29	S 27	Orwell (River)	23	X 28

Osborne House	10	Q 31	Owslebury	10	Q 30	Parbold	38	L 23
Osdale	65	A 11	Oxburgh Hall	30	V 26	Parc Cefn Onn	16	K 29
Osgaig (Loch)	72	E 9	Oxford	18	Q 28	Parham House	11	S 31
Osmington	8	M 32	Oxfordshire (County)	18	P 28	Park Gate	10	Q 31
Ossett	39	P 22	Oxted	21	T 30	Park of Pairc	70	A 9
Oswaldtwistle	39	M 22	Oxwich Bay	15	H 29	Parkeston	23	X 28
Oswestry	33	K 25	Oykel (Glen)	72	F 9	Parkhurst	10	Q 31
Otford	21	U 30	Oykel Bridge	72	F 10	Parnham House	8	L 31
Othery	8	L 30	Oyne	69	M 12	Parrett (River)	7	K 30
Otley (Suffolk)	23	X 27				Partney	37	U 24
Otley (West Yorks.)	39	O 22				Parton	43	J 20
Otterbourne	9	P 30				Partridge Green	11	T 31
Otterburn	51	N 18	**P**			Pass of LLanberis	32	H 24
Otterswick	75	Q 2				Patchway	17	M 29
Otterton	4	K 32	Pabay	65	C 12	Pateley Bridge	39	O 21
Ottery St. Mary	4	K 31	Pabbay (near Harris)	70	Y 10	Path of Condie	56	J 15
Oulton Park Circuit	34	M 24	Pabbay (near Mingulay)	58	X 13	Pathhead	56	L 16
Oulton Broad	31	Z 26	Pabbay (Sound of)	70	Y 10	Patna	48	G 17
Oundle	29	S 26	Padbury	28	R 28	Patrington	41	T 22
Ouse (River) (English Channel)	11	T 30	Paddock Wood	12	V 30	Patrixbourne	13	X 30
Ouse (River) (North Sea)	40	Q 21	Padiham	39	N 22	Patterdale	44	L 20
			Padstow	2	F 32	Pattingham	27	N 26
Out Skerries	75	R 2	Pagham	10	R 31	Paulerspury	28	R 27
Outer Hebrides	70	W 10	Paignton	4	J 32	Paull	41	T 22
Outwell	29	U 26	Painscastle	25	K 27	Paulton	17	M 30
Overseal	35	P 25	Painswick	17	N 28	Peacehaven	11	T 31
Overstrand	31	Y 25	Paisley	55	G 16	Peak District National Park	35	O 23
Overton (Wrexham)	34	L 25	Palnackie	43	I 19			
Overton (Hants.)	18	Q 30	Pangbourne	18	Q 29	Peasedown St. John	17	M 30
Overton (Lancs.)	38	L 21	Papa Stour	75	O 3	Peasenhall	31	Y 27
Overtown	55	I 16	Papa Westray	74	L 5	Peasmarsh	12	W 31
Ower	9	P 31	Paps of Jura	52	B 16	Peat Inn	56	L 15
Owermoigne	8	N 32	Parbh (The)	72	F 8	Peatknowe	69	M 11

OXFORD

Broad Street	**BZ** 3	Blue Boar Street	**BY** 2	Oriel Square	**BZ** 24
Clarendon Shopping Centre	**BZ**	Castle Street	**BZ** 5	Park End Street	**BZ** 30
Cornmarket Street	**BZ** 6	Hythe Bridge Street	**BZ** 12	Pembroke Street	**BZ** 31
George Street	**BZ** 9	Little Clarendon Street	**BY** 13	Queen's Lane	**BZ** 33
High Street	**BZ**	Logic Lane	**BZ** 14	Radcliffe Square	**BZ** 35
Queen Street	**BZ** 34	Magdalen Street	**BYZ** 16	St. Michael Street	**BZ** 40
Westgate Shopping Centre	**BZ**	Magpie Lane	**BZ** 17	Turl Street	**BZ** 41
		New Inn Hall Street	**BZ** 20	Walton Crescent	**BY** 42
		Norfolk Street	**BZ** 21	Worcester Street	**BZ** 47
		Old Greyfriars Street	**BZ** 23		

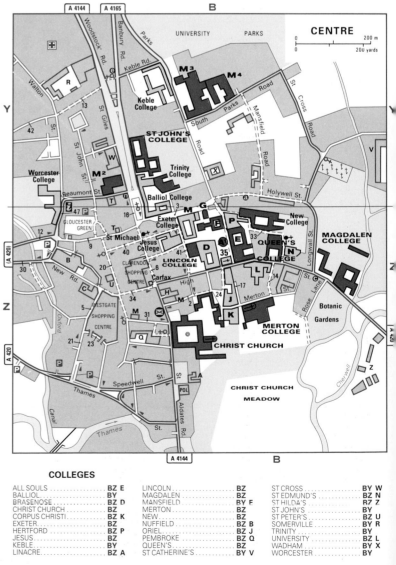

COLLEGES

ALL SOULS	**BZ** E	LINCOLN	**BZ**	ST CROSS	**BY** W
BALLIOL	**BY**	MAGDALEN	**BZ**	ST EDMUND'S	**BZ** N
BRASENOSE	**BZ** D	MANSFIELD	**BY** F	ST HILDA'S	**BZ**
CHRIST CHURCH	**BZ**	MERTON	**BZ**	ST JOHN'S	**BY**
CORPUS CHRISTI	**BZ** K	NEW	**BZ**	ST PETER'S	**BZ** U
EXETER	**BZ**	NUFFIELD	**BZ** B	SOMERVILLE	**BY** R
HERTFORD	**BZ** P	ORIEL	**BZ** J	TRINITY	**BY**
JESUS	**BZ**	PEMBROKE	**BZ** Q	UNIVERSITY	**BZ** L
KEBLE	**BY**	QUEEN'S	**BZ**	WADHAM	**BY** X
LINACRE	**BZ** A	ST CATHERINE'S	**BY** V	WORCESTER	**BY**

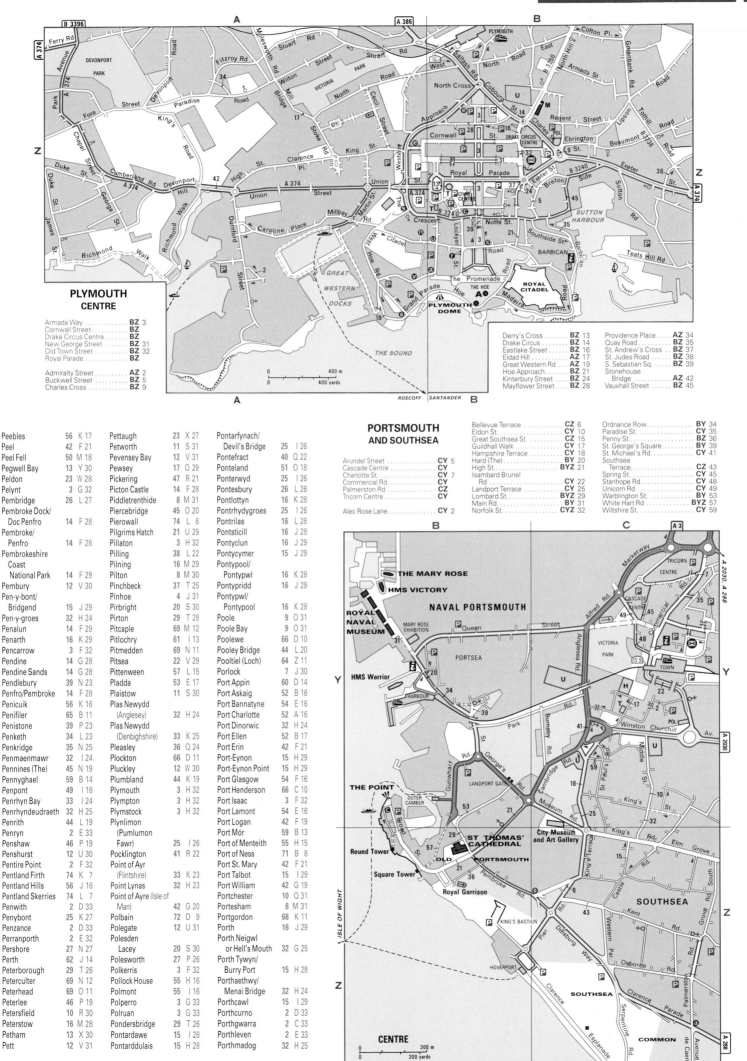

PLYMOUTH
CENTRE

Armada Way . . . . BZ 3
Cornwall Street . . . . BZ
Drake Circus Centre . . . . . BZ
New George Street . . . . . . BZ 31
Old Town Street . . . . BZ 32
Royal Parade . . . . BZ

Admiralty Street . . . . AZ 2
Buckwell Street . . . . BZ 5
Charles Cross . . . . BZ 9

Derry's Cross . . . . BZ 13
Drake Circus . . . . BZ 14
Eastlake Street . . . . . . BZ 16
Eldad Hill . . . . AZ 17
Great Western Rd . . . . AZ 19
Hoe Approach . . . . BZ 21
Kinterbury Street . . . . BZ 24
Mayflower Street . . . . . BZ 28

Providence Place . . . . AZ 34
Quay Road . . . . BZ 35
St. Andrew's Cross . . . . . . BZ 37
St. Judes Road . . . . BZ 38
S. Sebastian Sq. . . . . BZ 39
Stonehouse
   Bridge . . . . AZ 42
Vauxhall Street . . . . BZ 45

PORTSMOUTH
AND SOUTHSEA

Arundel Street . . . . CY 5
Cascade Centre . . . . CY
Charlotte St. . . . . CY 7
Commercial Rd. . . . . CY
Palmerston Rd. . . . . CZ
Tricorn Centre . . . . CY

Alec Rose Lane . . . . CY 2

Bellevue Terrace . . . . CZ 6
Eldon St. . . . . CY 10
Great Southsea St. . . . . CZ 15
Guildhall Walk . . . . CY 17
Hampshire Terrace . . . . CY 18
Hard (The) . . . . BY 20
High St. . . . . BYZ 21
Isambard Brunel
   Rd . . . . CY 22
Landport Terrace . . . . CY 25
Lombard St. . . . . BYZ 29
Main Rd. . . . . BY 31
Norfolk St. . . . . CYZ 32

Ordnance Row . . . . BY 34
Paradise St. . . . . CY 35
Penny St. . . . . BZ 36
St. George's Square . . . . BY 39
St. Michael's Rd. . . . . . . CY 41
Southsea
   Terrace . . . . CZ 43
Spring St. . . . . CY 45
Stanhope Rd. . . . . CY 48
Unicorn Rd. . . . . CY 49
Warblington St. . . . . BY 53
White Hart Rd . . . . BYZ 57
Wiltshire St. . . . . CY 59

Peebles	56 K 17	Pettaugh	23 X 27	Pontarfynach/	
Peel	42 F 21	Petworth	11 S 31	Devil's Bridge	25 I 26
Peel Fell	50 M 18	Pevensey Bay	12 V 31	Pontefract	40 Q 22
Pegwell Bay	13 Y 30	Pewsey	17 O 29	Ponteland	51 O 18
Peldon	23 W 28	Pickering	47 R 21	Ponterwyd	25 I 26
Pelynt	3 G 32	Picton Castle	14 F 28	Pontesbury	26 L 26
Pembridge	26 L 27	Piddletrenthide	8 M 31	Pontlottyn	16 K 28
Pembroke Dock/		Piercebridge	45 O 20	Pontrhydygroes	25 I 26
Doc Penfro	14 F 28	Pierowall	74 L 6	Pontrilas	16 L 28
Pembroke/		Pilgrims Hatch	21 U 29	Pontsticill	16 J 28
Penfro	14 F 28	Pillaton	3 H 32	Pontyclun	16 J 29
Pembrokeshire		Pilling	38 L 22	Pontycymer	15 J 29
Coast		Pilning	16 M 29	Pontypool/	
National Park	14 F 29	Pilton	8 M 30	Pontypwl	16 K 28
Pembury	12 V 30	Pinchbeck	37 T 25	Pontypridd	16 J 29
Pen-y-bont/		Pinhoe	4 J 31	Pontypwl/	
Bridgend	15 J 29	Pirbright	20 S 30	Pontypool	16 K 28
Pen-y-groes	32 H 24	Pirton	29 T 28	Poole	9 O 31
Penalun	14 F 29	Pitcaple	69 M 12	Poole Bay	9 O 31
Penarth	16 K 29	Pitlochry	61 I 13	Poolewe	66 D 10
Pencarrow	3 F 32	Pitmedden	69 N 11	Pooley Bridge	44 L 20
Pendine	14 G 28	Pitsea	22 V 29	Pooltiel (Loch)	64 Z 11
Pendine Sands	14 G 28	Pittenween	57 L 15	Porlock	7 J 30
Pendlebury	39 N 23	Pladda	53 E 17	Port Appin	60 D 14
Penfro/Pembroke	14 F 28	Plaistow	11 S 30	Port Askaig	52 B 16
Penicuik	56 K 16	Plas Newydd		Port Bannatyne	54 E 16
Penifiler	65 B 11	(Anglesey)	32 H 24	Port Charlotte	52 A 16
Penistone	39 P 23	Plas Newydd		Port Dinorwic	32 H 24
Penketh	34 L 23	(Denbighshire)	33 K 25	Port Ellen	52 B 17
Penkridge	35 N 25	Pleasley	36 Q 24	Port Erin	42 F 21
Penmaenmawr	32 I 24	Plockton	66 D 11	Port-Eynon	15 H 29
Pennines (The)	45 N 19	Pluckley	12 W 30	Port-Eynon Point	15 H 29
Pennyghael	59 B 14	Plumbland	44 K 19	Port Glasgow	54 F 16
Penpont	49 I 18	Plymouth	3 H 32	Port Henderson	66 C 10
Penrhyn Bay	33 I 24	Plympton	3 H 32	Port Isaac	3 F 32
Penrhyndeudraeth	32 H 25	Plymstock	3 H 32	Port Lamont	54 E 16
Penrith	44 L 19	Plynlimon		Port Logan	42 F 19
Penryn	2 E 33	(Pumlumon		Port Môr	59 B 13
Penshaw	46 P 19	Fawr)	25 I 26	Port of Menteith	55 H 15
Penshurst	12 U 30	Pocklington	41 R 22	Port of Ness	71 B 8
Pentire Point	2 F 32	Point of Ayr		Port St. Mary	42 F 21
Pentland Firth	74 K 7	(Flintshire)	33 K 23	Port Talbot	15 I 29
Pentland Hills	56 J 16	Point Lynas	32 H 23	Port William	42 G 19
Pentland Skerries	74 L 7	Point of Ayre (Isle of		Portchester	10 Q 31
Penwith	2 D 33	Man)	42 G 20	Portesham	8 M 31
Penybont	25 K 27	Polbain	72 D 9	Portgordon	68 K 11
Penzance	2 D 33	Polegate	12 U 31	Porth	16 J 29
Perranporth	2 E 32	Polesden		Porth Neigwl	
Pershore	27 N 27	Lacey	20 S 30	or Hell's Mouth	32 G 25
Perth	62 J 14	Polesworth	27 P 26	Porth Tywyn/	
Peterborough	29 T 26	Polkerris	3 F 32	Burry Port	15 H 28
Peterculter	69 N 12	Pollock House	55 H 16	Porthaethwy/	
Peterhead	69 O 11	Polmont	55 I 16	Menai Bridge	32 H 24
Peterlee	46 P 19	Polperro	3 G 33	Porthcawl	15 I 29
Petersfield	10 R 30	Polruan	3 G 33	Porthcurno	2 D 33
Peterstow	16 M 28	Pondersbridge	29 T 26	Porthgwarra	2 C 33
Petham	13 X 30	Pontardawe	15 I 28	Porthleven	2 E 33
Pett	12 V 31	Pontarddulais	15 H 28	Porthmadog	32 H 25

CENTRE

Porthyrhyd	15	H 28
Portinnisherrich	54	E 15
Portishead	16	L 29
Portknockie	68	L 10
Portland (Isle of)	8	M 32
Portlethen	63	N 12
Portmahomack	67	I 10
Portnacroish	60	D 14
Portnaguran	71	B 9
Portnahaven	52	A 16
Portobello	56	K 16
Portreath	2	E 33
Portree	65	B 11
Portscatho	2	F 33
Portskerra	73	I 8
Portskewett	16	L 29
Portslade	11	T 31
Portsmouth	10	Q 31
Portsoy	69	L 10
Portuairk	59	B 13
Postbridge	4	I 32
Potter Heigham	31	Y 25
Potter Street	22	U 28
Potterne	17	N 30
Potters Bar	20	T 28
Potterspury	28	R 27
Potton	29	T 27
Poughill	6	G 31
Poulton-le-Fylde	38	L 22
Poundstock	6	G 31
Powburn	51	O 17
Powerstock	8	L 31
Powick	27	N 27
Powis	25	K 26
Powmill	56	J 15
Powys (County)	25	J 26
Poynings	11	T 31
Poynton	35	N 23
Praa Sands	2	D 33
Praze-an-Beeble	2	E 33
Prees	34	M 25
Preesall	38	L 22
Prescot	34	L 23
Prestatyn	33	J 23
Prestbury	35	N 24
Presteigne	26	K 27
Preston (East Riding of Yorks.)	41	T 22
Preston (Kent)	13	X 30
Preston (Lancs.)	38	L 22
Preston (West Sussex)	11	S 31
Preston Candover	10	Q 30
Prestonpans	56	L 16
Prestwich	39	N 23
Prestwick	48	G 17
Prestwood	19	R 28
Priest Island	72	D 10
Princes Risborough	18	R 28
Princethorpe	27	P 26
Princetown	4	I 32
Priors Marston	28	Q 27
Probus	2	F 33
Prosen (Glen)	62	K 13
Prudhoe	51	O 19
Puckeridge	22	U 28
Puddletown	8	M 31
Pudsey	39	P 22
Pulborough	11	S 31
Pulham Market	31	X 26
Purbeck (Isle of)	8	N 32
Purbrook	10	Q 31
Purley	18	Q 29
Purse Caundle Manor	8	M 31
Purston Jaglin	40	P 22
Purton	17	O 29
Putsborough	6	H 30
Pwllheli	32	G 25
Pyecombe	11	T 31
Pyle	15	I 29

Q

Quainton	18	R 28
Quantock Hills	7	K 30
Quarr	10	Q 31
Quedgeley	17	N 28
Queen Camel	8	M 30
Queen Elizabeth Forest Park	55	G 15
Queenborough	12	W 29
Queensbury	39	O 22
Queensferry	33	K 24
Quinag	72	E 9

Quinish Point	59	B 14
Quiraing	65	B 11
Quoich (Loch)	60	E 12
Quorndon	36	Q 25
Quothquan	56	J 17

R

Raasay (Island of)	65	B 11
Raasay (Sound of)	65	B 11
Rackwick	74	J 7
Radcliffe	39	N 23
Radcliffe-on-Trent	36	Q 25
Radlett	20	T 29
Radnor Forest	25	K 27
Radstock	17	M 30
Radyr	16	K 29
Rafford	68	J 11
Raglan	16	L 28
Ragley Hall	27	O 27
Rainford	38	L 23
Rainham	12	V 29
Rainworth	36	Q 24
Ramsbottom	39	N 23
Ramsbury	18	P 29
Ramsey (Cambs.)	29	T 26
Ramsey (Isle of Man)	42	G 21
Ramsey Bay	42	G 21
Ramsey Island	14	D 28
Ramsey St. Mary's	29	T 26
Ramsgate	13	Y 29
Ramsgill	39	O 21
Ranfurly	55	G 16
Rannoch (Loch)	61	H 13
Rannoch Moor	60	F 14
Ranskill	36	Q 23
Ranworth	31	Y 25
Rapness	74	L 6
Rappach	72	F 10
Ratby	28	Q 26
Rathen	69	O 11
Rattray	62	K 14
Rattray Head	69	O 11
Raunds	29	S 26
Ravenglass	43	J 20
Ravenstonedale	45	M 20
Rawcliffe	41	R 22
Rawmarsh	40	P 23
Rawtenstall	39	N 22
Rayleigh	22	V 29
Read	39	M 22
Reading	18	R 29
Reay	73	I 8
Reay Forest	72	F 9
Reculver	13	X 29
Red Wharf Bay	32	H 24
Redbourn	19	S 28
Redbourne	41	S 23
Redbridge (London Borough)	21	U 29
Redcar	46	Q 20
Redcliff Bay	16	L 29
Redditch	27	O 27
Redford	63	L 14
Redhill	20	T 30
Redpoint	66	C 11
Redruth	2	E 33
Redwick	16	L 29
Reedham	31	Y 26
Reekie Linn	62	K 13
Reeth	45	O 20
Reigate	20	T 30
Reighton	41	T 21
Reiss	74	K 8
Rempstone	36	Q 25
Rendham	31	Y 27
Renfrew	55	G 16
Renish Point	70	Z 10
Renishaw	35	P 24
Renton	55	G 16
Resort (Loch)	70	Z 9
Restalrig	56	K 16
Restormel Castle	3	G 32
Retford	36	R 24
Rhaeadr/Rhayader	25	J 27
Rhaeadr Ddu	33	I 25
Rhayader/Rhaeadr	25	J 27
Rheidol (Vale of)	24	I 26
Rhiconich	72	F 8
Rhinns of Galloway (The)	42	E 19
Rhinns of Kells	48	G 18
Rhondda	16	J 29
Rhoose	16	J 29
Rhoscolyn	32	G 24

Rhoscrowther	14	E 28
Rhosllanerchrugog	33	K 24
Rhosneigr	32	G 24
Rhossili	15	H 29
Rhu	54	F 15
Rhuddlan	33	J 24
Rhum	59	A 13
Rhuthun/Ruthin	33	K 24
Rhyd-Ddu	32	H 24
Rhydaman/Ammanford	15	I 28
Rhydcymerau	24	H 27
Rhydd	27	N 27
Rhyddhywel	25	J 26
Rhydowen	24	H 27
Rhyl	33	J 24
Rhymney/Rhymmi	16	K 28
Rhynie	68	L 12
Ribble (River)	38	N 22
Ribblesdale	39	N 21
Ribchester	38	M 22
Riccall	40	Q 22
Riccarton	48	G 17
Richborough	13	X 30
Richmond	46	O 20
Richmond-upon-Thames (London Borough)	20	T 29
Rickmansworth	20	S 29
Ridgeway Path (The)	18	P 29
Rievaulx Abbey	46	Q 21
Rigside	49	I 17
Rillington	40	R 21
Rimsdale (Loch)	73	H 9
Ringford	43	H 19
Ringmer	12	U 31
Ringstead	29	S 26
Ringwood	9	O 31
Ringwould	13	Y 30
Rinnes (Glen)	68	K 11
Rinns of Islay	52	A 16
Rinns Point	52	A 16
Ripe	12	U 31
Ripley (Derbs.)	35	P 24
Ripley (North Yorks.)	39	P 21
Ripley (Surrey)	20	S 30
Ripon	40	P 21
Rippingale	37	S 25
Ripponden	39	O 22
Risca	16	K 29
Rishton	39	M 22
Ristol (Isle)	72	D 9
Roag (Loch)	70	Z 9
Roberton	50	L 17
Robertsbridge	12	V 31
Robin Hood's Bay	47	S 20
Roby	34	L 23
Rocester	35	O 25
Rochdale	39	N 23
Roche	3	F 32
Rochester	12	V 29
Rochford	22	W 29
Rock	3	F 32
Rockcliffe (Cumbria)	44	K 19
Rockcliffe (Dumfries and Galloway)	43	I 19
Rode	17	N 30
Rodel	70	Z 10
Rodmarton	17	N 28
Rogart	73	H 9
Rogerstone	16	K 29
Rolleston-on-Dove (Staffs.)	35	P 25
Rolleston (Notts.)	36	R 24
Rolvenden	12	V 30
Roman Villa	11	S 31
Romiley	35	N 23
Romney Marsh	12	W 30
Romsey	9	P 31
Romsley	27	N 26
Rona (Island of)	65	C 11
Ronaldsway	42	G 21
Ronas Voe	75	P 2
Ronay	64	Y 11
Roos	41	T 22
Rootpark	55	I 16
Ropsley	37	S 25
Rora Head	74	J 7
Rosedale Abbey	46	R 20
Rosehearty	69	N 10
Rosemarket	14	F 28
Rosemarkie	67	H 11
Roshven	59	C 13
Roslin	56	K 16
Ross of Mull	59	B 15

Ross-on-Wye	17	M 28
Rossall Point	38	K 22
Rossett	34	L 24
Rothbury	51	O 18
Rothbury Forest	51	O 18
Rotherfield	12	U 30
Rotherham	35	P 23
Rothes	68	K 11
Rothesay	54	E 16
Rothienorman	69	M 11
Rothiesholm	75	M 6
Rothwell (Northants.)	28	R 26
Rothwell (West Yorks.)	40	P 22
Rottingdean	11	T 31
Roughton	31	X 25
Rousay	74	K 6
Rowland's Castle	10	R 31
Rowland's Gill	51	O 19
Rownhams	9	P 31
Rowsley	35	P 24
Roxwell	22	V 28
Roy (Glen)	60	F 13
Royal Greenwich Observatory	12	V 31
Royal Leamington Spa	27	P 27
Royal Military Academy	19	R 29
Royal Tunbridge Wells	12	U 30
Roybridge	60	F 13
Roydon (Essex)	22	U 28
Roydon (Norfolk)	31	X 26
Royston (Herts.)	29	T 27
Royston (South Yorks.)	40	P 23
Royton	39	N 23
Ruabon	33	K 25
Ruan High Lanes	2	F 33
Ruan Minor	2	E 34
Ruardean	17	M 28
Rubha na Faing	52	A 16
Rubh'an Dùnain	65	A 12
Rubha a' Mhail	52	A 16
Rubha Còigeach	72	D 9
Rubha Dubh	58	Z 14
Rubha Hunish	65	A 10
Rubha na h-Easgainne	65	B 12
Rubha Réidh	66	C 10
Rubha Suisnish	65	B 12
Rudbaxton	14	F 28
Ruddington	36	Q 25
Rudgeway	17	M 29
Rudgwick	11	S 30
Rudston	41	T 21
Rufford	38	L 23
Rufford Old Hall	38	L 23
Rugby	28	Q 26
Rugeley	35	O 25
Rumney	16	K 29
Runcorn	34	L 23
Runwell	22	V 29
Rushden	29	S 27
Ruskington	37	S 24
Rusper	11	T 30
Rustington	11	S 31
Ruswarp	47	S 20
Rutherglen	55	H 16
Ruthin/Rhuthun	33	K 24
Ruthven	62	K 14
Ruthven (Loch)	67	H 12
Ruthwell	49	J 19
Rutland Water	28	S 26
Ruyton of the Eleven Towns	34	L 25
Ryan (Loch)	48	E 19
Rycote	18	Q 28
Rydal	44	L 20
Ryde	10	Q 31
Rye	12	W 31
Ryhall	29	S 25
Ryhill	40	P 23
Ryhope	46	P 19
Ryton	51	O 19

S

Sacrista	70	Y 10
Sadberge	46	P 20
Saddell Bay	53	D 17
Saddleworth	39	O 23
Saffron Walden	29	U 27

St. Abb's Head	57	N 16
St. Agnes	2	E 33
St. Albans	19	T 28
St. Aldhelm's Head	8	N 32
St. Andrews	57	L 14
St. Ann's Head	14	E 28
St. Arvans	16	L 29
St. Asaph	33	J 24
St. Athan	16	J 29
St. Austell	3	F 32
St. Bees	43	J 20
St. Bees Head	43	J 20
St. Blazey	3	F 32
St. Breock	3	F 32
St. Briavels	16	M 28
St. Brides Major	15	J 29
St. Brides-Super-Ely	16	K 29
St. Buryan	2	D 33
St. Catherine's Point	10	Q 32
St. Clears/Sanclêr	14	G 28
St. Cleer	3	G 32
St. Columb Major	2	F 32
St. Combs	69	O 11
St. Cyrus	63	M 13
St. David's Head	14	D 28
St. David's/Tyddewi	14	E 28
St. Day	2	E 33
St. Dennis	3	F 32
St. Dogmaels	24	F 27
St. Donats	15	J 29
St. Ewe	3	F 33
St. Fagans	16	K 29
St. Fergus	69	O 11
St. Fillans	61	H 14
St. Gennys	6	G 31
St. Germans	3	H 32
St. Govan's Head	14	F 29
St. Helens (I.O.W.)	10	Q 31
St. Helens (Merseyside)	38	L 23
St. Ishmael's	14	E 28
St. Issey	3	F 32
St. Ive	3	G 32
St. Ives (Cambs.)	29	T 27
St. Ives (Cornwall)	2	D 33
St. John's	42	G 21
St. John's Loch	73	J 8
St. John's Chapel	45	N 19
St. John's Town of Dalry	49	H 18
St. Just	2	C 33
St. Just in Roseland	2	E 33
St. Keverne	2	E 33
St. Kew	3	F 32
St. Leonards (Dorset)	9	O 31
St. Leonards (East Sussex)	12	V 31
St. Mabyn	3	F 32
St. Magnus Bay	75	P 2
St. Margaret's at Cliffe	13	Y 30
St. Margaret's Bay	13	Y 30
St. Margaret's Hope	74	L 7
St. Martin's	33	K 25
St. Mary in the Marsh	12	W 30
St. Mary's	74	L 7
St. Mary's Loch	50	K 17
St. Mawes	2	E 33
St. Mawgan	3	F 32
St. Mellion	3	H 32
St. Merryn	2	F 32
St. Michael's Mount	2	D 33
St. Michaels-on-Wyre	38	L 22
St. Monans	57	L 15
St. Neot	3	G 32
St. Neots	29	T 27
St. Nicholas-at-Wade	13	X 29
St. Ninian's Isle	75	P 4
St. Osyth	23	X 28
St. Patrick's Isle	42	F 21
St. Paul's Walden	19	T 28
St. Peter Port (Channel I.)	5	
St. Peter's	13	Y 29
St. Stephen	3	F 32
St. Teath	3	F 32
St. Tudwal's Islands	32	G 25
St. Tudy	3	F 32

St. Vigeans	63	M 14
Salcombe	4	I 33
Sale	34	N 23
Salen (Argyll and Bute)	59	C 14
Salen (Highland)	59	C 13
Salfleet	41	U 23
Salford	39	N 23
Salfords	19	T 30
Saline	56	J 15
Salisbury	9	O 30
Salisbury Plain	17	O 30
Saltash	3	H 32
Saltburn	67	H 10
Saltburn-by-the-Sea	46	R 20
Saltcoats	54	F 17
Saltford	17	M 29
Saltram House	3	H 32
Samala	64	X 11
Samlesbury Old Hall	38	M 22
Sampford Courtenay	6	I 31
Sampford Peverell	7	J 31
Sancreed	2	D 33
Sand Side	44	K 21
Sanda Island	53	D 18
Sanday (Highland)	65	A 12
Sanday (Orkney Islands)	75	M 6
Sandbach	34	M 24
Sandbank	54	F 16
Sandbanks	9	O 31
Sandend	68	L 10
Sandford	7	J 31
Sandford Orcas	8	M 31
Sandgate	13	X 30
Sandgreen	43	H 19
Sandhaven	69	N 10
Sandhurst (Berks.)	18	R 29
Sandhurst (Kent)	12	V 30
Sandleigh	18	Q 28
Sandlins	23	Y 27
Sandness	75	P 3
Sandon	35	N 25
Sandown	10	Q 32
Sandray	58	X 13
Sandridge	19	T 28
Sandringham House	30	V 25
Sandwell	27	O 26
Sandwich	13	Y 30
Sandwood Loch	72	E 8
Sandy	29	T 27
Sandygate	42	G 20
Sandyhills	43	I 19
Sanquhar	49	I 17
Santon Head	42	G 21
Sarisbury	10	Q 31
Sark (Channel I.)	5	
Sarre	13	X 29
Satterthwaite	44	K 21
Saundersfoot	14	F 28
Saunderton	18	R 28
Sawbridgeworth	22	U 28
Sawrey	44	L 20
Sawston	29	U 27
Sawtry	29	T 26
Saxilby	36	S 24
Saxlingham Nethergate	31	X 26
Saxmundham	23	Y 27
Saxtead Green	31	X 27
Scadavay (Loch)	64	Y 11
Scaddle (Glen)	60	D 13
Scafell Pikes	44	K 20
Scalasaig	52	B 15
Scalby	47	S 21
Scalloway	75	Q 3
Scalpay (Highland)	65	C 12
Scalpay (Western Isles)	70	A 10
Scampton	36	S 24
Scapa Flow	74	K 7
Scarba	52	C 15
Scarborough	47	S 21
Scarcliffe	36	Q 24
Scarisbrick	38	L 23
Scarista	70	Y 10
Scarp	70	Y 9
Scavaig (Loch)	65	B 12
Scilly (Isles of)	2	B 34
Scone Palace	62	J 14
Scopwick	37	S 24

Scorton	46	P 20
Scotch-Corner	46	P 20
Scothern	37	S 24
Scotlandwell	56	K 15
Scotney	12	V 30
Scotter	40	S 23
Scourie	72	E 8
Scousburgh	75	Q 4
Scrabster	73	J 8
Scridain (Loch)	59	B 14
Scunthorpe	40	S 23
Sea Palling	31	Y 25
Seaford	11	U 31
Seaforth (Loch)	70	Z 10
Seaham	46	P 19
Seale	19	R 30
Sealga (Loch na)	66	E 10
Seasalter	13	X 29
Seascale	43	J 20
Seaton	5	K 31
Seaton Carew	46	Q 20
Seaton Delaval	51	P 18
Seaton Delaval Hall	51	P 18
Seaview	10	Q 31
Sebergham	44	L 19
Sedbergh	45	M 21
Sedgebrook	36	R 25
Sedgley	27	N 26
Sedlescombe	12	V 31
Seend	17	N 29
Seething	31	Y 26
Seil (Isle of)	54	D 15
Seilich (Loch an t-)	61	H 13
Selborne	10	R 30
Selby	40	Q 22
Selker Bay	43	J 20
Selkirk	50	L 17
Sellindge	12	W 30
Selmeston	12	U 31
Selsey	10	R 31
Selworthy	7	J 30
Semley	8	N 30
Senghenydd	16	K 29
Sennen	2	C 33
Sennybridge	15	J 28
Settle	39	N 21
Seven Sisters (Neath and Port Talbot)	15	I 28
Seven Sisters (East Sussex)	12	U 31
Sevenoaks	21	U 30
Severn (River)	17	M 28
Severn Bridge	16	M 29
Sgibacleit (Loch)	70	A 9
Sgiwen	15	I 29
Sgurr Mór	66	E 10
Shaftesbury	8	N 30
Shalbourne	18	P 29
Shaldon	4	J 32
Shalford	19	S 30
Shandon	54	F 15
Shanklin	10	Q 32
Shap	45	L 20
Shapinsay	75	L 6
Sharnbrook	29	S 27
Sharpness	17	M 28
Shaw (Gtr. Mches.)	39	N 23
Shaw (Wilts.)	17	N 29
Shawbost	70	Z 9
Shawbury	34	M 25
Shawford	9	P 30
Shebbear	6	H 31
Shebster	73	I 8
Sheepwash	6	H 31
Sheering	22	U 28
Sheerness	12	W 29
Sheffield	35	P 23
Sheffield Park	12	T 31
Shefford	29	S 27
Sheldon	17	N 29
Sheldon Manor	17	N 29
Sheldwich	12	W 30
Shell or Sealg (Loch)	70	A 9
Shelley	39	O 23
Shenstone	27	O 26
Shenval	68	K 11
Shepley	39	O 23
Sheppey (Isle of)	12	W 29
Shepreth	29	U 27
Shepshed	36	Q 25
Shepton Mallet	8	M 30
Sherborne	8	M 31
Sherborne St. John	18	Q 30
Sherburn	47	S 21

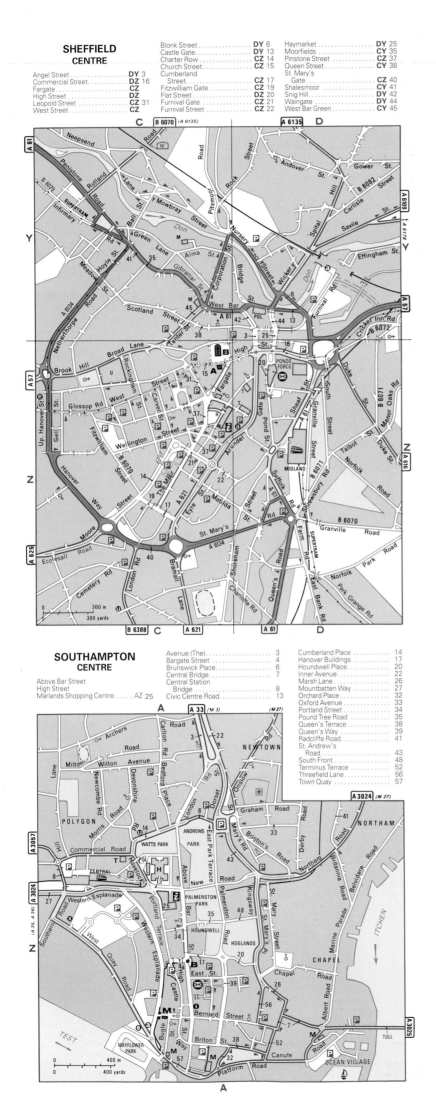

SHEFFIELD
CENTRE

Angel Street .... DY 3
Commercial Street .... DZ 16
Fargate .... CZ
High Street .... DZ
Leopold Street .... CZ 31
West Street .... CZ

Blonk Street .... DY 6
Castle Gate .... DY 13
Charter Row .... CZ 14
Church Street .... CZ 15
Cumberland
 Street .... CZ 17
Fitzwilliam Gate .... CZ 19
Flat Street .... DZ 20
Furnival Gate .... CZ 21
Furnival Street .... CZ 22

Haymarket .... DY 25
Moorfields .... CY 35
Pinstone Street .... CZ 37
Queen Street .... CY 38
St. Mary's
 Gate .... CZ 40
Shalesmoor .... CY 41
Snig Hill .... DY 42
Waingate .... DY 44
West Bar Green .... CY 45

SOUTHAMPTON
CENTRE

Above Bar Street
High Street
Marlands Shopping Centre ..... AZ 25

Avenue (The) 3
Bargate Street 4
Brunswick Place 6
Central Bridge 7
Central Station
 Bridge 8
Civic Centre Road 13

Cumberland Place 14
Hanover Buildings 17
Houndwell Place 20
Inner Avenue 22
Marsh Lane 26
Mountbatten Way 27
Orchard Place 32
Oxford Avenue 33
Portland Street 34
Pound Tree Road 35
Queen's Terrace 38
Queen's Way 39
Radcliffe Road 41
St. Andrew's
 Road 43
South Front 48
Terminus Terrace 52
Threefield Lane 56
Town Quay 57

Sherburn-in-Elmet	40	Q 22	Slaidburn	39	M 22	South Woodham	
Shere	20	S 30	Slaithwaite	39	O 23	Ferrers	22 V 29
Sheriff Hutton	40	Q 21	Slamannan	55	I 16	South Yorkshire	
Sheriffhales	34	M 25	Slapin (Loch)	65	B 12	(County)	39 O 23
Sheringham	31	X 26	Slapton	4	I 33	South Zeal	6 I 31
Sherston	17	N 29	Sleaford	37	S 25	Southam	28 P 27
Sherwood Forest	36	Q 24	Sleat (Sound)	65	C 12	Southampton	9 P 31
Shiant (Sound of)	70	A 10	Sledmere	40	S 21	Southborough	12 U 30
Shiel (Glen)	66	D 12	Sleekburn	51	P 18	Southbourne	
Shiel (Loch)	60	D 13	Sleights	47	S 20	(Dorset)	9 O 31
Shieldaig	66	D 11	Sligachan	65	B 12	Southbourne	
Shieldaig (Loch)	66	C 11	Sligachan (Loch)	65	B 12	(West Sussex)	10 R 31
Shifnal	26	M 25	Slimbridge	17	M 28	Southend	53 D 18
Shilbottle	51	O 17	Slindon	11	S 31	Southend-on-Sea	22 W 29
Shildon	46	P 20	Slockavullin	54	D 15	Southery	30 V 26
Shillingford	7	J 30	Slough	20	S 29	Southminster	23 W 29
Shillington	29	S 28	Sloy (Loch)	54	F 15	Southport	38 K 23
Shimpling	31	X 26	Small Hythe	12	W 30	Southsea	10 Q 31
Shin (Loch)	72	G 9	Smallfield	11	T 30	Southwark (London	
Shinfield	18	R 29	Smarden	12	W 30	Borough)	20 T 29
Shipdham	30	W 26	Smedmore	8	N 32	Southwater	11 S 30
Shipley (Salop)	27	N 26	Snaefell	42	G 21	Southwell	36 R 24
Shipley			Snainton	47	S 21	Southwick (West	
(West Yorks.)	39	O 22	Snaith	40	Q 22	Sussex)	11 T 31
Shipston-on-Stour	27	P 27	Snape	23	Y 27	Southwick (Wilts.)	17 N 30
Shipton	26	M 26	Snetterton Circuit	30	W 26	Southwick Widley	10 Q 31
Shipton-under-			Snettisham	30	V 25	Southwold	31 Z 27
Wychwood	18	P 28	Snizort (Loch)	65	A 11	Sowerby	
Shira (Lochan)	60	F 14	Snodland	12	V 30	Bridge	39 O 22
Shirebrook	36	Q 24	Snowdon/Yr			Spalding	37 T 25
Shirley	27	O 26	Wyddfa	32	H 24	Spaldwick	29 S 26
Shobdon	26	L 27	Snowdonia			Spanish Head	42 F 21
Shoeburyness	23	W 29	National Park	32	I 24	Sparkford	8 M 30
Shoreham	11	T 31	Snowshill	27	O 27	Spean (Glen)	60 F 13
Shorne	12	V 29	Soa	58	Z 14	Spean Bridge	60 F 13
Shorwell	9	P 32	Soa Island	59	A 15	Spelve (Loch)	59 C 14
Shotley Bridge	45	O 19	Soar (River)	36	Q 25	Spennymoor	46 P 19
Shotley Gate	23	X 28	Soay	65	B 12	Spey (River)	61 G 12
Shottermill	10	R 30	Soay Sound	65	B 12	Spey Bay	68 K 10
Shotton Colliery			Soham	30	V 26	Speymouth Forest	68 K 11
Thornley	46	P 19	Solent (The)	10	Q 31	Spilsby	37 U 24
Shotts	55	I 16	Solihull	27	O 26	Spinningdale	67 H 10
Shrewsbury	26	L 25	Sollas	64	X 11	Spithead	10 Q 31
Shrewton	17	O 30	Solva	14	E 28	Spittal (Highland)	73 J 8
Shrivenham	17	P 29	Solway Firth	43	J 19	Spittal (Northumb.)	57 O 16
Shropshire (County)	26	M 26	Somercotes	35	P 24	Spittal of Glenshee	62 J 13
Shuna Sound	54	D 15	Somerset (County)	8	M 30	Spofforth	40 P 22
Shurdington	17	N 28	Somersham	29	U 26	Spondon	35 P 25
Sible Hedingham	22	V 28	Somerton (Norfolk)	31	Y 25	Spreyton	6 I 31
Sibsey	37	U 24	Somerton (Oxon.)	28	Q 28	Springfield	56 K 15
Sidbury	5	K 31	Somerton			Sprotbrough	40 Q 23
Siddlington	35	N 24	(Somerset)	8	L 30	Spurn Head	41 U 23
Sidford	5	K 31	Sompting	11	S 31	St. Bride's Bay	14 E 28
Sidlaw Hills	62	K 14	Sonning	18	R 29	St. Nicholas	
Sidlesham	10	R 31	Sonning			(Pembrokes)	14 E 28
Sidmouth	5	K 31	Caversham	18	R 29	St. Nicholas (Vale of	
Sighthill	56	K 16	Sonning Common	18	R 29	Glamorgan)	16 K 29
Sileby	36	Q 25	Sopley	9	O 31	Stack (Loch)	72 F 8
Silecroft	44	K 21	Sorbie	42	G 19	Stack Island	64 Y 12
Silkstone	35	P 23	Sorn	48	H 17	Stack Rocks	14 E 28
Silloth	49	J 19	Sound (The)	3	H 32	Staffa	59 A 14
Silsden	39	O 22	South Brent	4	I 32	Staffin Bay	65 B 11
Silver End	22	V 28	South Cave	40	S 22	Stafford	35 N 25
Silverdale	38	L 21	South Cerney	17	O 28	Staffordshire	
Silverstone Circuit	28	Q 27	South Downs	10	R 31	(County)	35 N 25
Silverton	7	J 31	South Elmsall	40	Q 23	Staindrop	45 O 20
Simonsbath	7	I 30	South Esk (River)	63	L 13	Staines	20 S 29
Sinclair's Bay	74	K 8	South Foreland	13	Y 30	Stainforth (North	
Sionascaig (Loch)	72	E 9	South			Yorks.)	39 N 21
Sissinghurst	12	V 30	Hanningfield	22	V 29	Stainforth (South	
Sittingbourne	12	W 29	South Harris	70	Z 10	Yorks.)	40 Q 23
Skara Brae	74	J 6	South Harris			Staithes	47 R 20
Skares	48	H 17	Forest	70	Z 10	Stalbridge	8 M 31
Skeabost	65	B 11	South Hayling	10	R 31	Stalham	31 Y 25
Skegness	37	V 24	South Kelsey	41	S 23	Stalmine	38 L 22
Skellingthorpe	36	S 24	South Kirkby	40	Q 23	Stalybridge	39 N 23
Skelmanthorpe	35	P 23	South Lancing	11	T 31	Stamford	29 S 26
Skelmersdale	38	L 23	South Leverton	36	R 24	Stamford Bridge	40 R 22
Skelmorlie	54	F 16	South Lopham	30	X 26	Standing Stones	70 Z 9
Skelton (Cleveland)	46	R 20	South Mimms	20	T 28	Standish	38 M 23
Skelton (Cumbria)	44	L 19	South Molton	6	I 30	Standlake	18 P 28
Skelwith Bridge	44	K 20	South Morar	59	C 13	Standon	22 U 28
Skenfrith	16	L 28	South Normanton	35	P 24	Standford-	
Skerray	73	H 8	South			in-the-Vale	18 P 29
Skervuile			Ockendon	21	U 29	Stanford-le-Hope	22 V 29
Lighthouse	53	C 16	South Oxhey	20	S 29	Stanford-on-Avon	28 Q 26
Skidaw	44	K 20	South Petherton	8	L 31	Stanhope	45 N 19
Skilgate	7	J 30	South Petherwin	3	G 32	Stanley (Perthshire	
Skipness	53	D 16	South Queensferry	56	J 16	and Kinross)	62 J 14
Skipport (Loch)	64	Y 12	South Ronaldsay	74	L 7	Stanley (Durham)	46 O 19
Skipsea	41	T 22	South Shields	51	P 19	Stanley	
Skipton	39	N 22	South Stack	32	F 24	(West Yorks.)	40 P 22
Skirza	74	K 8	South Tawton	4	I 31	Stanmer Park	11 T 31
Skokholm Island	14	E 28	South Uist	64	X 12	Stanstead Abbotts	22 U 28
Skomer Island	14	E 28	South Walls	74	K 7	Stansted	
Skye (Isle of)	65	B 12	South			Mountfitchet	22 U 28
			Warnborough	18	R 30		

STOKE-ON-TRENT
BUILT UP AREA

Alexandra Road	U	3
Bedford Road	U	4
Brownhills Road	U	12
Church Lane	U	19
Cobridge Road	U	21
Davenport Street	U	23
Elder Road	U	24
Etruria Vale Road	U	27
Grove Road	V	30
Hanley Road	U	31
Heron Street	V	34
High Street	U	35
Higherland	V	37
Manor Street	V	44
Mayne Street	V	45
Moorland Road	U	48
Porthill Road	U	59
Snow Hill	U	63
Stoke Road	U	68
Strand (The)	V	69
Victoria Park Road	V	75
Victoria Park Link	V	76
Watlands View	U	77
Williamson Street	U	78

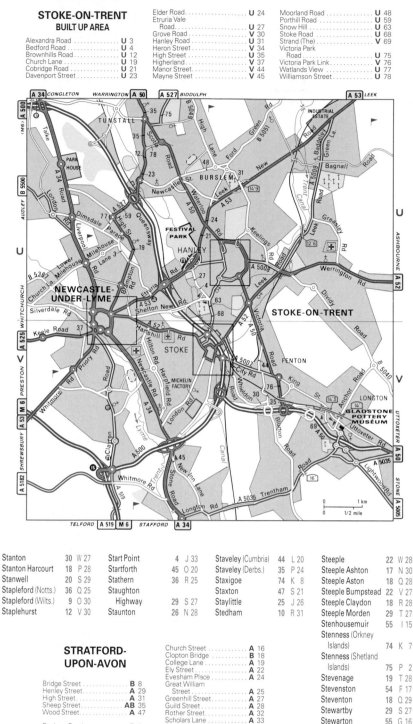

STOKE
Church Street

Campbell Place	14
Elenora Street	26
Fleming Road	28
Hartshill Road	33
London Road	42
Shelton Old Road	62
Station Road	66
Vale Street	72

STOKE

Stradbroke	31	X 27
Stradishall	22	V 29
Stradsett	30	V 26
Straiton	48	G 18
Straloch	62	J 13
Stranraer	42	E 19
Strata Florida Abbey	25	I 27
Stratfield Saye	18	Q 29
Stratford St. Mary	23	W 28
Stratford-upon-Avon	27	O 27
Strath Brora	73	H 9
Strath Dearn	67	I 11
Strath Halladale	73	I 8
Strath Isla	68	K 11
Strath More	66	E 10
Strath Mulzie	72	F 10
Strath of Kildonan	73	I 9
Strath Oykel	72	F 10
Strath Skinsdale	73	H 9
Strath Tay	62	J 14
Strathallan	55	I 15
Strathardle	62	J 13
Strathaven	55	H 16
Strathbeg (Loch of)	69	O 11
Strathblane	55	H 16
Strathbogie	68	L 11
Strathbraan	61	I 14
Strathcarron	66	D 11
Strathconon	66	F 11
Strathconon Forest	66	F 11
Strathdon	68	K 12
Strathearn	55	I 14
Stratherrick	67	G 12
Strathkinness	56	L 14
Strathmiglo	56	K 15
Strathmore	62	K 14
Strathnairn	67	H 11
Strathnaver	73	H 8
Strathpeffer	67	G 11
Strathspey	68	J 11
Strathvaich Lodge	66	F 10
Strathy	73	I 8
Strathy Point	73	H 8
Strathyre	55	H 15
Stratton (Cornwall)	6	G 31

Stoke Poges	20	S 29
Stoke sub Hamdon	8	L 31
Stokenchurch	18	R 29
Stokenham	4	I 33
Stokesay	26	L 26
Stokesley	46	Q 20
Stone (Bucks.)	18	R 28
Stone (Staffs.)	35	N 25
Stonehaven	63	N 13
Stonehenge	9	O 30
Stonehouse (South Lanarkshire)	55	I 16
Stonehouse (Devon)	3	H 32
Stonehouse (Glos.)	17	N 28
Stonesfield	18	P 28
Stoneybridge	64	X 12
Stoneykirk	42	E 19
Stoneywood	69	N 12
Stony Stratford	28	R 27
Stornoway	70	A 9
Storr (The)	65	B 11
Storrington	11	S 31
Stort (River)	22	U 28
Stotfold	29	T 27
Stottesdon	26	M 26
Stour (River) (English Channel)	8	N 31
Stour (River) (North Sea)	22	V 27
Stour (River) (R. Severn)	27	N 26
Stourbridge	27	N 26
Stourhead House	8	N 30
Stourport-on-Severn	27	N 26
Stow	56	L 16
Stow-on-the-Wold	17	O 28
Stowe School	28	Q 27
Stowmarket	23	W 27
Strachan	63	M 12
Strachur	54	E 15

Stanton	30	W 27
Stanton Harcourt	18	P 28
Stanwell	20	S 29
Stapleford (Notts.)	36	Q 25
Stapleford (Wilts.)	9	O 30
Staplehurst	12	V 30
Start Point	4	J 33
Startforth	45	O 20
Stathern	36	R 25
Staughton Highway	29	S 27
Staunton	26	N 28
Staveley (Cumbria)	44	L 20
Staveley (Derbs.)	35	P 24
Staxigoe	74	K 8
Staxton	47	S 21
Staylittle	25	J 26
Stedham	10	R 31
Steeple	22	W 28
Steeple Ashton	17	N 30
Steeple Aston	18	Q 28
Steeple Bumpstead	22	V 27
Steeple Claydon	18	R 28
Steeple Morden	29	T 27
Stenhousemuir	55	I 15
Stenness (Orkney Islands)	74	K 7
Stenness (Shetland Islands)	75	P 2
Stevenage	19	T 28
Stevenston	54	F 17
Steventon	18	Q 29
Stewartby	29	S 27
Stewarton	55	G 16
Stewkley	19	R 28
Steyning	11	T 31
Sticklepath	4	I 31
Stilligarry	64	X 12
Stillington	40	Q 21
Stilton	29	T 26
Stirling	55	I 15
Stithians	2	E 33
Stob Choire Claurigh	60	F 13
Stock	22	V 29
Stockbridge	9	P 30
Stockland	7	K 31
Stockport	35	N 23
Stocksbridge	39	P 23
Stockton Heath	34	M 23
Stockton-on-Tees	46	P 20
Stockton-on-Teme	26	M 27
Stoer	72	D 9
Stogumber	7	K 30
Stogursey	7	K 30
Stoke Albany	28	R 26
Stoke-by-Nayland	23	W 28
Stoke Climsland	3	H 32
Stoke Fleming	4	J 33
Stoke Gabriel	4	J 32
Stoke Lacy	26	M 27
Stoke Mandeville	18	R 28
Stoke-on-Trent	35	N 24

STRATFORD-UPON-AVON

Bridge Street	B	8
Henley Street	A	29
High Street	A	31
Sheep Street	AB	35
Wood Street	A	47
Banbury Road	B	2
Benson Road	B	3
Bridge Foot	B	6
Chapel Lane	A	13
Chapel Street	A	14
Church Street	A	16
Clopton Bridge	B	18
College Lane	A	19
Ely Street	A	22
Evesham Place	A	24
Great William Street	A	25
Greenhill Street	A	27
Guild Street	A	28
Rother Street	A	32
Scholars Lane	A	33
Tiddington Road	B	38
Trinity Street	A	40
Warwick Road	B	42
Waterside	B	43
Windsor Street	A	45

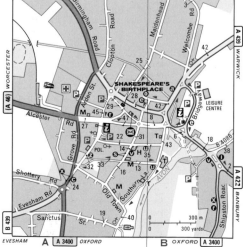

SUNDERLAND

Fawcett Street	
High Street West	15
Holmeside	
John Street	16
The Bridges	
Albion Place	2
Bedford Street	4
Borough Road	5
Bridge Street	6
Chester Road	10
Crowtree Road	11
Derwent Street	12
Livingstone Road	18
New Durham Road	19
Park Lane	23
St. Mary's Way	27
Southwick Road	30
Vine Place	36

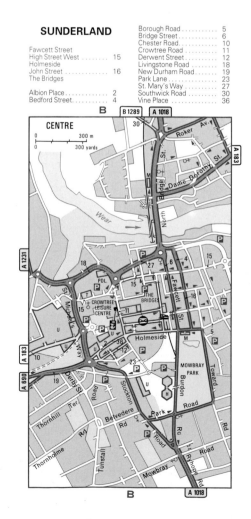

SWANSEA/ABERTAWE

College Street 13
Kingsway (The)
Oxford Street
Parc Tawe
  Shopping Centre
Princess Way
Quadrant Centre
St. David's Square

Alexandra Road 2
Belle Vue Way 4

Carmarthen Road 7
Christina Street 9
Clarence Terrace 10
De La Beche Street 14
Dillwyn Street 15
East Bank Way 16
Fabian Way 17
Grove Place 18
Nelson Street 20
New Cut Bridge 21
St. Mary's Square 28
Tawe Bridge 29
Union Street 37
Wellington Street 37
West Way 38
William Street 39

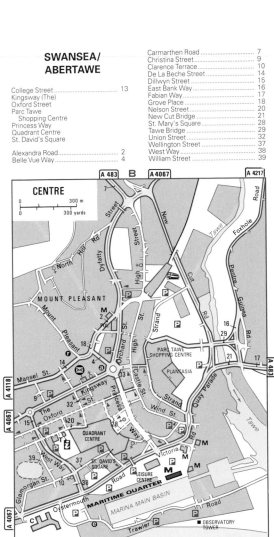

Stratton (Glos.)	17	O 28
Stratton-on-the-Fosse	17	M 30
Stratton-St. Margaret	17	O 29
Streatley	18	Q 29
Street	8	L 30
Strensall	40	Q 21
Stretford	39	N 23
Stretham	29	U 26
Stretton (Cheshire)	34	M 23
Stretton (Staffs.)	27	N 25
Strichen	69	N 11
Striven (Loch)	54	E 16
Stroma (Island of)	74	K 7
Stromeferry	66	D 11
Stromemore	66	D 11
Stromness	74	K 7
Stronachlachar	55	G 15
Stronchreggan	60	E 13
Stronsay	75	M 6
Stronsay Firth	74	L 6
Strontian	59	D 13
Stroud	17	N 28
Strumble Head	14	E 27
Stuart Castel	67	H 11
Stuartfield	69	N 11
Stubbington	10	Q 31
Studland	9	O 32
Studley (Warw.)	27	O 27
Studley (Wilts.)	17	N 29
Studley Royal Gardens	39	P 21
Stuley	64	Y 12
Sturminster Marshall	8	N 31
Sturminster Newton	8	N 31
Sturry	13	X 30
Sturton-le-Steeple	36	R 23
Suainaval (Loch)	70	Z 9
Sudbury (Derbs.)	35	O 25
Sudbury (Suffolk)	22	W 27
Sudbury Hall	35	O 25
Sudeley Castle	17	O 28

Suffolk (County)	30	X 27
Sùil Ghorm	59	A 13
Sulby	42	G 21
Sulgrave	28	Q 27
Sullom Voe	75	P 2
Summer Bridge	39	O 21
Summer Island	72	D 9
Summercourt	2	F 32
Sunart	59	D 13
Sunart (Loch)	59	C 13
Sunbury	20	S 29
Sunderland	46	P 19
Sunningdale	20	S 29
Sunninghill	20	S 29
Surfleet	37	T 25
Surrey (County)	11	S 30
Sutterton	37	T 25
Sutton Bank	46	Q 21
Sutton Benger	17	N 29
Sutton Bridge	37	U 25
Sutton Coldfield	27	O 26
Sutton Courtenay	18	Q 29
Sutton-in-Ashfield	36	Q 24
Sutton-on-Forest	40	Q 21
Sutton-on-Hull	41	T 22
Sutton-on-Sea	37	U 24
Sutton-on-Trent	36	R 24
Sutton Scotney	9	P 30
Sutton Valence	12	V 30
Swadlincote	35	P 25
Swaffham	30	W 26
Swaffham Bulbeck	29	U 27
Swale (River)	40	P 21
Swale (The)	12	W 29
Swale Dale	45	O 20
Swallow	41	T 23
Swallow Falls	33	I 24
Swanage	9	O 32

Swanland	41	S 22
Swanley	21	U 29
Swanscombe	21	U 29
Swansea/Abertawe	15	I 29
Swarbacks Minn	75	P 2
Sway	9	P 31
Swaythling	9	P 31
Swimbridge	6	I 30
Swinbrook	18	P 28
Swindon	17	O 29
Swineshead	37	T 25
Swinton (Scottish Borders)	57	N 16
Swinton (South Yorks.)	40	Q 23
Swynnerton	35	N 25
Symbister	75	Q 2
Symonds Yat	16	M 28
Symonds Yat Rock	16	M 28
Symondsbury	8	L 31
Syresham	28	Q 27
Syston	28	Q 25

T

Tadcaster	40	Q 22
Tadley	18	Q 29
Tadmarton	27	P 27
Tadworth	20	T 30
Taff (River)	16	K 29
Taibach	34	I 29
Tain	67	H 10
Takeley	22	U 28
Tal-y-bont (Dyfed)	24	I 26
Tal-y-Llyn Lake	33	I 25
Talgarth	25	K 28
Talke	34	N 24
Talladale	66	D 10
Talley	15	I 28
Talsarnau	32	H 25
Talybont-on-Usk (Powys)	16	K 28

Tamar (River)	6	G 31
Tamworth	27	O 26
Tan Hill	45	N 20
Tanera Beg	72	D 9
Tanera Mór	72	D 9
Tannadice	62	L 13
Tantallon Castle	57	M 15
Taransay	70	Y 10
Taransay (Sound of)	70	Z 10
Tarbat Ness	67	I 10
Tarbert (Argyll and Bute)	53	D 16
Tarbert (Western Isles)	70	Z 10
Tarbert (Loch)	53	C 16
Tarbet	54	F 15
Tarbolton	48	G 17
Tardy Gate	38	L 22
Tarland	68	L 12
Tarleton	38	L 22
Tarn (The)	44	L 20
Tarporley	34	M 24
Tarrant Hinton	8	N 31
Tarrant Keyneston	8	N 31
Tarrington	26	M 27
Tarskavaig Point	65	B 12
Tarves	69	N 11
Tarvin	34	L 24
Tattershall	37	T 24
Tatton Hall	34	M 24
Taunton	7	K 30
Taunton Deane	7	K 30
Taverham	31	X 25
Tavistock	3	H 32
Taw (River)	6	I 31
Tay (Firth of)	62	K 14
Tay (Loch)	61	H 14
Tay (River)	61	H 14
Tay Road Bridge	62	L 14
Taynuilt	60	E 14
Tayport	62	L 14
Tayvallich	54	D 15
Teacuis (Loch)	59	C 14
Tebay	45	M 20

Tedburn St. Mary	7	I 31
Tees (River)	46	P 20
Teesdale	45	N 20
Teifi (River)	24	G 27
Teignmouth	4	J 32
Telford	26	M 25
Teme (River)	26	M 27
Temple Ewell	13	X 30
Temple Sowerby	45	M 20
Templeton	14	F 28
Tempsford	29	T 27
Tenbury Wells	26	M 27
Tenby/Dinbych-y-pysgod	14	F 28
Tendring	23	X 28
Tenterden	12	W 30
Terling	22	V 28
Tern Hill	34	M 25
Terrington St. Clement	37	U 25
Test (River)	18	P 30
Tetbury	17	N 29
Tetford	37	T 24
Tetney	41	T 23
Tettenhall	27	N 26
Teviotdale	50	L 17
Tewin	19	T 28
Tewkesbury	27	N 28
Texa	52	B 17
Teynham	12	W 30
Thakeham	11	S 31
Thame	18	R 28
Thame (River)	18	R 28
Thames (River)	18	Q 29
Thanet (Isle of)	13	Y 29
Thatcham	18	Q 29
Thaxted	22	V 28
Theale (Berks.)	18	Q 29
Theale (Somerset)	16	L 30
Theddlethorpe St. Helen	37	U 23
Thetford	30	W 26
Theydon Bois	21	U 28
Thirsk	46	P 21
Thoralby	45	N 21
Thornaby-on-Tees	46	Q 20
Thornaganby	41	R 22
Thornbury (South Glos.)	17	M 29
Thornbury (Heref. and Worc.)	26	M 27
Thornby	28	Q 26
Thorne	41	R 23
Thorner	40	P 22
Thorney	29	T 26
Thornham	30	V 25
Thornhill (Stirling)	55	H 15
Thornhill (Dumfries and Galloway)	49	I 18
Thornley	46	P 19
Thornton (Fife)	56	K 15
Thornton (Lancs.)	38	K 22
Thornton Curtis	41	S 23
Thornton Dale	47	R 21
Thornton-in-Craven	39	N 22
Thornyhive Bay	63	N 13
Thorpe (Derbs.)	35	O 24
Thorpe (Essex)	23	W 29
Thorpe-le-Soken	23	X 28
Thorpe-on-the-Hill	36	S 24
Thorpeness	23	Y 27
Thorrington	23	X 28
Thrapston	29	S 26
Three Cocks	25	K 27
Threlkeld	44	K 20
Throckley	51	O 19
Throwleigh	4	I 31
Thruxton Circuit	18	P 30
Thundersley	22	V 29
Thurcroft	36	Q 23
Thurlby	37	S 25
Thurlestone	4	I 33
Thurlow	22	V 27
Thurmaston	28	Q 25
Thursby	44	K 19
Thurso	73	J 8
Thwaite	45	N 20
Tibberton (Glos.)	17	M 28
Tibberton (Salop)	34	M 25
Tibshelf	35	P 24
Ticehurst	12	V 30

Tickhill	36	Q 23
Ticknall	35	P 25
Tideswell	35	O 24
Tigerton	63	L 13
Tigharry	64	X 11
Tighnabruaich	54	E 16
Tilbury	21	V 29
Tillicoultry	55	I 15
Tillington	11	S 31
Tilshead	17	O 30
Tilt (Glen)	61	I 13
Tilton-on-the-Hill	28	R 26
Timberscombe	7	J 30
Timsbury	17	M 30
Tingwall (Loch)	75	P 3
Tintagel	3	F 32
Tintern Abbey	16	L 28
Tintinhull	8	L 31
Tipton	27	N 26
Tiptree	22	W 28
Tiree	58	Z 14
Tirga Mór	70	Z 10
Tiroran	59	B 14
Tisbury	8	N 30
Titchfield	10	Q 31
Tiumpan Head	71	B 9
Tiverton	7	J 31
Tobermory	59	B 14
Toberonochy	54	D 15
Tobson	70	Z 9
Toddington	19	S 28
Todmorden	39	N 22
Toe Head	70	Y 10
Toll of Birness	69	O 11
Tollerton	40	Q 21
Tollesbury	23	W 28
Tolleshunt d'Arcy	23	W 28
Tolpuddle	8	N 31
Tolsta	71	B 8
Tolsta Chaolais	70	Z 9
Tolsta Head	71	B 8
Tomatin	67	I 11
Tombreck	67	H 11
Tomintoul	68	J 12
Tonbridge	12	U 30
Tongland	43	H 19
Tongue	73	G 8
Tonna	15	I 28
Tonypandy	16	J 29
Tonyrefail	16	J 29
Topcliffe	46	P 21
Topsham	4	J 31
Tor Ness	74	K 7
Torbay	4	J 32
Torcross	4	J 33
Torksey	36	R 24
Torlundy	60	E 13
Torphichen	55	J 16
Torphins	69	M 12
Torpoint	3	H 32
Torquay	4	J 32
Torridon (Loch)	66	C 11
Torrisdale Bay	73	H 8
Torthorwald	49	J 18
Torver	44	K 20
Totland	9	P 31
Totnes	4	I 32
Totton	9	P 31
Tow Law	45	O 19
Towcester	28	R 27
Tower Hamlets (London Borough)	21	T 29
Town Yetholm	50	N 17
Towneley Hall	39	N 22
Traborton	48	G 17
Trallwng/Welshpool	25	K 26
Tranent	56	L 16
Traquair House	50	K 17
Trawden	39	N 22
Trawsfynydd	25	I 25
Trealaval (Loch)	70	A 9
Trearddur Bay	32	G 24
Trecastle	15	I 28
Trefaldwyn/Montgomery	25	K 26
Treffynnon/Holywell	33	K 24
Trefnant	33	J 24
Trefyclawdd/Knighton	25	K 26
Trefynwy/Monmouth	16	L 28
Tregaron	24	I 27
Tregony	3	F 33
Treharris	16	K 29

Treherbert	15	J 28
Treig (Loch)	60	F 13
Trelech	14	G 28
Trelissick Gardens	2	E 33
Trelleck	16	L 28
Tremadog	32	H 25
Tremadog Bay	32	H 25
Trengwainton Garden	2	D 33
Trent (River)	36	N 25
Trentham	35	N 25
Treorchy	15	J 29
Trerice	2	E 32
Treshnish Isles	59	A 14
Treshnish Point	59	A 14
Tretower	16	K 28
Trevone	2	F 32
Trevor	32	G 25
Trevose Head	2	E 32
Trewithen	3	F 33
Trimdon	46	P 19
Trimley Heath	23	X 28
Trimsaran	15	H 28
Tring	19	R 28
Trispen	2	E 33
Trochry	62	J 14
Troedyrhiw	16	J 28
Trollamarig (Loch)	70	Z 10
Tromie (Glen)	61	H 12
Troon	48	G 17
Trossachs (The)	55	G 15
Trotternish	65	B 11
Troutbeck	44	L 20
Trowbridge	17	N 30
Truim (Glen)	61	H 13
Trull	7	K 31
Trumpington	29	U 27
Truro	2	E 33
Trwyn Cilan	32	G 25
Tuath (Loch)	59	B 14
Tuddenham	30	V 27
Tudweiliog	32	G 25
Tugford	26	M 26
Tulla (Loch)	60	F 14
Tullibody	55	I 15
Tumble	15	H 28
Tummel (Loch)	61	I 13
Tunstall (Staffs.)	35	N 24
Tunstall (Suffolk)	31	Y 25
Turnberry	48	F 18
Turnditch	35	P 24
Turret (Loch and Reservoir)	61	I 14
Turriff	69	M 11
Turvey	29	S 27
Tusker Rock	15	I 29
Tutbury	35	O 25
Tuxford	36	R 24
Twatt	74	K 6
Tweed (River)	49	J 17
Tweeddale	49	J 17
Tweedmouth	57	N 16
Tweedsmuir Hills	49	J 17
Twickenham	20	S 29
Twyford (Berks.)	18	R 29
Twyford (Hants.)	10	Q 30
Twyford (Leics.)	28	R 25
Twynholm	43	H 19
Tyddewi/St. David's	14	E 28
Tyldesley	34	M 23
Tyne (River)	51	P 19
Tyne and Wear (Metropolitan County Newcastle)	51	P 19
Tynemouth	51	P 18
Tynewydd	15	J 28
Tytherington	17	M 29
Tywardreath	3	F 32
Tywi (River)	25	I 27
Tywyn	24	H 26

U

Uckfield	12	U 31
Uddingston	55	H 16
Uffculme	7	K 31
Ufford	23	Y 27
Ugadale Bay	53	D 17
Ugborough	4	I 32
Uig (Highland)	65	A 11
Uig (Western Isles)	70	Y 9
Uisg (Loch)	59	C 14
Uiskevagh (Loch)	64	Y 11

Uley 17 N 28
Ullapool 72 E 10
Ulleskelf 40 Q 22
Ullesthorpe 28 Q 26
Ullswater 44 L 20
Ulpha 44 K 21
Ulsta 75 Q 2
Ulva 59 B 14
Ulverston 44 K 21
Unapool 72 E 9
Unst 75 R 1
Upavon 17 O 30
Uphall 56 J 16
Uphill 16 L 30
Uplyme 7 L 31
Upottery 7 K 31
Upper Badcall 72 E 9
Upper Beeding 11 T 31
Upper Chapel 25 J 27
Upper Dicker 12 U 31
Upper Knockando 68 J 11
Upper Loch
Torridon 66 D 11
Upper Poppleton 40 Q 22
Upper Tean 35 O 25
Uppertown 74 K 7
Uppingham 28 R 26
Upton (Dorset) 8 N 31
Upton (Notts.) 36 R 24
Upton Grey 18 Q 30
Upton House 27 P 27
Upton Magna 26 M 25
Upton-upon-
Severn 27 N 27
Upwell 29 U 26
Urchfont 17 O 30
Ure (River) 40 Q 21
Urigill (Loch) 72 F 9
Urmston 39 M 23
Urquhart Castle 67 G 12
Urquhart (Glen) 67 G 11
Urrahag (Loch) 70 A 8
Urswick 38 K 21
Usk (River) 15 J 28
Usk/Brynbuga 16 L 28
Uttoxeter 35 O 25
Uyea 75 R 2
Uyeasound 75 R 1

V

Vallay Strand 64 X 11
Valle Crucis 33 K 25
Valley 32 G 24
Valtos 70 Z 9
Vatersay 58 X 13
Ve Skerries 75 O 2
Venachar (Loch) 55 H 15
Ventnor 10 Q 32
Verwood 9 O 31
Veryan 2 F 33
Veyatie (Loch) 72 E 9
Vindolanda 50 M 19
Voe 75 Q 2
Voil (Loch) 61 G 14
Vowchurch 26 L 27
Vyrnwy (Lake) 33 J 25

W

Waddesdon 18 R 28
Waddington
(Lancs.) 39 M 22
Waddington (Lincs.) 36 S 24
Wadebridge 3 F 32
Wadhurst 12 U 30
Wainfleet All Saints 37 U 24
Wakefield 40 P 22
Wakes Colne 22 W 28
Walberswick 31 Y 27
Walderslade 12 V 29
Walkden 39 M 23
Walkeringham 36 R 23
Walkern 19 T 28
Wall 27 O 26
Wallace Monument 55 I 15
Wallasey 34 K 23
Wallingford 18 Q 29
Wallington House 54 O 18
Walls 75 P 3
Wallsend 51 P 18
Walney (Isle of) 38 K 21
Walpole St. Andrew 37 U 25
Walpole St. Peter 37 U 25

Walsall 27 O 26
Waltham (North
East Lincs.) 41 T 23
Waltham (Kent) 13 X 30
Waltham
Abbey 21 U 28
Waltham Forest
(London Borough) 21 T 29
Waltham-
on-the-Wolds 36 R 25
Walton-le-Dale 38 M 22
Walton-
on-Thames 20 S 29
Walton-on-the-
Naze 23 X 28
Wanborough 17 O 29
Wandsworth
(London Borough) 20 T 29
Wanlockhead 49 I 17
Wansford 29 S 26
Wanstrow 8 M 30
Wantage 18 P 29
Wappenham 28 Q 27
Warboys 29 T 26
Wardington 28 Q 27
Wardour Castle 8 N 30
Ware 19 T 28
Wareham 8 N 31
Wargrave 18 R 29
Wark 57 N 17
Wark Forest 50 M 18
Warkworth 51 P 17
Warley 27 O 26
Warlingham 21 T 30
Warmington 28 P 27
Warminster 17 N 30
Warmsworth 40 Q 23
Warren (The) 13 X 30
Warrington 38 M 23
Warsash 10 Q 31
Warsop 36 Q 24
Warton (near
Morecambe) 38 L 21
Warton (near
Preston) 38 L 22
Warwick 27 P 27
Warwickshire
(County) 27 P 27
Warwickshire
(County) 27 P 27
Wasbister 74 K 6
Wasdale Head 44 K 20
Wash (The) 37 U 25
Washington
(Tyne and Wear) 51 P 19
Washington (West
Sussex) 11 S 31
Wast Water 44 K 20
Watchet 7 K 30
Watchfield 17 P 29
Watchgate 44 L 20
Water Orton 27 O 26
Waterbeach 29 U 27
Watergate Bay 2 E 32
Waterhouses 35 O 24
Wateringbury 12 V 30
Waterlooville 10 Q 31
Waternish Point 65 A 11
Waters Upton 34 M 25
Waterside 54 G 17
Watford 20 S 29
Wath-upon-Dearne 40 P 23
Watlington 18 Q 29
Watten 74 K 8
Watton 30 W 26
Watton at Stone 19 T 28
Waunfawr 32 H 24
Waveney (River) 31 Y 26
Weald (The) 12 U 30
Wear (River) 45 O 20
Weardale 45 N 19
Weaver (River) 34 M 24
Weaverthorpe 41 S 21
Wedmore 16 L 30
Wednesbury 27 N 26
Wednesfield 27 N 26
Weedon-Bec 28 Q 27
Week St. Mary 6 G 31
Weeley 23 X 28
Weem 61 I 14
Welcombe 6 G 31
Welham Green 19 T 28
Welland 26 N 27
Welland (River) 37 T 25
Wellesbourne 27 P 27
Wellingborough 28 R 27

Wellington (Salop) 26 M 25
Wellington
(Somerset) 7 K 31
Wells 16 M 30
Wells-
next-the-Sea 30 W 25
Welshpool/
Trallwng 25 K 26
Welton 37 S 24
Welwyn 19 T 28
Welwyn Garden
City 19 T 28
Wem 34 L 25
Wembdon 7 K 30
Wembley 20 T 29
Wembury 3 H 33
Wembworthy 6 I 31
Wemyss Bay 54 F 16
Wendens Ambo 29 U 27
Wendover 19 R 28
Wendron 2 E 33
Wenlock Edge 26 L 26
Wennington 38 M 21
Wensley 45 O 21
Wensleydale 45 O 21
Wentbridge 40 Q 23
Weobley (Hereford
and Worcester) 26 L 27
Wereham 30 V 26
West Alvington 4 I 33
West Auckland 45 O 20
West Bay 8 M 32
West Bergholt 23 W 28
West Bridgford 36 Q 25
West
Bromwich 27 O 26
West Calder 56 J 16
West Camel 8 M 30
West Charleton 4 I 33
West Chiltington 11 S 31
West Coker 8 L 31
West Dean 9 P 30
West Down 6 H 30
West End 10 Q 31
West Farleigh 12 V 30
West Geirinish 64 X 11
West Harptree 16 M 30
West Hoathly 11 T 30
West Kilbride 54 F 16
West
Kingsdown 21 U 29
West Kirby 34 K 23
West Linton 56 J 16
West Loch Roag 70 Z 9
West Loch Tarbert
(Argyll and Bute) 53 D 16
West Loch Tarbert
(Western Isles) 70 Z 10
West Looe 3 G 32
West Lulworth 8 N 32
West Malling 12 V 30
West Malvern 26 M 27
West Meon 10 Q 30
West Mersea 23 W 28
West Midlands
(Metropolitan
County
Birmingham) 27 O 26
West Moors 9 O 31
West Runton 31 X 25
West Sussex
(County) 11 S 30
West Tanfield 46 P 21
West Thorney 10 R 31
West Walton 37 U 25
West Wellow 9 P 31
West Wittering 10 R 31
West Witton 45 O 21
West Wycombe 18 R 29
West Yorkshire
(Metropolitan
County Leeds) 39 O 23
Westbourne 10 R 31
Westbury (Cheshire) 26 L 25
Westbury (Wilts.) 17 N 30
Westbury-on-
Severn 17 M 28
Westcliff 22 W 29
Westcott 20 S 30
Wester Ross 66 D 11
Westerham 21 U 30
Western Cleddau 14 E 28
Westfield 12 V 31
Westgate-on-Sea 13 Y 29
Westham 12 U 31
Westhoughton 38 M 23

Westleton 31 Y 27
Westmill 19 T 28
Westminster
(London Borough) 20 T 29
Westnewton 44 J 19
Weston (Devon) 7 K 31
Weston (Staffs.) 35 N 25
Westonbirt 17 N 29
Weston-on-the-
Green 18 Q 28
Weston-on-Trent 35 P 25
Weston-super-
Mare 16 L 29
Weston Turville 19 R 28
Weston-under-
Lizard 27 N 25
Weston-
under-Penyard 17 M 28
Westonzoyland 7 L 30
Westray 74 K 6
Westruther 57 M 16
Westward Ho 6 H 30
Westwood 17 N 30
Westwood Manor 8 N 31
Wetheral 44 L 19
Wetherby 40 P 22
Wethersfield 22 V 28
Wetwang 40 S 21
Wey (River) 18 R 30
Weybourne 31 X 25
Weybridge 20 S 29
Weyhill 18 P 30
Weymouth 8 M 32
Whaley Bridge 35 O 23
Whalley 39 M 22
Whalsay 75 R 2
Whaplode 37 T 25
Wharfe (River) 40 Q 22
Wharfedale 39 O 22
Whauphill 42 G 19
Whauphill 42 G 21
Wheathampstead 19 T 28
Wheatley (Notts.) 36 R 23

Wheatley
(Oxon.) 18 Q 28
Wheatley Hill 46 P 19
Wheaton Aston 27 N 25
Wheldrake 41 R 22
Whernside 38 M 21
Wherwell 9 P 30
Whickham 51 O 19

Whimple 4 J 31
Whipsnade 19 S 28
Whissendine 36 R 25
Whitburn (West
Lothian) 55 I 16
Whitburn
(Tyne and Wear) 51 P 19
Whitby 47 S 20

Whitchurch (Bath
and N.E.
Somerset) 17 M 29
Whitchurch (Bucks.) 18 R 28
Whitchurch (Devon) 3 H 32
Whitchurch
(Heref. and Worc.) 16 M 28
Whitchurch (Oxon.) 18 Q 29

WINCHESTER

Brooks Shopping Centre. **B** 8
High Street

Andover Road 3
Bridge Street 6
Broadway (The) 7
City Road 10
Clifton Terrace 12
East Hill 15

Eastgate Street 16
Friarsgate 19
Magdalen Hill 23
Middle Brook Street 24
St. George's Street 32
St. Paul's Hill 33
St. Peter's Street 34
Southgate Street 35
Stockbridge Road 37
Sussex Street 38
Union Street 39
Upper High Street 40

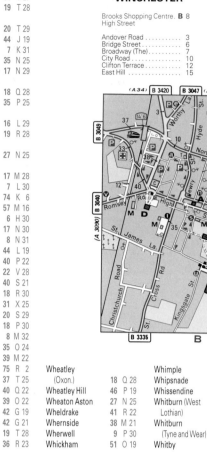

WOLVERHAMPTON

Darlington Street
Mander Centre
Victoria Street 24

Wulfrun Centre
Cleveland
Street 7
Garrick Street 8
Lichfield Street 12

Market Street 14
Princess
Street 15
Queen Square 17
Railway Drive 20
Salop Street 22

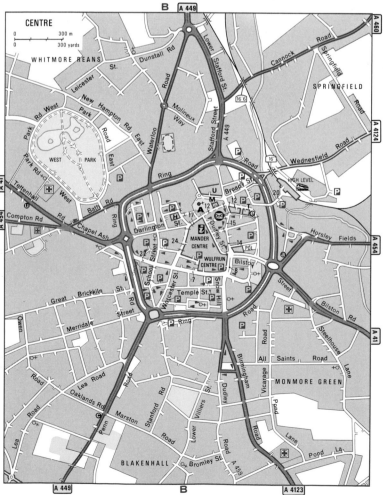

Whitchurch (Salop)	34	L	25
White Coomb	50	K	17
White Horse Hill	18	P	29
White Waltham	19	R	29
Whitebridge	67	G	12
Whitefield	39	N	23
Whitehaven	43	J	20
Whitehill	10	R	30
Whitehills	69	M	10
Whitehouse	53	D	16
Whiten Head	72	G	8
Whiteness Sands	67	I	10
Whiteparish	9	P	30
Whiterashes	69	N	12
Whitesand Bay (Pembrokes)	14	E	28
Whitesand Bay (Cornwall)	2	C	33
Whitewell	38	M	22
Whitfield	13	X	30
Whithorn	42	G	19
Whiting Bay	53	E	17
Whitland	14	G	28
Whitley	18	R	29
Whitley Bay	51	P	18
Whitsand Bay	3	H	32
Whitstable	13	X	29
Whitstone	6	G	31
Whittingham	51	O	17
Whittington (Derbs.)	35	P	24
Whittington (Lancs.)	38	L	21
Whittington (Salop)	34	L	25
Whittle le Woods	38	M	22
Whittlebury	28	R	27
Whittlesey	29	T	26
Whitton (Powys)	25	K	27
Whitton (Suffolk)	23	X	27
Whittonstall	51	O	19
Whitwell (Derbs.)	36	Q	24
Whitwell (I.O.W.)	10	Q	32
Whitwell-on-the-Hill	40	R	21
Whitwick	35	P	25
Whitworth	39	N	23
Wiay (Highland)	65	A	11
Wiay (Western Isles)	64	Y	11
Wick (South Glos.)	17	M	29
Wick (Highland)	74	K	8
Wicken (Cambs.)	28	R	27
Wicken (Northants.)	29	U	27
Wickenby	37	S	24
Wickford	22	V	29
Wickham	10	Q	31
Wickhambrook	22	V	27
Wickham Market	23	Y	27
Wickwar	17	M	29
Widecombe-in-the-Moor	4	I	32
Wideford Hill Cairn	74	K	7
Widford	22	U	28
Widnes	34	L	23
Wigan	38	M	23
Wiggenhall St. Mary Magdalen	30	V	25
Wight (Isle of) (County)	9	P	32
Wigmore	12	V	29
Wigston	28	Q	26
Wigton	44	K	19
Wigtown	42	G	19
Wigtown Bay	43	H	19
Wilberfoss	41	R	22
Wilcot	17	O	29
Wild Animal Kingdom	29	S	28
Willand	7	J	31
Willenhall	27	N	26
Willerby	41	S	22
Willersey	27	O	27
Willingdon	12	U	31
Willingham	29	U	27
Willingham Forest	37	T	23
Willington (Beds.)	29	S	27
Willington (Derbs.)	35	P	25
Willington (Durham)	45	O	19
Williton	7	K	30
Wilmcote	27	O	27
Wilmington (East Essex)	12	U	31
Wilmington (Kent)	21	U	29
Wilmslow	34	N	24
Wilton	9	O	30
Wiltshire (County)	17	O	30
Wimbledon	20	T	29
Wimblington	29	U	26
Wimborne Minster	9	O	31
Wimborne St. Giles	9	O	31
Wincanton	8	M	30
Winchcombe	27	O	28
Winchelsea	12	W	31
Winchester	9	O	30
Windermere	44	L	20
Windlesham	20	S	29
Windrush	17	O	28
Windrush (River)	17	O	28
Windsor	20	S	29
Windsor Great Park	20	S	29
Windygates	56	K	15
Winfarthing	30	X	26
Winfrith Newburgh	8	N	32
Wing	19	R	28
Wingate	46	P	19
Wingfield	35	P	24
Wingham	13	X	30
Wingrave	19	R	28
Winkfield	19	R	29
Winkleigh	6	I	31
Winnersh	18	R	29
Winscombe	16	L	30
Winsford (Cheshire)	34	M	24
Winsford (Somerset)	7	J	30
Winshill	35	P	25
Winslow	28	R	28
Winster	35	P	24
Winterborne Kingston	8	N	31
Winterborne Stickland	8	N	31
Winterborne Whitechurch	8	N	31
Winterbourne	17	M	29
Winterbourne Abbas	8	M	31
Winterbourne Stoke	9	O	30
Winteringham	40	S	22
Winterton	40	S	23
Winterton-on-Sea	31	Z	25
Winton	45	N	20
Winwick	29	S	26
Wirksworth	35	P	24
Wirral	33	K	24
Wisbech	29	U	25
Wisborough Green	11	S	30
Wishaw	55	I	16
Wisley	20	S	30
Wissey (River)	30	V	26
Witchford	29	U	26
Witham	22	V	28
Witham (River)	37	T	24
Witheridge	7	I	31
Withernsea	41	U	22
Withington	17	O	28
Withycombe	4	J	32
Withypool	7	J	30
Witley	11	S	30
Witney	18	P	28
Wittering	29	S	26
Wittersham	12	W	30
Wiveliscombe	7	K	30
Wivenhoe	23	W	28
Woburn	29	S	28
Woburn Abbey	29	S	28
Woburn Sands	28	S	27
Woking	20	S	30
Wokingham	18	R	29
Woldingham	21	T	30
Wollaston	28	U	30
Wollaton Hall	36	Q	25
Wolsingham	45	O	19
Wolvercote	18	Q	28
Wolverhampton	27	N	26
Wolverton	28	R	27
Wolviston	46	Q	20
Wombourn	27	N	26
Wombwell	40	P	23
Womersley	40	Q	22
Wonersh	19	S	30
Wood Dalling	31	X	25
Woodbridge	23	X	27
Woodbury	4	J	31
Woodchurch	12	W	30
Woodcote	18	Q	29
Woodford Halse	28	Q	27
Woodhall Spa	37	T	24
Woodham Ferrers	22	V	29
Woodingdean	11	T	31
Woodnesborough	13	X	30
Woodseaves	34	N	25
Woodstock	18	P	28
Woodton	31	Y	26
Woody Bay	6	I	30
Wookey Hole	16	L	30
Wool	8	N	31
Woolacombe	6	H	30
Wooler	51	N	17
Woolfardisworthy	6	G	31
Woolpit	23	X	27
Woolsthorpe	36	R	25
Woore	34	M	25
Wootton Bassett	17	O	29
Wootton Courtenay	7	J	30
Wootton-Wawen	27	O	27
Worcester	27	N	27
Workington	43	J	20
Worksop	36	Q	24
Worle	16	L	29
Wormit	62	L	14
Worms Head	15	H	29
Worplesdon	20	S	30
Worsbrough	40	P	23
Worsley	39	M	23
Worthen	26	L	26
Worthing	11	S	31
Wortwell	31	Y	26
Wotton-under-Edge	17	M	29
Wragby	37	T	24
Wrangle	37	U	24
Wrawby	41	S	23
Wray	38	M	21
Wrea Green	38	L	22
Wrecsam/Wrexham	34	L	24
Wremtham	31	Z	26
Wrexham/Wrecsam	34	L	24
Wrington	16	L	29
Writtle	22	V	28
Wrotham	21	U	30
Wroughton	17	O	29
Wroxham	31	Y	25
Wroxton	27	P	27
Wyche	26	M	27
Wye	12	W	30
Wye (River)	16	M	28
Wylam	51	O	19
Wylye	9	O	30
Wymondham (Leics.)	36	R	25
Wymondham (Norfolk)	31	X	26
Wyre	74	L	6

YORK CENTRE

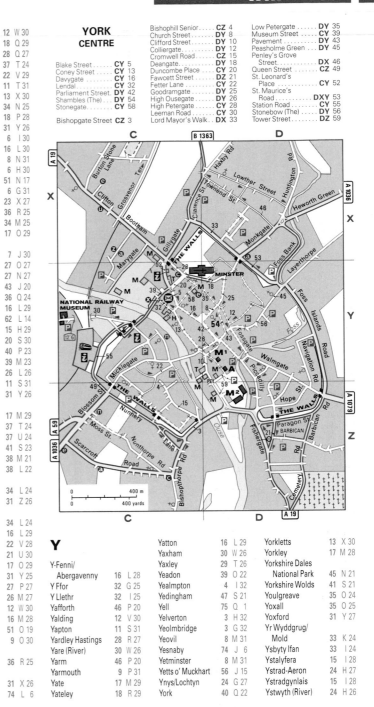

Street	Ref	
Blake Street	CY	5
Coney Street	CY	13
Davygate	CY	16
Lendal	CY	32
Parliament Street	DY	42
Shambles (The)	DY	54
Stonegate	CY	58
Bishopgate Street	CZ	3
Bishophill Senior	CZ	4
Church Street	DY	8
Clifford Street	DY	10
Colliergate	DY	12
Cromwell Road	CZ	15
Deangate	DY	18
Duncombe Place	CY	20
Fawcett Street	DZ	21
Fetter Lane	CY	22
Goodramgate	DY	25
High Ousegate	DY	26
High Petergate	CY	28
Leeman Road	CY	30
Lord Mayor's Walk	DX	33
Low Petergate	DY	35
Museum Street	CY	39
Pavement	DY	43
Peasholme Green	DY	45
Penley's Grove Street	DX	46
Queen Street	CZ	49
St. Leonard's Place	CY	52
St. Maurice's Road	DXY	53
Station Road	CY	55
Stonebow (The)	DY	56
Tower Street	DZ	59

Y

Y-Fenni/Abergavenny	16	L	28
Y Ffor	32	G	25
Y Llethr	32	I	25
Yafforth	46	P	20
Yalding	12	V	30
Yapton	11	S	31
Yardley Hastings	28	R	27
Yare (River)	30	W	26
Yarm	46	P	20
Yarmouth	9	P	31
Yate	17	M	29
Yateley	18	R	29
Yatton	16	L	29
Yaxham	30	W	26
Yaxley	29	T	26
Yeadon	39	O	22
Yealmpton	4	I	32
Yedingham	47	S	21
Yell	75	Q	1
Yelverton	3	H	32
Yeolmbridge	3	G	32
Yeovil	8	M	31
Yesnaby	74	J	6
Yetminster	8	M	31
Yetts o' Muckhart	56	J	15
Ynys/Lochtyn	24	G	27
York	40	Q	22
Yorkletts	13	X	30
Yorkley	17	M	28
Yorkshire Dales National Park	45	N	21
Yorkshire Wolds	41	S	21
Youlgreave	35	O	24
Yoxall	35	O	25
Yoxford	31	Y	27
Yr Wyddgrug/Mold	33	K	24
Ysbyty Ifan	33	I	24
Ystalyfera	15	I	28
Ystrad-Aeron	24	H	27
Ystradgynlais	15	I	28
Ystwyth (River)	24	H	26

Ireland

A

Abbeydorney	82	C 10
Abbeyfeale	83	E 10
Abbeylara	91	J 6
Abbeyleix /		
Mainistir Laoise	86	J 9
Achill Head	94	B 6
Achill Island	94	B 6
Achill Sound /		
Gob an Choire	94	C 6
Achillbeg Island	94	C 6
Aclare	95	F 5
Acoose (Lough)	76	C 11
Adamstown	81	L 10
Adare	84	F 10
Adrigole	76	C 12
Aghaboe	86	J 9
Aghabullogue	78	F 12
Aghada	79	H 12
Aghalee	98	N 4
Aghavannagh	87	M 9
Aghaville	77	D 13
Aghla Mountain	100	H 3
Aglish	79	I 11
Ahakista	77	D 13
Ahalia (Loughs)	88	D 7
Ahascragh	89	G 7
Ahenny	80	J 10
Aherlow (Glen of)	85	H 10
Ahoghill	102	M 3
Aillwee Cave	89	E 8
Ailt an Chorráin /		
Burtonport	100	G 3
Aird Mhór /		
Ardmore	79	I 12
Allen (Bog of)	86	K 8
Allen (Lough)	96	H 5
Allenwood	86	L 8
Allihies	76	B 13
Allua (Lough)	77	E 12
Altan Lough	100	H 2
An Blascaod Mór /		
Blasket Islands	82	A 11
An Bun Beag /		
Bunbeg	100	H 2
An Cabhán / Cavan	97	J 6
An Caiseal / Cashel		
(Galway)	88	C 7
An Caisleán Nua /		
Newcastle West	83	E 10
An Caisleán		
Riabhach /		
Castlerea	96	G 6
An Charraig /		
Carrick	100	G 4
An Chathair / Caher	85	I 10
An Cheathrú Rua /		
Carraroe	88	D 8
An Chloich		
Mhóir /		
Cloghmore	94	C 6
An Clochán /		
Clifden	88	B 7
An Clochán /		
Cloghan		
(Donegal)	100	I 3
An Clochán Liath /		
Dunglow	100	G 3
An Cloigeann /		
Cleegan	88	B 7
An Cóbh / Cobh	78	H 12
An Coimín /		
Commeen	100	I 3
An Coireán /		
Waterville	76	B 12
An Corrán / Currane	94	C 6
An Creagán /		
Mount Bellew	89	G 7
An Daingean /		
Dingle	82	B 11
An Droichead Nua /		
Newbridge	86	L 8
An Dúchoraidh /		
Doocharry	100	H 3
An Fál Carrach /		
Falcarragh	100	H 2
An Fhairche /		
Clonbur	88	D 7
An Geata Mór	94	B 5
An Gleann Garbh /		
Glengarriff	77	D 12

An Gort / Gort	89	F 8
An Gort Mór /		
Gortmore	88	D 7
An Leacht / Lahinch	88	D 9
An Longfort /		
Longford	91	I 6
An Mám /		
Maam Cross	88	D 7
An Mhala		
Raithní/Mulrany	94	C 6
An Móta / Moate	91	I 7
An Muileann		
gCearr/Mullingar	91	J 7
An Nás / Naas	87	M 8
An Ráth /		
Charleville	84	F 10
An Ráth / Rath Luirc		
(Charleville)	84	F 10
An Ros / Rush	93	N 7
An Scairbh /		
Scarriff	84	G 9
An Sciobairín /		
Skibbereen	77	E 13
An Seanchaisleán /		
Oldcastle	91	K 6
An Spidéal /		
Spiddal	88	E 8
An tAonach /		
Nenagh	84	H 9
An Teampall Mór /		
Templemore	85	I 9
An Tearmann /		
Termon	101	I 2

An tInbhear Mór /		
Arklow	87	N 9
An tSraith / Srah	95	E 6
An Tulach / Tullow	86	L 9
An Uaimh / Navan	92	L 7
Anascaul	82	B 11
Annacarriga	84	G 9
Annacotty	84	G 9
Annagary	100	H 2
Annagassan	93	M 6
Annageeragh	83	D 9
Annagh Head	94	B 5
Annaghdown	89	E 7
Annaghmore		
Lough	90	H 6
Annalee	97	J 5
Annalong	99	O 5
Annamoe	87	N 8
Annestown	80	K 11
Antrim	103	N 3
Antrim (County)	102	M 3
Antrim Coast	103	O 2
Antrim (Glens of)	103	N 2
Antrim Mountains	103	N 2
Anure (Lough)	100	H 3
Araglin	79	H 11
Árainn Mhór / Aran		
or Aranmore		
Island	100	G 2
Árainn (Oiléain) /		
Aran Islands	88	C 8
Aran Islands /		
Oiléáin Árainn	88	C 8

Aran or Aranmore		
Island / Árainn		
Mhór	100	G 2
Archdale (Castle)	97	I 4
Ardagh	83	E 10
Ardara	100	G 3
Ardboe	98	M 4
Ardcath	93	M 7
Ardcrony	85	H 9
Ardea	76	C 12
Ardee / Baile		
Átha Fhirdhia	93	M 6
Ardfert	82	C 11
Ardfinnan	85	I 11
Ardglass	99	P 5
Ardgroom	76	C 12
Ardkeen	99	P 4
Ardmore / Aird		
Mhór	79	I 12
Ardrahan	89	F 8
Ardress House	98	M 4
Ards Forest Park	101	I 2
Ards Peninsula	99	P 4
Argideen	78	F 13
Argory (The)	98	M 4
Arigna	96	H 5
Arklow /		
An tInbhear Mór	87	N 9
Armagh	98	M 4
Armagh (County)	98	L 5
Armoy	103	N 2
Arney	97	I 5
Arrow (Lough)	96	H 5

Arthurstown	80	L 11
Arvagh	97	J 6
Ashbourne	93	M 7
Ashford	87	N 8
Ashford Castle	89	E 7
Askeaton	84	F 10
Astee	83	D 10
Áth Cinn / Headford	89	E 7
Athassel Abbey	85	I 10
Athboy	92	L 7
Athea	83	E 10
Athenry /		
Baile Átha an Rí	89	F 8
Athleague	90	H 7
Athlone /		
Baile Átha Luain	90	I 7
Athy / Baile Átha	86	L 9
Attymon	89	G 8
Audley's Castle	99	P 4
Augher	97	K 4
Aughils	82	C 11
Aughnacloy	97	L 4
Aughnanure Castle	89	E 7
Aughrim (Galway)	90	H 8
Aughrim		
(Wicklow)	87	N 9
Aughris Head	95	F 5
Avoca	87	N 9
Avoca (River)	87	N 9
Avoca (Valle of)	87	N 9
Avonbeg	87	M 9
Avondale Forest		
Park	87	N 9

B

Bagenalstown	86	L 9
Baile an		
Fheirtéaraigh /		
Ballyferriter	82	A 11
Baile an Mhóta /		
Ballymote	96	G 5
Baile an Róba /		
Ballinrobe	89	E 7
Baile an Sceilg /		
Ballinskelligs	76	B 12
Baile Átha an Rí /		
Athenry	89	F 8
Baile Átha Cliath /		
Dublin	87	N 8
Baile Átha Fhirdhia /		
Ardee	93	M 6
Baile Átha / Athy	86	L 9
Baile Átha Luain /		
Athlone	90	I 7
Baile Átha Troim /		
Trim	92	L 7
Baile Bhuirne /		
Ballyvourney	77	E 12
Baile Brigín /		
Balbriggan	93	N 7
Baile Chláir /		
Claregalway	89	F 7
Baile Locha Riach /		
Loughrea	89	G 8
Baile Mhic Andáin /		
Thomastown	80	K 10

Baile Mhic íre /		
Ballymakeery	77	E 12
Baile Mhistéala /		
Mitchelstown	79	H 11
Baile na Finne /		
Fintown	100	H 3
Baile na Lorgan /		
Castleblayney	98	L 5
Baile Uí Fhiacháin /		
Newport	94	D 6
Baile Uí Mhatháin /		
Ballymahon	91	I 7
Bailieborough /		
Coill an		
Chollaigh	97	L 6
Balbriggan /		
Baile Brigín	92	N 7
Baldoyle	93	N 7
Balla	95	E 6
Ballagan Point	99	N 5
Ballaghaderreen /		
Bealach an		
Doirín	96	G 6
Ballaghbeama Gap	76	C 12
Ballaghisheen Pass	76	C 12
Ballina / Béal an		
Átha	95	E 5
Ballina (Tipperary)	84	G 9
Ballinaboy	88	B 7
Ballinadee	78	G 12
Ballinafad	96	G 5
Ballinagar	86	J 8
Ballinakill	86	K 9

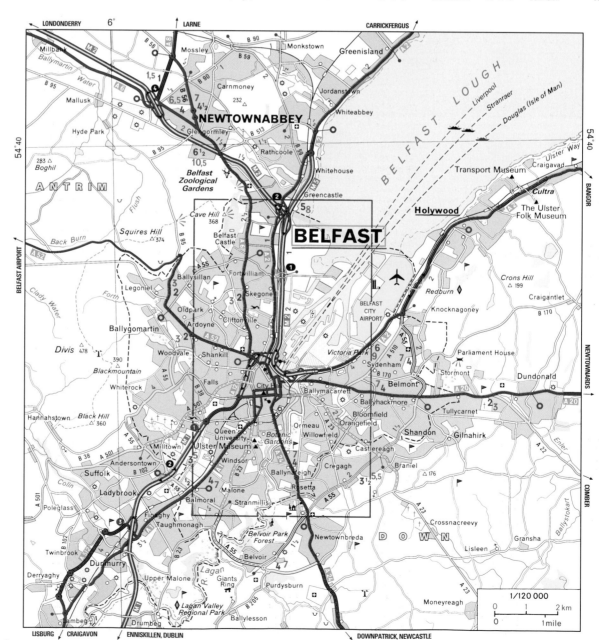

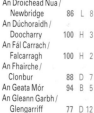

1/120 000

0   1   2 km

0   1 mile

BELFAST

Castlecourt Shopping Centre . . BYZ
Castle Place . . BZ
Donegal Place . . BZ
Royal Avenue . . BYZ
Albert Square . . BY 3
Ann Street . . BZ 5
Bridge Street . . BZ 12
Clifton Street . . BY 15
Corporation Square . . BY 16
Donegall Quay . . BYZ 19
Donegall Square . . BZ 20
Great Victoria Street . . BZ 26
High Street . . BYZ 28
Howard Street . . BZ 29
Lagan Bridge . . BY 32
Queen Elizabeth Bridge . . BZ 40
Queen's Bridge . . BZ 41
Queen's Square . . BZ 42
Rosemary Street . . BZ 44
Waring Street . . BY 54
Wellington Place . . BZ 55

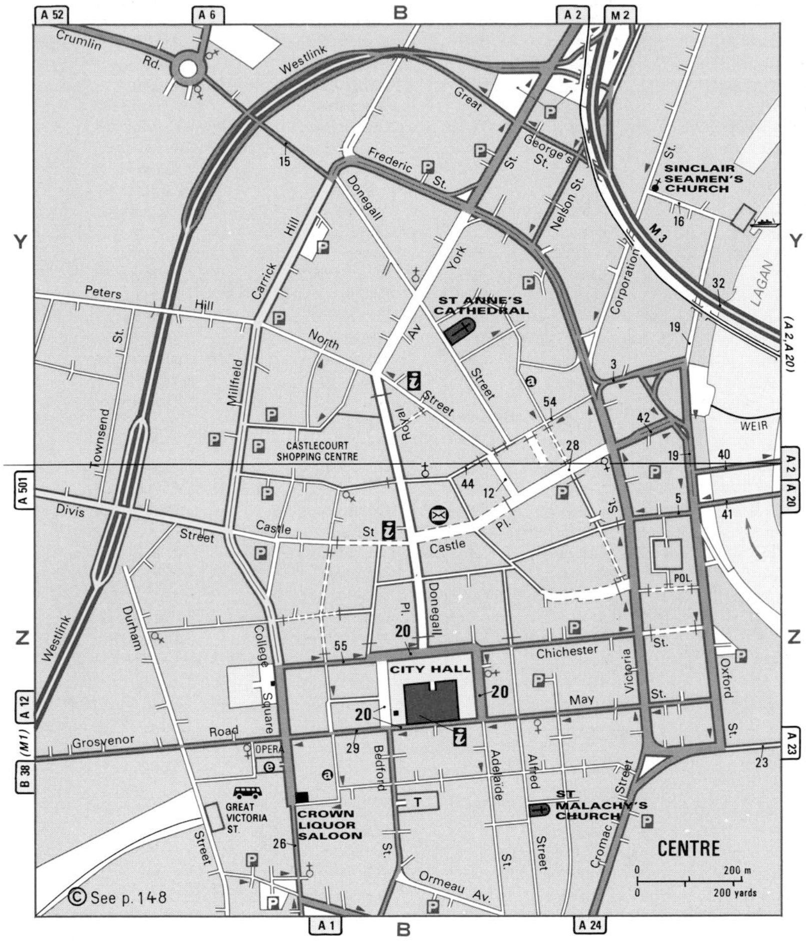

A 52
A 6
B
A 2
M 2
Crumlin Rd.
Westlink
Great
George's St.
Frederic St.
Donegall
SINCLAIR SEAMEN'S CHURCH
M 3
York
Nelson St.
Corporation
LAGAN
Peters Hill
Carrick Hill
St. Anne's Cathedral
North Street
Millfield
Townsend St.
Royal Av.
CASTLECOURT SHOPPING CENTRE
Divis Street
Castle St.
Castle Pl.
WEIR
POL
Westlink
Durham
College Square
Donegall Pl.
Chichester
Victoria
Oxford St.
CITY HALL
May St.
Grosvenor Road
OPERA
Bedford
Adelaide
Alfred
ST MALACHY'S CHURCH
Cromac Street
GREAT VICTORIA ST.
CROWN LIQUOR SALOON
Ormeau Av.
CENTRE
200 m
200 yards
See p. 148
A 1
A 24
A 23
A 501
A 12
(M1)
B 38
A 2
A 20
(A 2, A 20)
Y
Z

Ballinalack 91 J 7
Ballinalea 87 N 8
Ballinalee 91 J 6
Ballinamallard 97 J 4
Ballinamore / Béal an Átha Mhóir 96 I 5
Ballinamore Bridge 89 G 7
Ballinascarty 78 F 12
Ballinasloe / Béal Átha na Sluaighe 90 H 8
Ballincollig 78 G 12
Ballincrea 80 K 11
Ballincurrig 79 H 12
Ballindarragh 97 J 5
Ballinderry 85 H 8
Ballindine 95 F 6
Ballineen 78 F 12
Ballingarry (Galway) 85 H 8
Ballingarry (Limerick) 84 F 10
Ballingarry (Tipperary) 80 J 10
Ballingeary / Béal Átha an Ghaorthaidh 77 E 12
Ballinhassig 78 G 12
Ballinlough 96 G 6
Ballinrobe / Baile an Róba 89 E 7
Ballinskelligs / Baile an Sceilg 76 B 12
Ballinskelligs Bay 76 B 12
Ballinspittle 78 G 12
Ballintober (Roscommon) 96 G 6
Ballintogher 96 G 5
Ballintoy 103 M 2
Ballintra 96 H 4
Ballinure 85 I 10
Ballitore 86 L 8
Ballivor 92 L 7
Ballon 86 L 9
Ballyagran 84 F 10
Ballybay 97 L 5
Ballybofey / Bealach Féich 101 I 3
Ballyboghil 93 N 7
Ballyboy 91 I 8
Ballybrittas 86 K 8
Ballybrophy 86 J 9
Ballybunnion 83 D 10
Ballycanew 81 N 10
Ballycarney 81 M 10
Ballycastle (Antrim) 103 N 2
Ballycastle (Mayo) 95 D 5
Ballycastle Bay 103 N 2
Ballyclare (Antrim) 103 N 3
Ballyclare (Roscommon) 90 I 6
Ballyclogh 78 F 11
Ballycolla 86 J 9
Ballyconneely 88 B 7
Ballyconneely Bay 88 B 7
Ballyconnell 97 J 5
Ballycopeland 103 P 4
Ballycotton 79 H 12
Ballycotton Bay 79 H 12
Ballycroy 94 C 5
Ballydavid 82 A 11
Ballydavid Head 82 A 11
Ballydavis 86 K 8
Ballydehob 77 D 13
Ballydesmond 83 E 11
Ballydonegan 76 B 13
Ballyduff (Dingle) 82 B 11
Ballyduff (Kerry) 83 D 10
Ballyduff (Waterford) 79 H 11
Ballyeighter Loughs 84 F 9
Ballyfarnan 96 H 5
Ballyferriter/Baile an Fheirtéaraigh 82 A 11
Ballyforan 90 H 7
Ballygalley 103 O 3
Ballygalley Head 103 O 3
Ballygar 90 H 7
Ballygawley (Sligo) 96 G 5
Ballygawley (Tyrone) 97 K 4
Ballygorman 101 K 1
Ballygowan (near Belfast) 99 O 4
Ballyhack 80 L 11
Ballyhahill 83 E 10
Ballyhaise 97 K 5
Ballyhalbert 99 P 4
Ballyhale 80 K 10
Ballyhaunis / Béal Átha hAmhnais 95 F 6
Ballyhean 95 E 6
Ballyheige 82 C 10
Ballyheige Bay 82 C 10
Ballyhoe Lough 92 L 6
Ballyhooly 78 G 11
Ballyhoura Mountains 84 G 11
Ballyjamesduff 91 K 6
Ballykeeran 90 I 7
Ballykelly 102 K 2
Ballylanders 84 G 10
Ballylickey 77 D 12
Ballyliffin 101 J 2
Ballylongford 83 D 10
Ballylongford Bay 83 D 10
Ballylynan 86 K 9
Ballymacarbry 79 I 11
Ballymacoda 79 I 12
Ballymagorry 101 J 3
Ballymahon / Baile Uí Mhatháin 91 I 7
Ballymakeery / Baile Mhic Íre 77 E 12
Ballymartin 99 O 5
Ballymena 103 N 3
Ballymoe 96 G 6
Ballymoney (Antrim) 102 M 2
Ballymore 91 I 7
Ballymore Eustace 87 M 8
Ballymote / Baile an Mhóta 96 G 5
Ballymurphy 81 L 10
Ballynabola 81 L 10
Ballynacarrigy 91 J 7
Ballynacorra 79 H 12
Ballynagore 91 J 7
Ballynagree 78 F 12
Ballynahinch 99 O 4
Ballynahinch Lake 88 C 7
Ballynahown 88 D 8
Ballynakill Harbour 88 B 7
Ballyneety 84 G 10
Ballynoe 79 H 11
Ballynure 103 O 3
Ballyorgan 84 G 11
Ballypatrick 80 J 10
Ballyporeen 79 H 11
Ballyquintin Point 99 P 5
Ballyragget 86 J 9
Ballyroan 86 K 9
Ballyronan 102 M 3
Ballyroney 99 N 5
Ballysadare 96 G 5
Ballyshannon / Béal Átha Seanaidh 96 H 4
Ballysteen 84 F 10
Ballyteige Bay 81 L 11
Ballyvaughan 89 E 8
Ballyvaughan Bay 89 E 8
Ballyvourney / Baile Bhuirne 77 E 12
Ballywalter 99 P 4
Ballywilliam 81 L 10
Balrath 93 M 7
Baltimore 77 D 13
Baltinglass / Bealach Conglais 87 L 9
Baltray 93 N 6
Banagher 90 I 8
Banbridge 98 N 4
Bandon / Droichead na Bandan 78 F 12
Bandon River 77 F 12
Bangor (Down) 103 O 4
Bangor (Mayo) 94 C 5
Bann (River) (Lough Neagh) 99 N 5
Bann (River) (R. Slaney) 81 M 10
Banna Strand 82 C 11
Bannow 81 L 11
Bansha 85 H 10
Banteer 78 F 11
Bantry / Beanntrai 77 D 12
Bantry Bay 76 C 13
Barefield 84 F 9
Barley Cove 76 C 13
Barna / Bearna 89 E 8
Barnaderg 89 F 7
Barnatra / Barr na Trá 94 C 5
Barnesmore Gap 100 I 3
Baronscourt Forest 101 J 3
Barra (Lough) 100 H 3
Barraduff 77 D 11
Barr na Trá / Barnatra 94 C 5
Barrow 86 J 8
Barrow Harbour 82 C 11
Barrow (River) 86 K 8
Beagh (Lough) 101 I 2
Béal an Átha / Ballina 95 E 5
Béal an Átha Mhóir / Ballinamore 96 I 5
Béal an Mhuirthead / Belmullet 94 C 5
Béal Átha an Ghaorthaidh / Ballingeary 77 E 12
Béal Átha hAmhnais / Ballyhaunis 95 F 6
Béal Átha na Muice / Swinford 95 F 6
Béal Átha na Sluaighe / Ballinasloe 90 H 8
Béal Átha Seanaidh / Ballyshannon 96 H 4
Béal Deirg / Belderrig 94 D 5
Béal Tairbirt / Belturbet 97 J 5
Bealach an Doirín / Ballaghaderreen 96 G 6
Bealach Conglais / Baltinglass 87 L 9
Bealach Féich / Ballybofey 101 I 3
Bealaclugga 89 E 8
Bealadangan 88 D 8
Bealaha 83 D 9
Beanntraí / Bantry 77 D 12
Beara 76 C 12
Bearna / Barna 89 E 8
Beaufort 77 D 11
Beehive Huts 82 A 11
Beenoskee 82 B 11
Beg (Lough) 102 M 3
Behy 76 C 11
Belcarra 95 E 6
Belclare 89 F 7
Belcoo 96 I 5
Belderrig / Béal Deirg 94 D 5
Belfast 103 O 4
Belfast Lough 103 O 3
Belgooly 78 G 12
Belhavel Lough 96 H 5
Bellacorick 94 D 5
Bellaghy 102 M 3
Bellanagare 96 G 6
Bellanaleck 97 J 5
Bellananagh 97 J 6
Bellavary 95 E 6
Belleek (Armagh) 98 M 5
Belleek (Fermanagh) 96 H 4
Belmullet / Béal an Mhuirthead 94 C 5
Beltra 95 D 6
Beltra Lough 94 D 6
Belturbet / Béal Tairbirt 97 J 5
Benbane Head 102 M 2
Benbrack 96 I 5
Benbulben 96 G 4
Benburb 98 L 4
Bencroy or Gubnaveagh 96 I 5
Benmore or Fair Head 103 N 2
Benettsbridge 80 K 10
Benwee Head 94 C 4
Beragh 97 K 4
Bere Island 76 C 13
Bernish Rock 98 M 5
Bertraghboy Bay 88 C 7
Bessbrook 98 M 5
Bettystown 93 N 6
Binevenagh 102 L 2
Binn Éadair / Howth 93 N 7
Biorra / Birr 90 I 8
Birdhill 84 G 9
Birr / Biorra 90 I 8
Black Head (Antrim) 103 O 3
Black Head (Clare) 89 E 8
Black Ball Head 76 B 13
Black Bull 93 M 7
Black Gap (The) 96 I 4
Blacklion 96 I 5
Blackrock 87 N 8
Blackrock (Louth) 98 M 6
Blacksod Bay 94 B 5
Blacksod Point 94 B 5
Blackstairs Mountains 81 L 10
Blackwater 81 M 10
Blackwater Bridge 76 C 12
Blackwater (River) (Cork) 78 F 11
Blackwater (River) (Lough Neagh) 98 L 4
Blackwater (River) (R. Boyne) 92 L 6
Blarney 78 G 12
Blasket Islands / An Blascaod Mór 82 A 11
Blennerville 83 C 11
Blessington 87 M 8
Bloody Foreland 100 H 2
Blue Ball 86 J 8
Blue Stack Mountains 100 H 3
Boderg (Lough) 96 I 6
Bodyke 84 G 9
Bofin (Lough) (Galway) 88 D 7
Bofin (Lough) (Roscommon) 96 I 6
Boggeragh Mountains 77 E 12
Boheraphuca 85 I 8
Boherboy 77 E 11
Bohermeen 92 L 7
Bola (Lough) 88 C 7
Boley 86 L 8
Boliska Lough 88 E 8
Bolus Head 76 A 12
Bonet 96 H 5
Boobyglass 80 K 10
Borris 80 L 10
Borris in Ossory 86 J 9
Borrisokane / Buiríos Uí Chéin 85 H 9
Borrisoleigh 85 I 9
Bouladuff 85 I 9
Boyle / Mainistir na Búille 96 H 6
Boyle (River) 96 H 6
Boyne (River) 91 K 7
Bracklin 91 K 7
Brandon / Cé Bhréanainn 82 B 11
Brandon Bay 82 B 11
Brandon Head 82 B 11
Brandon Hill 81 L 10
Bray / Bré 87 N 8
Bray Head (Kerry) 76 A 12
Bray Head (Wicklow) 87 N 8
Bré / Bray 87 N 8
Breenagh 100 I 3
Bride (River) 79 I 11
Bridebridge 79 H 11
Bridgend 101 J 2
Bridgeland 87 M 9
Bridget Lough 84 G 9
Bridgetown 81 M 11
Briensbridge 84 G 9
Brinlack / Bun na Leaca 100 H 2
Brittas 87 M 8
Brittas Bay 87 N 9
Broad Haven 94 C 5
Broad Meadow 93 N 7
Broadford (Clare) 84 G 9
Broadford (Limerick) 84 F 10
Broadway 81 M 11
Brookeborough 97 J 5
Brosna (River) 90 I 8
Brosna 83 E 11
Broughshane 103 N 3
Brow Head 76 C 13
Brown Flesk 83 D 11
Brownstown Head 80 K 11
Bruff 84 G 10
Bruree 84 G 10
Buckode 96 H 4
Buiriós Uí Chéin / Borrisokane 85 H 9
Bull Point 103 N 2
Bull's Head 82 B 11
Bullaun 89 G 8
Bun an Phobail / Moville 101 K 2
Bun Cranncha / Buncrana 101 J 2
Bun Dobhráin / Bundoran 96 H 4
Bun na hAbhna / Bunnahowen 94 C 5
Bun na Leaca / Brinlack 100 H 2
Bunacurry 94 C 6
Bunbeg / An Bun Beag 100 H 2
Bunclody 81 M 10
Buncrana / Bun Cranncha 101 J 2
Bundoran / Bun Dobhráin 96 H 4
Bunmahon 80 J 11
Bunnahowen / Bun na hAbhna 94 C 5
Bunnanaddan 96 G 5
Bunny (Lough) 89 F 8
Bunnyconnellan 95 E 5
Bunowen 94 C 6
Bunratty 84 F 9
Burncourt 85 H 11
Burnfort 78 G 11
Burren (The) 89 E 8
Burrishoole Abbey 94 D 6
Burtonport / Ailt an Chorráin 100 G 3
Bush 102 M 2
Bushfield 84 G 9
Bushmills 102 M 2
Butler's Bridge 97 J 5
Butlerstown 78 F 13
Buttevant 84 F 11
Bweeng 78 F 11

C

Caha Mountains 76 C 12
Caher / An Chathair 85 I 10
Caher Island 94 B 6
Caherbarnagh 77 E 11
Caherconlish 84 G 10
Caherdaniel 76 B 12
Cahersiveen / Cathair Saidhbhín 76 B 12
Cahore Point 81 N 10
Caiseal / Cashel 85 I 10
Caiseal / Cashel (Tipperary) 88 I 10
Caisleán an Bharraigh / Castlebar 95 E 6
Caisleán an Chomair / Castlecomer 86 K 9
Calafort Ros Láir / Rosslare Harbour 81 M 11
Caledon 98 L 4
Callainn / Callan 80 J 10
Callan / Callainn 80 J 10
Caltra 89 G 7
Camlough 98 M 5
Camolin 81 M 10

Camp	82 C 11
Campile	80 L 11
Canglass Point	76 B 12
Canningstown	97 K 6
Cappagh White	84 H 10
Cappamore	84 G 10
Cappoquin / Ceapach Choinn	79 I 11
Car (Slieve)	94 D 5
Caragh (Lough)	76 C 11
Caragh (River)	76 C 12
Carbery's Hundred Isles	77 D 13
Carbury	92 L 7
Carhan House	76 B 12
Cark Mountain	101 I 3
Carlanstown	92 L 6
Carlingford	98 N 5
Carlingford Lough	98 N 5
Carlow / Ceatharlach	86 L 9
Carlow (County)	86 L 9
Carn Domhnach / Carndonagh	101 K 2
Carna	88 C 8
Carncastle	103 O 3
Carndonagh / Carn Domhnach	101 K 2
Carnew	87 M 9
Carney	96 G 4
Carnlough	103 O 3
Carnlough Bay	103 O 3
Carnsore Point	81 M 11
Carra (Lough)	95 E 6
Carraig Airt / Carrigart	101 I 2
Carraig Mhachaire Rois / Carrickmacross	98 L 6
Carraig na Siúire / Carrick-on-Suir	80 J 10
Carran	89 E 8
Carrantuohill	76 C 11
Carraroe / An Cheathrú Rua	88 D 8
Carrick-a-Rede Rope Bridge	103 M 2
Carrick / An Charraig (Donegal)	100 G 4
Carrick (Wexford)	81 L 11
Carrick-on-Shannon-Cora Droma Rúisc	96 H 6
Carrick-on-Suir / Carraig na Siúire	80 J 10
Carrickboy	91 I 7
Carrickfergus	103 O 3
Carrickmacross / Carraig Mhachaire Rois	98 L 6
Carrickmore	97 K 4
Carrigafoyle Castle	83 D 10
Carrigaholt	82 C 10
Carrigaline	78 G 12
Carrigallen	97 J 6
Carriganimmy	77 E 12
Carrigans	101 J 3
Carrigart / Carraig Airt	101 I 2
Carrigkerry	83 E 10
Carriglass Manor	90 I 6
Carrigtohill	78 H 12
Carrowkeel	101 J 2
Carrowmore	96 G 5
Carrowmore Lake	94 C 5
Carrownisky	94 C 6
Carrowteige / Ceathrú Thaidhg	94 C 5
Carrybeg	80 J 10
Carryduff	99 O 4
Cashel / An Caiseal (Galway)	88 C 7
Cashel / Caiseal (Tipperary)	85 I 10
Cashel (Rock of)	85 I 10
Cashen River	83 D 10
Cashla Bay	88 D 8
Casla / Costelloe	88 D 8
Castle Coole	101 J 4
Castle coole	101 J 4
Castle Espie Centre	99 O 4
Castle Espie Centre	99 O 4
Castle Gardens	78 F 13
Castle Haven	77 E 13
Castle Point	82 C 10
Castlebaldwin	96 G 5
Castlebar / Caisleán an Bharraigh	95 E 6
Castlebellingham	93 M 6
Castleblakeney	89 G 7
Castleblayney / Baile na Lorgan	98 L 5
Castlebridge	81 M 10
Castlecaulfield	98 L 4
Castleconnell	84 G 9
Castlecove	76 B 12
Castledawson	102 M 3
Castlederg	101 J 3
Castledermot	86 L 9
Castlefinn	101 J 3
Castlefreke	78 F 13
Castlegal	96 G 4
Castlegregory	82 B 11
Castlehill	94 C 6
Castleisland / Oileán Ciarraí	83 D 11
Castlelyons	79 H 11
Castlemaine	83 C 11
Castlemaine Harbour	82 C 11
Castlemartyr	79 H 12
Castleplunket	96 G 6
Casltepollard	91 K 6
Castlerea / An Caisleán Riabhach	96 G 6
Castlerock	102 L 2
Castletown (Laois)	86 J 9
Castletown (Westmeath)	91 J 7
Castletown (Wexford)	87 N 9
Castletownbere	76 C 13
Castletownroche	78 G 11
Castletownshend	77 E 13
Castleward House	99 P 4
Castlewellan	99 O 5
Castlewellan Forest Park	99 O 5
Cathair na Mart / Westport	94 D 6
Cathair Saidhbhín / Cahersiveen	76 B 12
Causeway	82 C 10
Cavan / An Cabhán	97 J 6
Cavan (County)	97 J 6
Cé Bhréanainn / Brandon	82 B 11
Ceanannas / Ceanannus Mór (Kells)	92 L 6
Ceanannus Mór (Kells)	92 L 6
Ceanannas	92 L 6
Ceann Toirc / Kanturk	78 F 11
Ceapach Choinn / Cappoquin	79 I 11
Ceatharlach / Carlow	86 L 9
Ceathrú Thaidhg / Carrowteige	94 C 5
Cecilstown	78 F 11
Celbridge	93 M 7
Chapeltown	99 P 5
Charlestown (Armagh)	98 M 4
Charlestown (Mayo)	95 F 6
Charleville (Ráth Luirc) / An Ráth	84 F 10
Church Hill	101 I 3
Church Quarter	103 N 2
Churchtown	80 L 11
Cill Airne / Killarney	77 D 11
Cill Chainnigh / Kilkenny	80 K 10
Cill Chaoi / Kilkee	83 D 9
Cill Chiaráin / Kilkieran	88 C 8
Cill Dalua / Killaloe	84 G 9
Cill Dara / Kildare	86 L 8
Cill Mhantáin / Wicklow	87 N 9
Cill Mocheallóg / Kilmallock	84 G 10
Cill Orglan / Killorglin	76 C 11
Cill Rois / Kilrush	83 D 10
Cill Rónáin / Kilronan	88 C 8
Cionn tSáile / Kinsale	78 G 12
Clady	101 J 3
Clane	87 L 8
Clár Chlainne Mhuiris / Claremorris	95 F 6
Clara / Clóirtheach (Offaly)	91 J 7
Clara (Wicklow)	87 N 9
Clare (County)	84 F 9
Clare (River)	89 F 7
Clare Island	94 B 6
Clarecastle	84 F 9
Claregalway / Baile Chláir	89 F 7
Claremorris / Clár Chlainne Mhuiris	95 F 6
Clarinbridge	89 F 8
Clashmore	79 I 11
Claudy	102 K 3
Clear (Cape)	77 D 13
Clear Island / Cléire (Oileán)	77 D 13
Cleegan Bay	88 B 7
Cleggan / An Cloigeann	88 B 7
Cléire (Oilean) / Clear Island	77 D 13
Clew Bay	94 C 6
Clifden / An Clochán	88 B 7
Cliffony	96 G 4
Clogh (Antrim)	103 N 3
Clogh (Kilkenny)	86 K 9
Clogh (Wexford)	81 M 10
Clogh Mills	103 N 3
Cloghan / An Clochán (Donegal)	100 I 3
Cloghan (Offaly)	90 I 8
Cloghan (Westmeath)	91 K 7
Cloghane	82 B 11
Cloghaneely	100 H 2
Cloghbrack	88 D 7
Clogheen	79 I 11
Clogher	97 K 4
Clogher Head (Kerry)	82 A 11
Clogher Head	93 N 6
Clogherhead	93 N 6
Cloghjordan	85 H 9
Cloghmore / An Chloich Mhóir	94 C 6
Cloghy	99 P 4
Clohamon	81 M 10
Cod's Head	76 B 13
Coill an Chollaigh / Bailieborough	97 L 6
Colgan Lough	96 G 5
Colligan	79 I 11
Collinstown	91 K 7
Collon	93 M 6
Collooney	96 G 5
Comber	99 O 4
Comeragh Mountains	80 J 11
Commeen / An Coimín	100 I 3
Cong / Conga	89 E 7
Conga / Cong	89 E 7
Conlig	103 O 4
Conn (Lough)	95 E 5
Conna	79 H 11
Connemara	88 C 7
Connemara National Park	88 C 7
Connor Pass	82 B 11
Convoy	101 I 3
Cookstown	98 L 4
Coola	96 G 5
Coolaney	96 G 5
Coole	97 K 6
Coole (Castle)	101 J 4
Coolea / Cúil Aodha	77 E 12
Coolgreany	87 N 9
Coolmore	96 H 4
Coolrain	86 J 9
Coomacarrea	76 B 12
Coomhola	77 D 12
Cooraclare	83 D 9
Cootehill / Muinchille	97 K 5
Copeland Island	99 P 3
Cora Droma Rúisc / Carrick-on-Shannon	96 H 6
Corbally	95 E 5
Corcaigh / Cork	78 G 12
Corcomroe Abbey	89 E 8
Cork / Corcaigh	78 G 12
Cork (County)	78 F 12
Cork Harbour	78 H 12
Corkscrew Hill	89 E 8
Cornamona	88 D 7
Corrandulla	89 F 7
Coachford	78 F 12
Coagh	98 M 4
Coalisland	98 L 4
Cobh / An Cóbh	78 H 12
Coleraine	102 L 2
Corraun Peninsula	94 C 6
Corrib (Lough)	89 E 7
Corrigeenroe	96 H 5
Corrofin	89 E 9
Costelloe / Casla	88 D 8
Cottoners	76 C 11
Coulagh Bay	76 B 12
Courtmacsherry	78 F 13
Courtmacsherry Bay	78 F 13
Courtown	81 N 10
Cousane Gap	77 E 12
Crag Cave	83 D 11
Craggaunowen Megalithic Centre	84 F 9
Craigavon	98 M 4
Crana	101 J 2
Cranfield Point	99 N 5
Cranford	101 I 2
Cratloe	84 F 9
Craughwell	89 F 8
Crawfordsburn	99 O 4
Creeslough	101 I 2
Creevykeel	96 G 4
Creggs	89 G 7
Croagh	84 F 10
Croagh Patrick	94 C 6
Croaghnageer	100 I 3
Croaghnakeela Island	88 C 8
Croangar (Lough)	100 H 3
Croghan	96 H 6
Crohy Head	100 G 3
Crois Mhaoilíona / Crossmolina	95 E 5
Croithlí / Crolly	100 H 2
Crolly / Croithlí	100 H 2
Cromane	76 C 11
Crookedwood	91 K 7
Crookhaven	76 C 13
Crookstown	78 F 12
Croom	84 F 10
Croos	90 H 7
Cross	89 E 7
Cross Barry	78 G 12
Cross (River)	88 D 7
Crossakeel	91 K 6
Crossdoney	97 J 6
Crossgar	99 O 4
Crosshaven	78 H 12
Crossmaglen	98 M 5
Crossmolina / Crois Mhaoilíona	95 E 5
Crow Head	76 B 13
Cruit Island	100 G 2
Crumlin	98 N 4
Crusheen	84 F 9
Cúil an tSúdaire / Portarlington	86 K 8
Cúil Aodha / Coolea	77 E 12
Cuilcagh	96 I 5
Culdaff	101 K 2
Culdaff Bay	101 K 2
Culleens	95 F 5
Cullenagh	88 E 9
Cullin (Lough)	95 E 6
Cullybackey	102 M 3
Cummeragh	76 B 12
Curlew Mountains	96 G 5
Curracloe	81 M 10
Curragh (The)	86 L 8
Curraghmore Gardens	80 J 11
Curraghroe	90 H 6
Currahchase Forest Park	84 F 10
Currane / An Corran	94 C 6
Currane (Lough)	76 B 12
Currans	83 D 11
Curreel (Lough)	88 C 7
Curry	95 F 6
Cushendall	103 N 2
Cushendun	103 N 2
Cushina	86 K 8
Cutra (Lough)	89 F 8

D

Daingean	86 K 8
Dalkey	87 N 8
Dan (Lough)	87 N 8
Darragh	83 E 9
Dartry Mountains	96 G 4
Davagh Forest Park	102 L 3
Dawros Head	100 G 3
Deel	84 F 10
Deel (Mayo)	94 D 5
Delamont	99 O 4
Delgany	87 N 8
Delphi	88 C 7
Delvin	91 K 7
Delvin (River)	93 N 7
Derg	101 J 3
Derg (Lough)	84 H 9
Derg (Lough) (Donegal)	97 I 4
Dernagree	77 E 11
Derravaragh (Lough)	91 J 7
Derreeny Bridge	77 E 13

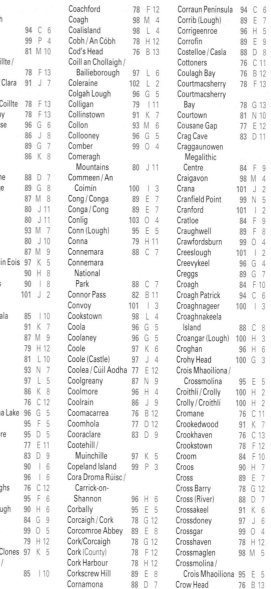

CORK / CORGAICH

Merchant's Quay Shopping Centre	Y
Oliver Plunkett Street	Z
St. Patrick's Street	Z
Camden Place	Y 5
Coburg Street	Y 10
Corn Market Street	Y 13
Dominick Street	Y 15
Eason's Hill	Y 17
Emmet Place	Y 18
Gerald Griffin St.	Y 21
Infirmary Road	Z 24
John Redmond Street	Y 26
Lancaster Quay	Z 28
Langford Row	Z 29
Lower Glanmire Road	Y 30
Merchant's Quay	Y 32
Newsom's Quay	Y 34
North Mall	Y 35
O'Connell's Square	Y 36
Parnell Place	Z 38
Pembroke Street	Z 39
Proby's Quay	Z 40
Roman Street	Y 42
St Patrick's Quay	Y 44
Southern Road	Z 45
South Link	Z 46
South Main Street	Z 47
Summer Hill	Y 48
Wolfe Tone Street	Y 56

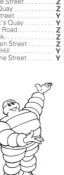

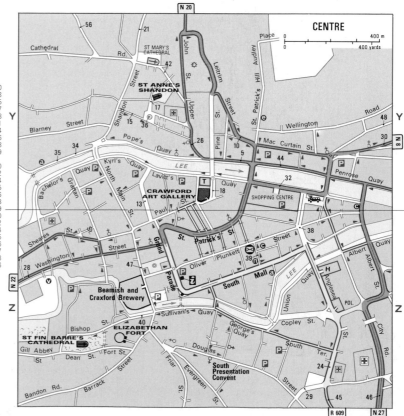

Derriana Lough	76	C	12
Derrybeg	100	H	2
Derryclare Lough	88	C	7
Derrycraff	94	D	6
Derrygonnelly	97	I	4
Derrylin	97	J	5
Derrynane House	76	B	12
Derrynane National Historic Park	76	B	12
Derrynasaggart Mountains	83	E	11
Derryveagh Mountains	100	H	3
Dervock	102	M	2
Devenish Island	97	J	4
Devilsbit	85	I	9
Dingle / An Daingean	82	B	11
Dingle Bay	76	B	11
Dingle Harbour	82	B	11
Divis	98	N	4
Doagh	101	I	2
Doagh Beg / Dumhaigh Bhig	101	J	2
Doe Castle	101	I	2
Dolla	84	H	9
Domhnach Phádraig / Donaghpatrick	92	L	6
Donabate	93	N	7
Donagh	97	J	5
Donaghadee	99	P	4
Donaghmore	98	L	4
Donaghpatrick / Domhnach Phádraig	92	L	6
Donard	87	M	8
Donard (Slieve)	99	O	5
Donegal / Dún na nGall	100	H	4
Donegal (County)	100	H	3
Donegal Bay	96	G	5
Doneraile	78	G	11
Donoughmore	78	F	12
Doo Lough	88	C	7
Dooagh	94	B	6
Doocharry / An Dúchoraidh	100	H	3
Dooega / Dumha Éige	94	B	6
Dooega Head	94	B	6
Doogort	94	B	5
Doohooma	94	C	5
Doon Lough	84	F	9
Doonaha	83	D	9
Doonbeg	83	D	9
Douglas	78	G	12
Doulus Head	76	A	12
Down (County)	99	N	4
Downhill	102	L	2
Downings / Na Dúnaibh	101	I	2
Downpatrick	99	O	5
Downpatrick Head	94	D	5
Downs (The)	91	K	7
Dowra	96	H	5
Dowth	93	M	6
Drangan	80	J	10
Draperstown	102	L	3
Drimoleague	77	E	13
Drinagh	77	E	13
Dripsey	78	F	12
Drishane Bridge	77	D	13
Drogheda / Droichead Átha	93	M	6
Droichead Átha / Drogheda	92	M	6
Droichead na Bandan / Bandon	78	F	12
Dromahair	96	H	5
Dromara	99	N	4
Dromcolliher	84	F	10
Dromin	93	M	6
Dromina	84	F	11
Dromineer	84	H	9
Dromiskin	98	M	6
Dromod	96	I	6
Dromore (Down)	99	N	4
Dromore (Tyrone)	97	J	4
Dromore West	95	F	5
Drum	97	K	5
Drum Hills	79	I	11
Drum Manor Forest Park	98	L	4
Drumbeg	99	O	4
Drumcliff	96	G	5
Drumcondra	92	M	6
Drumena Cashel	99	O	5
Drumfin	96	G	5
Drumfree	101	J	2
Drumgoft	87	M	9
Drumkeeran	96	H	5
Drumlaheen Lough	96	I	5
Drumlish	91	I	6
Drumone	91	K	6
Drumquin	97	J	4
Drumshanbo	96	H	5
Drumsna	96	H	6
Dublin / Baile Átha Cliath	87	N	8
Dublin Bay	93	N	7
Dublin (County)	93	N	7
Duff	96	H	4
Duleek	93	M	7
Dumha Éige / Dooega	94	B	6
Dumhaigh Bhig / Doagh Beg	101	J	2
Dún Á Rí Forest Park	98	L	6
Dún Aengus	88	C	8
Dún Chaoin / Dunquin	82	A	11
Dún Dealgan / Dundalk	98	M	5
Dún Garbhán / Dungarvan	80	J	11
Dún Mánmhaí / Dunmanway	77	E	12
Dún Mór / Dunmore	89	F	7
Dún na nGall / Donegal	100	H	4
Dunaff Head	101	J	2
Dunamase (Rock of)	86	K	8
Dunany Point	93	N	6
Dunboyne	93	M	7
Dunbrody Abbey	80	L	11
Duncannon	80	L	11
Duncormick	81	M	11
Dundalk / Dún Dealgan	98	M	5
Dundalk Bay	98	N	6
Dundonald	99	O	4
Dundrum (Down)	99	O	5
Dundrum (Dublin)	87	N	8
Dundrum (Tipperary)	85	H	10
Dundrum Bay	99	O	5
Dunfanaghy	100	I	2
Dungannon	98	L	4
Dunganstown	81	L	10
Dungarvan / Dún Garbhán	80	J	11
Dungarvan Harbour	80	J	11
Dungiven	102	L	3
Dunglow / An Clochán Liath	100	G	3
Dungonnell Dam	103	N	3
Dungourney	79	H	12
Dunguaire Castle	89	F	8
Dunkerrin	85	I	9
Dunkineely	100	G	4
Dunlavin	87	L	8
Dunleer	93	M	6
Dunlewy	100	H	2
Dunloe Castle	77	D	11
Dunloe (Gap of)	77	D	11
Dunluce Castle	102	M	2
Dunmanus Bay	76	C	13
Dunmanway / Dún Mánmhaí	77	E	12
Dunmore / Dún Mór	89	F	7
Dunmore Cave	86	K	9
Dunmore Head	82	A	11
Dunmore East	80	L	11
Dunmurry	99	N	4
Dunnamanagh	102	K	3
Dunowen Head	78	F	13
Dunquin / Dún Chaoin	82	A	11
Dunshaughlin	93	M	7
Durlas / Thurles	85	I	9
Durrow	86	J	9
Durrus	77	D	13
Dursey Head	76	B	13
Dursey Island	76	B	13
Duvillaun More	94	B	5
Dysert O'Dea	83	E	9

E

Éadan Doire / Édenderry	91	K	7
Eany	100	H	3
Eanymore	100	H	3
Easky	95	F	5
East Ferry	79	H	12
Édenderry / Éadan Doire	91	K	7
Ederny	97	J	4
Edgeworthstown	91	J	6
Egish (Lough)	98	L	5
Eglinton	102	K	2
Emly	84	G	10
Emo	86	K	8
Emyvale	97	L	4
Ennel (Lough)	91	J	7
Ennis / Inis	84	F	9
Enniscorthy / Inis Córthaidh	81	M	10
Enniskean	78	F	12
Enniskerry	87	N	8
Enniskillen	97	J	4
Ennistimon / Inis Díomáin	88	E	9
Eochaill / Youghal	79	I	12
Erne (Lower Lough)	96	I	4
Erne (River)	97	J	6
Erne (Upper Lough)	97	J	5
Errew Abbey	95	E	5
Erriff	88	D	7
Errigal Mountain	100	H	2
Erris Head	94	B	5
Eske (Lough)	100	H	3
Eyeries	76	C	12

F

Fahan	101	J	2
Fairy Glen	98	N	5
Fairymount	96	G	6
Falcarragh / An Fál Carrach	100	H	2
Fanad	101	I	2
Fanad Head	101	I	2
Fane River	98	M	5
Fanore	88	E	8
Farnanes Cross Roads	78	F	12
Farran Forest Park	78	F	12
Farranfore	83	D	11
Fastnet Rock	76	D	13
Feakle	84	G	9
Feale (River)	83	D	10
Fedamore	84	G	10
Fee (Lough)	88	C	7
Feeagh (Lough)	94	D	6
Feeny	102	K	3
Fenagh	96	I	5
Fenit	82	C	11
Feohanagh (River)	82	B	11
Ferbane	90	I	8
Fergus (River)	83	E	9
Fermanagh (County)	97	I	4
Fermoy / Mainistir Fhear Maí	78	H	11
Fern (Lough)	101	I	2
Ferns	81	M	10
Ferrycarrig	81	M	10
Ferta	76	B	12
Fethard / Fiodh Ard (Tipperary)	85	I	10
Fethard (Wexford)	80	L	11
Fiddown	80	K	10

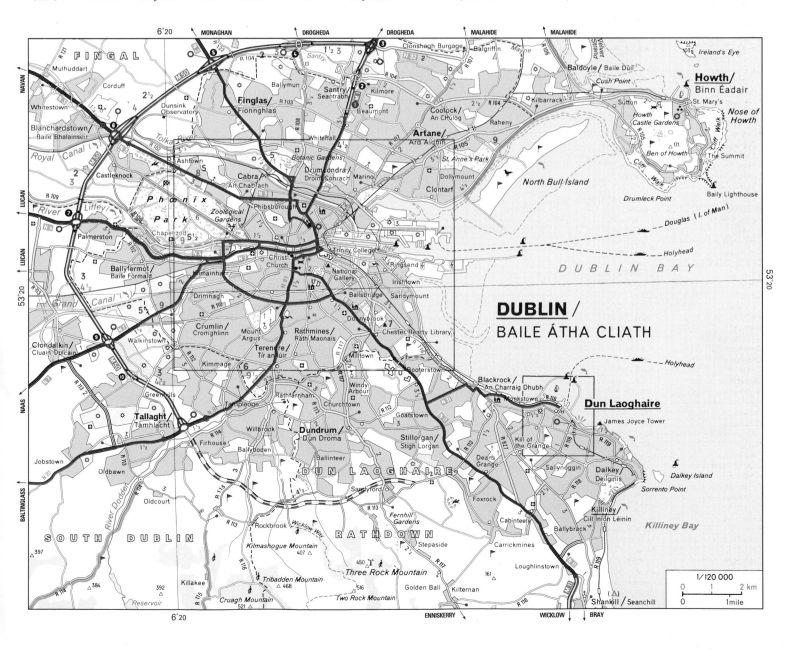

DUBLIN / BAILE ÁTHA CLIATH

DUBLIN/ BAILE ÁTHA CLIATH CENTRE

Anne Street South . . . . JYZ 6
Dawson Street . . . . JYZ
Duke Street . . . . JY 58
Grafton Street . . . . JYZ
Henry Street . . . . JX
Ilac Centre . . . . HJX
Irish Life Mall Centre . . . . . JKX
O'Connell Street . . . . JX

Brunswick Street North . . . . . HX 24
Buckingham Street . . . . KX 25
Bull Alley . . . . HZ 27
Chancery Street . . . . HY 33
Clanbrassil Street . . . . HZ 40
College Green . . . . JY 45
College Street . . . . HY 46
Cornmarket . . . . HY 49
D'Olier Street . . . . JY 51
Earlsfort Terrace . . . . JZ 60
Essex Quay . . . . HY 65
Essex Street . . . . HY 66
Fishamble Street . . . . HY 67
George's Quay . . . . KY 69
Golden Lane . . . . HZ 70
Henrietta Street . . . . HX 75
High Street . . . . HY 78
Kevin Street Upper . . . . HZ 85
Kildare Street . . . . JKZ 87
King Street South . . . . JZ 88
Marlborough Street . . . . JX 100
Merchants Quay . . . . HY 103
Montague Street . . . . JZ 106
Mount Street Upper . . . . KZ 112
Nicholas Street . . . . HY 118
North Great Georges Street . . . JX 119
Parnell Square East . . . . . . JX 126
Parnell Squatre North . . . . . JX 127
Parnell Square West . . . . . . HJX 129
St Mary's Abbey Street . . . . . HY 148
St Patrick Close . . . . HZ 150
Stephen Street . . . . HJY 165
Tara Street . . . . KY 171
Wellington Quay . . . . HJY 181
Werburgh Street . . . . HY 183
Westland Row . . . . KY 186
Westmoreland Street . . . . . . JY 187
Wexford Street . . . . HZ 189
Winetavern Street . . . . HY 193
Wood Quay . . . . HY 196

Town plans : the names of main shopping streets are indicated in red at the beginning of the list of streets.

Finglas	93 N 7
Finglass	76 C 11
Finn (Lough)	100 H 3
Finn (River)	101 J 3
Finnea	91 J 6
Finny / Fionnaithe	88 D 7
Fintona	97 K 4
Fintown / Baile na Finne	100 H 3
Fintragh Bay	100 G 4
Fiodh Ard / Fethard	85 I 10
Fionnaithe / Finny	88 D 7
Fiveabley	90 I 8
Fivemiletown	97 K 4
Flat Head	78 G 12
Flesk	77 D 11
Florence Court	97 I 5
Florence Court Forest Park	97 I 5
Foaty Island	79 H 12
Fontstown	86 L 8
Forbes (Lough)	90 I 6
Fore	91 K 6
Forkill	98 M 5
Forlorn Point	81 M 11
Formoyle (Lough)	88 D 7
Fota Island	78 H 12
Foul Sound	88 D 8
Foulksmills	81 L 11
Four Mile House	90 H 6
Fourknocks	93 N 7

Foxford	95 E 6
Foxhall	89 E 7
Foyle (Lough)	101 K 2
Foynes	83 E 10
Freemount	84 F 11
Frenchpark	96 G 6
Freshford	86 J 9
Fuerty	90 H 7
Furnace	88 D 7
Furnace Lough	94 D 6

G

Gabhla / Gola Island	100 G 2
Gabriel (Mount)	77 D 13
Gaddagh	76 C 11
Gaillimh / Galway	89 E 8
Galbally	84 H 10
Galey	83 D 10
Gallarus Oratory	82 A 11
Galley head	78 F 13
Gallion (Slieve)	102 L 3
Galty Mountains	84 H 10
Galtymore Mountain	84 H 10
Galway / Gaillimh	89 E 8
Galway (County)	89 F 7
Galway Bay	88 D 8
Galways Bridge	77 D 12

Gaoth Dobhair / Gweedore	100 H 2
Gaoth Sáile / Geesala	94 C 5
Gara (Lough)	96 G 6
Garadice Lough	97 I 5
Garrane	77 E 12
Garrison	96 H 4
Garristown	93 M 7
Garron Point	103 O 2
Garryvoe	79 H 12
Gartan Lough	100 I 3
Garty Lough	97 J 6
Garvagh	96 I 6
Garvagh	102 L 3
Gearagh (The)	78 F 12
Geashill	86 K 8
Geesala / Gaoth Sáile	94 C 5
Geevagh	96 H 5
Gerahies	77 D 13
Giant's Causeway	102 M 2
Giles Quay	98 N 6
Gilford	98 M 4
Gill (Lough)	96 G 5
Glanaruddery Mountains	83 D 11
Glandore	77 E 13
Glandore Harbour	77 E 13
Glanevin	96 I 5
Glanmire	78 G 12

Glantane	78 F 11
Glanworth	78 G 11
Glasdrumman	99 O 5
Glaslough	97 L 5
Glassan	90 I 7
Glasshouse Lake	97 J 5
Gleann Bhairr / Glenvar	101 J 2
Gleann na Muaidhe / Glenamoy	94 C 5
Gleann Cholm Cille / Glencolumbkille	100 F 3
Gleann Domhain / Glendowan	100 I 3
Glen	101 I 2
Glen Bay	100 F 3
Glen Head	100 F 3
Glen Lough (Donegal)	100 I 2
Glen Lough (Westmeath)	91 J 7
Glen (River) (Donegal)	100 G 3
Glenade Lough	96 H 4
Glenamoy / Gleann na Muaidhe	94 C 5
Glenamoy (River)	94 D 5
Glenariff	103 N 2
Glenariff Forest Park	103 N 2

Glenariff or Waterfoot	103 N 2
Glenarm	103 O 3
Glenavy	98 N 4
Glenbeigh	76 C 11
Glenbrook	78 G 12
Glencar	76 C 11
Glencar Lough	96 G 4
Glencolumbkille / Gleann Cholm Cille	100 F 3
Glencree	87 N 8
Glendalough	87 M 8
Glendovan Mountains	100 H 3
Glendowan / Gleann Domhain	100 I 3
Glenealy	87 N 9
Glenelly	101 K 2
Glenelly Valley	102 K 3
Glenfarne	96 I 5
Glenflesk	77 D 11
Glengad Head	101 K 1
Glengarriff / An Gleann Garbh	77 D 12
Glengarriff Harbour	77 D 12
Glengarriff (River)	76 D 12
Glengesh Pass	100 G 3
Glengormley	103 O 3
Glenicmurrin Lough	88 D 8

Glenmalur	87 M 9
Glenmore (Clare)	83 E 9
Glenmore (Kilkenny)	80 K 10
Glennamaddy	89 G 7
Glennamong	94 D 6
Glenoe	103 O 3
Glenshane Pass	102 L 3
Glenties	100 H 3
Glenvar / Gleann Bhairr	101 J 2
Glenveagh National Park	100 I 2
Glenville	78 G 11
Glin	83 E 10
Glin Castle	83 E 10
Glinsce / Glinsk	88 C 7
Glinsk / Glinsce	88 C 7
Glyde	98 M 6
Glynn	103 O 3
Gob an Choire / Achill Sound	94 C 6
Gobbins (The)	103 O 3
Gola Island / Gabhla	100 G 2
Golden	85 I 10
Golden Vale	85 H 10
Goleen	76 C 13
Goold's Cross	85 I 10
Gorey / Guaire	87 N 9
Gormanston	93 N 7

Gort / An Gort	89 F 8
Gort an Choirce / Gortahork	100 H 2
Gortahork / Gort an Choirce	100 H 2
Gorteen	96 G 6
Gortin	102 K 3
Gortin Glen Forest Park	102 K 3
Gortmore / An Gort Mór	88 D 7
Gorumna Island	88 C 8
Gosford Forest Park	98 M 5
Gougane Barra Forest Park	77 D 12
Gougane Barra Lake	77 E 12
Gowla	88 C 7
Gowna (Lough)	91 J 6
Gráig na Manach / Graiguena-managh	80 L 10
Graiguenamanagh / Gráig na Manach	80 L 10
Gránard / Granard	91 J 6
Grand Canal	90 I 8
Graney	86 L 9
Grange (Kilkenny)	80 K 10
Grange (Louth)	98 N 5
Grange (Sligo)	96 G 4
Gransha	103 O 3

Great Island	78	H 12
Great Blasket Island	82	A 11
Great Newtown Head	80	K 11
Great Skellig	76	A 12
Greenan	87	N 9
Greencastle (Donegal)	101	L 2
Greencastle (Down)	99	N 5
Greencastle (Tyrone)	102	K 3
Greenfield	89	E 7
Greenisland	103	O 3
Greenore	99	N 5
Greenore Point	81	N 11
Grey Point	103	O 3
Greyabbey	99	P 4
Greystones / Na Clocha Liatha	87	N 8
Grianan of Aileach	101	J 2
Groomsport	99	P 3
Guaire / Gorey	87	N 9
Gulladoo Lough	97	J 6
Gullion (Slieve)	98	M 5
Gur (Lough)	84	G 10
Gurteen	96	G 6
Gwebarra Bridge	100	H 3
Gweebarra Bay	100	G 3
Gweedore / Gaoth Dobhair	100	H 2
Gweestin	77	D 11
Gyleen	79	H 12

H

Hacketstown	87	M 9
Hags Head	88	D 9
Headford / Áth Cinn	89	E 7
Healy Pass	76	C 12
Helvick Head	80	J 11
Herbertstown	84	G 10
Hillsborough	99	N 4
Hilltown	99	N 5
Hog's Head	76	B 12
Hollyford	85	H 10
Hollyfort	87	M 9
Hollymount	89	E 7
Hollywood	87	M 8
Holy Cross	85	I 10
Holy Island	84	G 9
Holycross	84	G 10
Holywood	103	O 4
Hook Head	80	L 11
Hore Abbey	85	I 10
Horn Head	100	I 2
Horseleap	91	J 7
Hospital	84	G 10
Howth / Binn Éadair	93	N 7
Hugginstown	80	K 10
Hungry Hill	76	C 12
Hurlers Cross	84	F 9
Hyne (Lough)	77	E 13

I

Ilen	77	E 13
Inagh	83	E 9
Inagh (Lough)	88	C 7
Inch	82	C 11
Inch Abbey	99	O 4
Inch Island	101	J 2
Inchigeelagh	77	E 12
Inchiquin Lough (Kerry)	77	D 12
Inchydoney Island	78	F 13
Indreabhán / Inverin	88	D 8
Inis / Ennis	84	F 9
Inis Bó Finne / Inishbofin	100	H 2
Inis Córthaidh / Enniscorthy	81	M 10
Inis Díomáin / Ennistimon	88	E 9
Inis Meáin / Inishmaan	88	D 8
Inis Mór / Inishmore	88	C 8
Inis Oírr / Inisheer	88	D 8
Inishannon	78	G 12
Inishbofin / Inis Bó Finne (Donegal)	100	H 2
Inishbofin (Galway)	88	B 7

Inishcarra Reservoir	78	F 12
Inishcrone	95	E 5
Inisheer / Inis Oírr	88	D 8
Inishfree Bay	100	G 2
Inishglora	94	A 5
Inishkea North	94	B 5
Inishkea South	94	B 5
Inishmaan / Inis Meáin	88	D 8
Inishmore / Inis Mór	88	C 8
Inishmurray	96	G 4
Inishnabro	82	A 11
Inishowen	101	J 2
Inishowen Head	102	L 2
Inishshark	88	B 7
Inishtrahull	101	K 1
Inishtrahull Sound	101	K 1
Inishturk	94	B 6
Inistioge	80	K 10
Innfield	92	L 7
Inniskeen	98	M 5
Inny (River)	91	J 6
Inver	100	H 4
Inver (Mayo)	94	C 5
Inverin / Indreabhán	88	D 8
Ireland's Eye	93	N 7
Irishtown	89	F 7
Iron (Lough)	91	J 7
Iron Mountains	96	I 5
Irvinestown	97	J 4
Iveragh	76	B 12

J

Jamestown	96	H 6
Japanese Gardens	86	L 8
Jerpoint Abbey	80	K 10
Johnstown	86	J 9
Johnstown Castle	81	M 11
Jonesborough	98	M 5
Joyce	88	D 7
Joyce Country	88	C 7
Julianstown	93	N 6

K

Kanturk / Ceann Toirc	78	F 11
Katesbridge	98	N 5
Keadew	96	H 5
Keady	98	L 5
Kealduff	76	C 12
Kealkill	77	D 12
Kearney	99	P 4
Keel	94	B 6
Keel Lough	94	B 6
Keem Strand	94	B 6
Keimaneigh (The pass of)	77	E 12
Kells (Antrim)	103	N 3
Kells (Kerry)	76	B 12
Kells (Ceanannus Mor)/ Ceanannas (Meath)	92	L 6
Kells Bay	76	B 11
Kenmare / Neidín	77	D 12
Kenmare River	76	B 12
J. F. Kennedy Park	80	L 11
Kerry (County)	77	D 11
Kerry Head	82	C 10
Kerry (Ring of)	76	B 12
Kesh	97	I 4
Key (Lough)	96	H 5
Key (Lough) Forest Park	96	H 6
Kilbaha	82	C 10
Kilbeggan	91	J 7
Kilbeheny	84	H 11
Kilberry	92	L 6
Kilbricken	86	J 9
Kilbride (near Blessington)	87	M 8
Kilbrittain	78	F 12
Kilcar	100	G 4
Kilchreest	89	G 8
Kilclief	99	P 5
Kilcock	92	L 7
Kilcolgan	89	F 8
Kilconly (Galway)	89	F 7
Kilcoo	99	N 5

Kilcormac	90	I 8
Kilcrohane	76	C 13
Kilcullen	86	L 8
Kilcummin (Kerry)	82	B 11
Kildare / Cill Dara	86	L 8
Kildare (County)	86	L 8
Kildorrery	78	G 11
Kilfenora	89	E 9
Kilfinnane	84	G 10
Kilgarvan	77	D 12
Kilglass	95	E 5
Kilglass Lough	90	H 6
Kilgobnet	76	C 11
Kilgory Lough	84	F 9
Kilkee / Cill Chaoi	83	D 9
Kilkeel	98	N 5
Kilkeeran High Crosses	80	J 10
Kilkenny / Cill Chainnigh	80	K 10
Kilkenny (County)	80	J 10
Kilkieran / Cill Chiaráin	88	C 8
Kilkishen	84	F 9
Kill	80	J 11
Killadoon	94	C 6
Killadysert	83	E 9
Killala	95	E 5
Killala Bay	95	E 5
Killaloe / Cill Dalua	84	G 9
Killamery	80	J 10
Killann	81	L 10
Killard Point	99	P 5
Killarga	96	H 5
Killarney / Cill Airne	77	D 11
Killarney National Park	83	D 11
Killary Harbour	88	C 7
Killashandra	97	J 5
Killavally	95	D 6
Killavullen	78	G 11
Killeagh	79	H 12
Killeigh	86	J 8
Killenagh	81	N 10
Killenaule	85	I 10
Killerrig	86	L 9
Killeshin	86	K 9
Killeter	101	I 3
Killeter Forest	101	I 3
Killevy Churches	98	M 5
Killimer	83	D 10
Killimor	90	H 8
Killinaboy	89	E 9
Killiney Bay	87	N 8
Killiney (Dublin)	87	N 8
Killinick	81	M 11
Killinure Lough	90	I 7
Killkelly	95	F 6
Killmuckbridge	81	N 10
Killorglin / Cill Orglan	76	C 11
Killough	99	P 5
Killucan	91	K 7
Killurin	81	M 10
Killybegs / Na Cealla Beaga	100	G 4
Killygordon	101	I 3
Killykeen Forest Park	97	J 5
Killylea	98	L 4
Killyleagh	99	P 4
Kilmacduagh Monastery	89	F 8
Kilmacow	80	K 11
Kilmacrenan	101	I 2
Kilmacthomas	80	J 11
Kilmaganny	80	K 10
Kilmaine	89	E 7
Kilmalkedar	82	B 11
Kilmallock / Cill Mocheallóg	84	G 10
Kilmanagh	80	J 10
Kilmeage	86	L 8
Kilmeedy	84	F 10
Kilmessan	93	M 7
Kilmichael	77	E 12
Kilmichael Point	87	N 9
Kilmihil	83	D 9
Kilmore	81	M 11
Kilmore Quay	81	M 11
Kilmurry (near Kilkishen)	84	F 9
Kilmurvy	88	C 8
Kilnaleck	91	K 6

Kilpode	87	N 9
Kilrane	81	M 11
Kilrea	102	M 3
Kilreekill	89	G 8
Kilronan / Cill Rónáin	88	C 8
Kilrush / Cill Rois	83	D 10
Kilshanny	88	E 9
Kilsheelan	80	J 10
Kiltealy	81	L 10
Kiltegan	87	M 9
Kilternan	87	N 8
Kiltimagh	95	E 6
Kiltoom	90	H 7
Kiltormer	90	H 8
Kiltyclogher	96	H 4
Kilworth	79	H 11
Kilworth Mountains	79	H 11
Kinale (Lough)	91	J 6
Kincasslagh	100	G 2
Kings River	80	J 10
Kingscourt	97	L 6
Kinlough	96	H 4
Kinnegad	91	K 7
Kinnitty	90	I 8
Kinsale / Cionn tSáile	78	G 12
Kinsale (Old Head of)	78	G 13
Kinvarra	89	F 8
Kinvarra Bay	89	F 8
Kinvarra (near Screeb)	88	D 7
Kippure	87	N 8
Kircubbin	99	P 4
Kitconnell	89	G 8
Knappagh	94	D 6
Knappogue Castle	84	F 9

Knight's Town	76	B 12
Knock (Clare)	83	E 10
Knock (Mayo)	95	F 6
Knockadoon Head	79	I 12
Knockainy	84	G 10
Knockalongy	95	F 5
Knockcroghery	90	H 7
Knockferry	89	E 7
Knocklayd	103	N 2
Knocklong	84	G 10
Knockmealdown	79	I 11
Knockmealdown Mountains	79	I 11
Knockmoy Abbey	89	F 7
Knocknadobar	76	B 12
Knocknagree	77	E 11
Knockraha	78	G 12
Knocktopher	80	K 10
Knowth	93	M 6
Kylemore Abbey	88	C 7
Kylemore Lough	88	C 7

L

Labasheeda	83	E 10
Lack	97	J 4
Ladies View	77	D 12
Lady's Island Lake	81	M 11
Ladysbridge	79	H 12
Lagan (River)	99	N 4
Lagan Valley	99	O 4
Laghy	100	H 4
Lahinch / An Leacht	88	D 9
Lamb's Head	76	B 12
Lambay Island	93	N 7
Lanesborough	90	I 6

Laois (County)	86	J 9
Laragh	87	N 8
Larne	103	O 3
Larne Lough	103	O 3
Lauragh	76	C 12
Laurencetown	90	H 8
Lavagh More	100	H 3
Lawrencetown	98	N 4
Laytown	99	N 6
League (Slieve)	100	F 4
Leamaneh Castle	89	E 9
Leane (Lough)	77	D 11
Leannan	101	I 2
Leap	77	E 13
Leap (The)	81	M 10
Lecarrow (Leitrim)	96	H 5
Lecarrow (Roscommon)	90	H 7
Leckanvy	94	C 6
Leckavrea Mountain	88	D 7
Lee	82	C 11
Lee (River)	78	G 12
Leenane	88	C 7
Legananny Dolmen	99	N 5
Leighlinbridge	86	L 9
Leinster (Mount)	81	L 10
Leitir Ceanainn / Letterkenny	101	I 3
Leitir Meálláin / Lettermullan	88	C 8
Leitir Mhic an Bhaird / Lettermacaward	100	H 3
Leitrim	96	H 6

Leitrim (County)	96	I 6
Leixlip	93	M 7
Lemybrien	80	J 11
Lene (Lough)	91	K 7
Letterfrack	88	C 7
Letterkenny / Leitir Ceanainn	101	I 3
Lettermacaward / Leitir Mhic an Bhaird	100	H 3
Lettermore	88	D 8
Lettermore Island	88	C 8
Lettermullan / Leitir Meálláin	88	C 8
Licky	79	I 11
Liffey (River)	87	M 8
Lifford	101	J 3
Limavady	102	L 2
Limerick / Luimneach	84	G 9
Limerick (County)	84	F 10
Limerick Junction	84	H 10
Lios Dúin Bhearna / Lisdoonvarna	88	E 8
Lios Mór / Lismore	79	I 11
Lios Póil / Lispole	82	B 11
Lios Tuathail / Listowel	83	D 10
Lisbellaw	97	J 5
Lisburn	99	N 4
Liscannor	88	D 9
Liscannor Bay	83	D 9
Liscarroll	84	F 11
Lisdoonvarna / Lios Dúin Bhearna	88	E 8

LIMERICK/ LUIMNEACH

Arthur Quay Shopping Centre		Y
O'Connell Street		Z
Patrick Street		YZ 32
Roches Street		Z
Sarfield Street		Y 39
William Street		Z
Arthur Quay		Y 2
Baal's Bridge		Y 4
Bank Place		Y 5
Barrington Street		Z 6
Bridge Street		Y 7
Broad Street		Y 8
Castle Street		Y 10
Cathedral Place		Z 12
Charlotte's Quay		Y 13
The Crescent		Z 14
Cruises Street		Z 15
Gerald Griffen St.		Z 16
Grattan Street		Y 17
High Street		Y 18
Honan's Quay		Y 19
John Square		Y 20
Lock Quay		Y 21
Lower Cecil Street		Z 22
Lower Mallow Street		Z 23
Mathew Bridge		Y 24
Mount Kenneth		Z 26
Newtown Mahon		Z 28
North Circular Rd.		Y 29
O'Dwyer Bridge		Y 30
Penniwell Road		Z 33
Rutland Street		Y 34
St Alphonsus St.		Z 35
St Gerard St.		Z 36
St Lelia Street		YZ 37
Sexton Street North		Y 40
Shannon Street		Z 42
South Circular Rd		Z 43
Thomond Bridge		Y 45
Wickham Street		Z 47

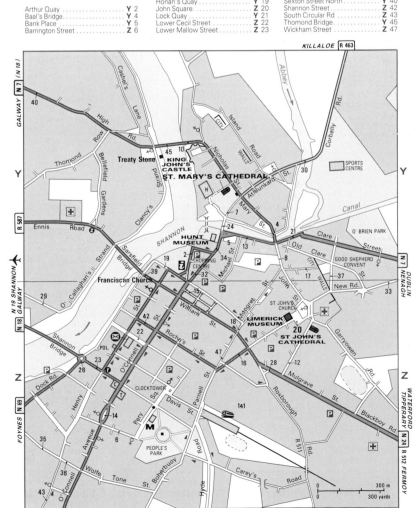

LONDONDERRY

Orchard Lane X 25

Barrack Street X 2
Clooney Terrace X 5
Creggan Street X 6
Custom House Street X 7
Dungiven Road X 8
Duke Street X 9
Foyle Road X 10
Foyle Street X 12
Francis Street X 13
Glendermott Road X 14
Harbour Square X 15
Infirmary Road X 17
John Street X 18
Lecky Road X 19
Limavady Road X 20
Long Tower Street X 22
Lower James Street X 23
Sackville Street X 26
Simpsons Brae X 29
Water Street X 32
William Street X 34

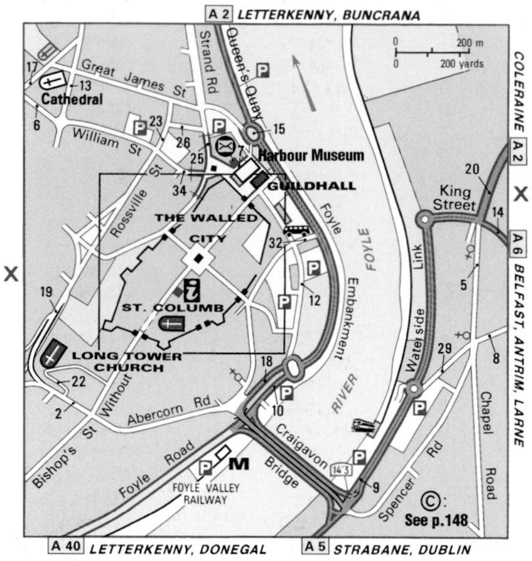
A 2 LETTERKENNY, BUNCRANA
COLERAINE A 2
A 6 BELFAST, ANTRIM, LARNE
A 40 LETTERKENNY, DONEGAL
A 5 STRABANE, DUBLIN
200 m
200 yards
Great James St
Cathedral
William St
Harbour Museum
GUILDHALL
THE WALLED CITY
ST. COLUMB
LONG TOWER CHURCH
Rossville St
Strand Rd
Queen's Quay
Foyle Embankment
RIVER FOYLE
King Street
Link
Waterside
Chapel Road
Spencer Rd
Craigavon Bridge
Foyle Road
Bishop's St
Without
Abercorn Rd
FOYLE VALLEY RAILWAY
See p.148

Lismacaffry 91 J 6
Lismore / Lios Mór 79 I 11
Lisnacree 99 N 5
Lisnarrick 97 I 4
Lisnaskea 97 J 5
Lispole / Lios Póil 82 B 11
Lissadell House 96 G 4
Lissatinnig Bridge 76 C 12
Lisselton 83 D 10
Lissycasey 83 E 9
Listowel / Lios Tuathail 83 D 10
Little Island 78 G 12
Little Skellig 76 A 12
Littleton 85 I 10
Lixnaw 83 D 10
Loch Garman / Wexford 81 M 10
Loghill 83 E 10
Londonderry 102 K 3
Londonderry (County) 102 K 3
Long Island 77 D 13
Longford (County) 90 I 6
Longford / An Longfort (Longford) 91 I 6
Longford (Offaly) 85 I 8
Loo Bridge 77 D 12
Loop Head 82 C 10
Lorrha 90 H 8
Lough Gowna 97 J 6
Loughgall 98 M 4
Loughbrickland 98 N 5
Loughglinn 96 G 6
Loughinisland 99 O 4
Loughrea / Baile Locha Riach 89 G 8
Loughros More Bay 100 G 3
Loughshinny 93 N 7
Louisburgh 94 C 6
Loup (The) 102 M 3
Louth 98 M 6
Louth (County) 98 M 6
Lower Lake 81 N 8
Lower Ballinderry 98 N 4
Lucan 93 M 7
Lugnaquillia Mountain 87 M 9
Luimneach / Limerick 84 G 10
Lullymore 86 L 8
Lung 96 G 6
Lurgan 98 N 4
Lusk 93 N 7
Lyracrumpane 83 D 10

M

Maam Cross / An Teach Dóite 88 D 7
Maas 100 G 3
Macgillycuddy's Reeks 76 C 12
Macnean Upper (Lough) 96 I 5
Macroom / Maigh Chromtha 78 F 12
Maganey 86 L 9
Magee (Island) 103 O 3
Maghera (Donegal) 100 G 3
Maghera (Down) 99 O 5
Maghera (Londonderry) 102 L 3
Magherafelt 102 M 3
Magheralin 98 N 4
Maghery 98 M 4
Magilligan 102 L 2
Magilligan Strand 102 L 2
Maguiresbridge 97 J 5
Mahee Island 99 P 4
Mahon 80 J 11
Mahoonagh 83 E 10
Maigh Chromtha / Macroom 78 F 12
Maigh Cuilinn / Moycullen 89 E 7
Maigh Nuad / Maynooth 93 M 7
Maigue (River) 84 F 10
Main 103 N 3
Maine (River) 82 C 11
Mainistir Fhear Maí / Fermoy 78 H 11
Mainistir Laoise / Abbey Leix 86 J 9
Mainistir na Búille / Boyle 96 H 6
Mainistir na Corann / Midleton 79 H 12
Máistir Gaoithe / Mastergeehy 76 B 12
Mal Bay 83 D 9
Mala / Mallow 78 G 11
Malahide / Mullach Íde 93 N 7
Málainn Bhig / Malin Beg 100 F 3
Malin 101 K 2
Malin Bay 100 F 3
Malin Beg / Málainn Bhig 100 F 3
Malin Head 101 J 1
Malin More 100 F 3
Mallow / Mala 78 G 11
Mamore (Gap of) 101 J 2
Mangerton Mountain 77 D 12
Mannin Bay 88 B 7
Mannin Lake 95 F 6
Manorcunningham 101 J 3
Manorhamilton / Cluainín 96 H 5
Mansfieldstown 92 M 6
Manulla 95 E 6
Maothail / Mohill 96 I 6
Marble Arch Caves 96 I 5
Marble Hill 101 I 2
Markethill 98 M 5
Mask (Lough) 88 D 7
Mastergeehy / Máistir Gaoithe 76 B 12
Matrix (Castle) 84 F 10
Mattock 93 M 6
Maum 88 D 7
Maumeen Lough 88 B 7
Maumtrasna 88 D 7
Maumturk Mountains 88 C 7
Maynooth / Maigh Nuad 93 M 7
Mayo 95 E 6
Mayo (County) 95 E 6
Mayo (Plains of) 95 E 6
Mealagh 77 D 12
Meath (County) 92 L 7
Meela (Lough) 100 G 3
Meenaneary / Mín na Aoire 100 G 3
Meenavean 100 F 3
Meeting of the Waters 87 N 9
Mellifont Abbey 93 M 6
Melmore Head 101 I 2
Melvin (Lough) 96 H 4
Menlough 89 G 7
Mew Island 99 P 3
Middletown (Armagh) 98 L 5
Middletown (Donegal) 100 H 2
Midleton / Mainistir na Corann 79 H 12
Milestone 85 H 9
Milford 84 F 10
Millford 101 I 2
Millisle 99 P 4
Millstreet 77 E 11
Milltown (Cavan) 97 J 5
Milltown (Galway) 89 F 7
Milltown (Kerry) 77 C 11
Milltown Malbay / Sráid na Cathrach 83 D 9
Mín na Aoire / Meenaneary 100 G 3
Minane Bridge 78 G 12
Minard Head 82 B 11
Mine Head 80 J 12
Mitchelstown / Baile Mhistéala 79 H 11
Mizen Head 76 C 13
Moate / An Móta 91 I 7
Moher (Cliffs of) 88 D 9
Moher Lough 94 D 6
Mohill / Maothail 96 I 6
Móinteach Mílic / Mountmellick 86 K 8
Moll's Gap 77 D 12
Monaghan / Muineachán 97 L 5
Monaghan (County) 97 K 5
Monasteraden 96 G 6
Monasteranenagh Abbey 84 G 10
Monasterboice 93 M 6
Monasterevin 86 K 8
Monavullagh Mountains 80 J 11
Mondello Park 86 L 8
Monea 97 I 4
Moneygall 85 I 9
Moneymore 102 L 3
Monivea 89 F 7
Monkstown (Antrim) 103 O 3
Monkstown (Cork) 78 G 12
Mooncoin 80 K 11
Moone 86 L 9
Moore Bay 83 C 9
Moorfields 103 N 3
Morley's Bridge 77 D 12
Mosney 93 N 7
Moss-Side 102 M 2
Mossley 103 O 3
Mostrim 91 J 6
Motte Stone 87 N 9
Mount Bellew / An Creagán 89 G 7
Mount Melleray Monastery 79 I 11
Mount Norris 98 M 5
Mount Nuggent 91 K 6
Mount Stewart Gardens 99 P 4
Mount Usher Gardens 87 N 8
Mountcharles 100 H 4
Mountfield 97 K 4
Mountmellick / Móinteach Mílic 86 K 8
Mountrath 86 J 8
Mountshannon 84 G 9
Mourne (Lough) 103 O 3
Mourne Mountains 99 N 5
Mourne River 101 J 3
Moville / Bun an Phobail 101 K 2
Moy 98 L 4
Moy (River) 95 E 5
Moyard 88 B 7
Moyasta 83 D 9
Moycullen / Maigh Cuilinn 89 E 7
Moylough 89 G 7
Moynalty 92 L 6
Moyne Abbey 95 E 5
Moyvally 92 L 7
Moyvore 91 J 7
Muck (Isle of) 103 O 3
Muckamore 103 N 3
Muckanagh Lough 84 F 9
Muckish Mountain 100 H 2
Muckno Lake 98 L 5
Muckros Head 100 G 4
Muckross 77 D 11
Muff 101 K 2
Muggort's Bay 80 J 11
Muinchille / Cootehill 97 K 5
Muineachán / Monaghan 97 L 5
Muine Bheag 86 L 9
Muing 94 D 5
Muingnabo 94 C 5
Mulkear 84 G 10
Mullach Íde / Malahide 93 N 7
Mullagh (Cavan) 92 L 6
Mullagh (Meath) 93 M 7
Mullaghareirk Mountains 83 E 10
Mullaghcleevaun 87 M 8
Mullaghmore 96 G 4
Mullet Peninsula 94 B 5
Mullinahone 80 J 10
Mullinavat 80 K 10
Mullingar / An Muileann gCearr 91 J 7
Mulrany / An Mhala Raithní 94 C 6
Mulroy Bay 101 I 2
Multyfarnham 91 J 7
Mungret 84 F 10
Muntervary or Sheep's Head 76 C 13
Murlough Bay 103 N 2
Murntown 81 M 11
Murrisk 94 D 6
Murroe 84 G 10
Mussenden Temple 102 L 2
Mutton Island 83 D 9
Mweelrea Mountains 88 C 7
Myshall 86 L 9

N

Na Cealla Beaga / Killybegs 100 G 4
Na Clocha Liatha / Greystones 87 N 8
Na Dúnaibh / Downings 101 I 2
Na Sceirí / Skerries 93 N 7
Naas / An Nás 87 L 8
Nacung (Lough) 100 H 2
Nad 78 F 11
Nafooey (Lough) 88 D 7
Nagles Mountains 78 G 11
Naminn (Lough) 101 J 2
Namona (Lough) 76 B 12
Nanny 93 M 7
Naran 100 G 3
Narrow Water Castle 98 N 5
Naul 93 N 7
Navan / An Uaimh 92 L 7
Neagh (Lough) 98 M 4
Neale 89 E 7
Neidín / Kenmare 77 D 12
Nenagh / An tAonach 84 H 9
Nephin 95 D 5
Nephin (Glen) 95 D 6
Nephin Beg 94 D 5
Nephin Beg Range 94 C 5
New Inn (Cavan) 97 K 6
New Inn (Galway) 89 G 8
New Kildimo 84 F 10
New Ross / Ros Mhic Thriúin 80 L 10
Newbawn 81 L 10
New Birmingham 80 J 10
Newbliss 97 K 5
Newbridge 93 N 7
Newbridge / An Droichead Nua 86 L 8
Newcastle (Down) 99 O 5
Newcastle (Dublin) 87 M 8
Newcastle (Tipperary) 79 I 11
Newcastle (Wicklow) 87 N 8
Newcastle West / An Caisleán Nua 83 E 10
Newgrange 93 M 6
Newinn 85 I 10
Newmarket 84 F 11
Newmarket on Fergus 84 F 9
Newport / Baile Uí Fhiacháin (Mayo) 94 D 6
Newport (Tipperary) 84 G 9
Newport Bay 94 C 6
Newry 98 M 5
Newtown Cashel 90 I 7
Newtown-Crommelin 103 N 3
Newtown (Laois) 86 K 9
Newtown (Offaly) 90 H 8
Newtownabbey 103 O 4
Newtown Forbes 90 I 6
Newtown Gore 96 I 5
Newtown Mount Kennedy 87 N 8
Newtownards 99 O 4
Newtownbutler 97 J 5
Newtownhamilton 98 M 5
Newtown-shandrum 84 F 10
Newtownstewart 101 J 3
Nier 80 J 11
Ninemilehouse 80 J 10
Nobber 92 L 6
Nohaval 78 G 12
Nore 86 J 9
Nore (River) 80 K 10
North Sound 88 C 8
North Ring 78 F 13
Nurney 86 L 8
Nurney (Carlow) 86 L 9

O

O'Brien's Tower 88 D 9
Offaly (County) 90 I 8
O'Grady (Lough) 84 G 9
Oileán Ciarraí / Castleisland 83 D 11
Oilgate 81 M 10
Oily 100 G 4
Old Head 94 C 6
Old Kildimo 84 F 10
Oldcastle / An Seanchaisleán 91 K 6
Oldleighlin 86 K 9
Old Ross 81 L 10
Omagh 97 K 4
Omeath 98 N 5
Omey Island 88 B 7
Oola 84 H 10
Oorid Lough 88 D 7
Oranmore 89 F 8
Ossian's Grave 103 N 2
Oughterard / Uachtar Ard 89 E 7
Ougther (Lough) 97 J 6
Ovens 78 G 12
Owel (Lough) 91 J 7
Owenascaul 82 B 11
Owenator 100 H 3
Owenavorragh 81 M 10
Owenbeg (River) 96 G 5
Owenboliska 88 E 8
Owencarrow 101 I 2
Owenea 100 G 3
Owengarve 94 D 6
Owenglin 88 C 7
Oweniny 94 D 5
Owenkillew 101 J 2
Owenkillew 102 K 3
Owenriff 88 D 7
Owentocker 100 H 3
Owey Island / Uaigh 100 G 2
Owvane 77 D 12
Oysterhaven 78 G 12

P

Pallasgreen 84 G 10
Pallaskenry 84 F 10
Paps (The) 77 E 11
Parke's Castle 96 H 5
Parkmore Point 82 A 11
Parknasilla 76 C 12
Partry 95 E 6
Partry Mountains 88 D 7
Passage East 80 L 11
Passage West 78 G 12
Patrickswell 84 F 10
Peake 78 F 12
Peatlands 98 M 4
Pettigoe 97 I 4
Phoenix Park 93 M 7
Piltown 80 K 10
Pluck 101 J 3
Plumbridge 102 K 3
Pomeroy 97 L 4
Pontoon 95 E 6
Port Durlainne / Porturlin 94 C 5
Port Láirge / Waterford 80 K 11
Port Laoise / Portlaoise 86 K 8
Port Omna / Portumna 90 H 8
Portacloy 94 C 5
Portadown 98 M 4
Portaferry 99 P 4
Portarlington / Cúil an tSúdaire 86 K 8
Portavogie 99 P 4
Port Ballintrae 102 M 2
Portglenone 102 M 3
Portlaoise / Port Laoise 86 K 8
Portlaw 80 K 11
Portmagee 76 A 12
Portmagee Channel 76 A 12
Portmarnock 93 N 7
Portmuck 103 O 3
Portnablagh 101 I 2
Portnoo 100 G 3
Portrane 93 N 7
Portroe 84 G 9
Portrush 102 M 2
Portsalon 101 J 2
Portstewart 102 L 2
Portumna / Port Omna 90 H 8
Porturlin / Port Durlainne 94 C 5
Poulaphouca Reservoir 87 M 8
Poulnasherry Bay 83 D 10
Powerscourt Demesne 87 N 8
Poyntz Pass 98 M 5
Prosperous 87 L 8
Puckaun 84 H 9
Puffin Island 76 A 12

Q

Quigley's Point 101 K 2
Quilty 83 D 9
Quin 84 F 9

R

Rae na nDoirí / Reananeree 77 E 12
Raghly 96 G 5
Raharney 91 K 7
Ram Head 79 I 12
Ramor (Lough) 91 K 6
Randalstown 103 N 3
Raphoe 101 J 3
Rasharkin 102 M 3
Rath 90 I 8
Ráth Caola / Rathkeale 84 F 10
Ráth Droma / Rathdrum 87 N 9
Rath Luirc (Charleville) / An Ráth 84 F 10
Rathangan 86 L 8
Rathcool 78 F 11
Rathcoole 87 M 8
Rathcormack 78 H 11
Rathcroghan 90 H 6
Rathdangan 87 M 9
Rathdowney 86 J 9
Rathdrum / Ráth Droma 87 N 9
Rathfriland 99 N 5
Rathgormuck 80 J 11
Rathkeale / Ráth Caola 84 F 10
Rathlackan 95 E 5
Rathlin Island 103 N 2
Rathlin Sound 103 N 2
Rathmelton 101 J 2
Rathmolyon 92 L 7
Rathmore 83 E 11
Rathmullan 101 J 2
Rathnew 87 N 9
Rathowen 91 J 7
Rathvilla 86 K 8
Rathvilly 87 L 9
Ratoath 93 M 7
Raven Point (The) 81 M 10
Ray 100 H 2
Rea (Lough) 89 G 8
Reananeree / Rae na nDoirí 77 E 12
Rear Cross 84 H 9

Recess /
  Straith Salach 88 C 7
Red Bay 103 N 2
Redcastle 101 K 2
Redcross 87 N 9
Redhills 97 K 5
Ree (Lough) 90 I 7
Reelan 100 H 3
Relaghbeg 92 L 6
Rhode 91 K 7
Richhill 98 M 4
Ringabella Bay 78 H 12
Ringsend 102 L 2
Ringville / An Rinn 80 J 11
Rinn Lough 96 I 6
Rinvyle 88 C 7
Rinvyle Castle 88 B 7
Riverstown 96 G 5
Roadford 88 D 8
Roaringwater Bay 77 D 13
Robert's Head 78 H 12
Robertstown 86 L 8
Rochestown 80 K 11
Rochfortbridge 91 K 7
Rockabill 93 N 7
Rockchapel 83 E 11
Rockcorry 97 K 5
Rockhill 84 F 10
Rockmills 78 G 11
Roe 102 L 3
Roonah Quay 94 C 6
Roosky 90 I 6
Ros an Mhil /
  Rossaveel 88 D 8
Ros Comáin /
  Roscommon 90 H 7
Ros Cré / Roscrea 85 I 9
Ros Láir / Rosslare 81 M 11
Ros Mhic
  Thriúin/New
  Ross 80 L 10
Rosapenna 101 I 2
Roscommon /
  Ros Comáin 90 H 7
Roscommon
  (County) 96 G 6
Roscrea / Ros Cré 85 I 9
Rosegreen 85 I 10
Rosenallis 86 J 8
Rosmuck 88 D 7
Rosnakill 101 I 2
Ross Abbey 89 E 7
Ross Port 94 C 5
Ross Lake 89 E 7
Rossaveel /
  Ros an Mhil 88 D 8
Rossbeg 100 G 3
Rossbeigh Creek 76 C 11
Rosscarbery 77 E 13
Rosscarbery Bay 77 E 13
Rosserk Abbey 95 E 5
Rosses (The) 100 G 2
Rosses Point 96 G 5
Rossinver 96 H 4
Rosslare / Ros Láir 81 M 11
Rosslare Bay 81 M 11
Rosslare Harbour/
  Calafort Ros Láir 81 M 11
Rosslare Point 81 M 11

Rosslea 97 K 5
Rossmore Forest
  Park 97 L 5
Rossnowlagh 96 H 4
Rostrevor 98 N 5
Rough Point 82 B 11
Roughty 77 D 12
Roundstone 88 C 7
Roundwood 87 N 8
Rower (The) 80 L 10
Royal Canal 90 I 7
Royaloak 86 L 9
Rue Point 103 N 2
Runabay Head 103 N 2
Rush / An Ros 93 N 7
Russborough
  House 87 M 8
Rylane Cross 78 F 12

S
Saggart 87 M 8
St. Columbkille 100 F 3
St. Fachtnan's 88 E 9
St. Finan's Bay 76 A 12
St. John's Lough 96 I 5
St. John's Point
  (Donegal) 100 G 4
St. John's Point
  (Down) 99 P 5
St. Johnstown 101 J 3
St. Macdara's
  Island 88 C 8
St. Mochta's House 98 M 6
Saintfield 99 O 4
Sallins 87 M 8
Sally Gap 87 N 8
Sallybrook 78 G 12
Saltee Islands 81 M 11
Salthill 89 E 8
Santry 93 N 7
Saul 99 O 4
Sawel Mountain 102 K 3
Scarriff / An
  Scairbh 84 G 9
Scarriff Island 76 B 12
Scartaglin 83 D 11
Scarva 98 M 5
Schull / Skull 77 D 13
Scolban (Lough) 96 H 4
Scotshouse 97 K 5
Scotstown 97 K 5
Scrabo Hill 99 O 4
Scramoge 90 H 6
Screeb / Scriob 88 D 7
Screen 81 M 10
Scriob / Screeb 88 D 7
Scur (Lough) 96 I 5
Seaforde 99 O 5
Seven Heads 78 F 13
Seven Hogs or
  Magharee
  Islands
  (The) 82 B 11
Shanagarry 79 H 12
Shanagolden 83 E 10
Shanballymore 78 G 11
Shanes Castle 103 N 3

Shankill 87 N 8
Shannagh (Lough) 99 N 5
Shannon 84 F 9
Shannon Airport 84 F 9
Shannon
  (River) 90 H 8
Shannonbridge 90 H 8
Shannon Harbour 90 I 8
Shantonagh 98 L 5
Sheddings (The) 103 N 3
Sheeffry Hills 94 C 6
Sheelin (Lough) 91 K 6
Sheep Haven 101 I 2
Sheever (Lough) 91 K 7
Shehy Mountains 77 D 12
Shercock 97 L 6
Sherkin Island 77 D 13
Shillelagh 87 M 9
Shinrone 85 I 9
Shrule 89 E 7
Silent Valley 99 O 5
Sillan (Lough) 97 L 5
Silver Strand 94 C 6
Silvermine
  Mountains 84 H 9
Silvermines 84 H 9
Sion Mills 101 J 3
Six Towns (The) 102 L 3
Sixmilebridge 84 F 9
Sixmilecross 97 K 4
Skannive (Lough) 88 C 8
Skerries / Na Sceirí 93 N 7
Skibbereen /
  An Sciobairín 77 E 13
Skreen 95 F 5
Skull / Schull 77 D 13
Sky Road 88 B 7
Slade 80 L 11
Slane 93 M 6
Slane (Hill of) 93 M 6
Slaney (River) 81 M 10
Slea Head 82 A 11
Slemish
  Mountain 103 N 3
Slieve Anierin 96 I 5
Slieve Aught
  Mountains 89 G 8
Slieve Bernagh 84 G 9
Slieve Bloom
  Mountains 86 J 8
Slieve Gamph or
  the Ox
  Mountains 95 F 5
Slieve Mish
  Mountains 82 C 11
Slieve Miskish
  Mountains 76 C 13
Slieveanorra 103 N 2
Slievefelim
  Mountains 84 H 9
Slievenamon 80 J 10
Slievetooey 100 G 3
Sligeach / Sligo 96 G 5
Sligo / Sligeach 96 G 5
Sligo Bay 95 F 5
Sligo (County) 95 F 5
Sliveardagh Hills 80 J 10
Slyne Head 88 B 7
Smearlagh 83 D 11

Smerwick 82 A 11
Smerwick Harbour 82 A 11
Smithborough 97 K 5
Snaght (Slieve)
  (Derryveagh Mts.) 100 H 3
Snaght (Slieve)
  (Inishowen) 101 J 2
Snave 77 D 12
Sneem 76 C 12
Sord / Swords 93 N 7
South Sound 88 D 8
Spa 82 C 11
Spanish Point 83 D 9
Spelga Dam 99 N 5
Sperrin Mountains 102 K 3
Spiddal / An
  Spidéal 88 E 8
Spink 86 K 9
Springhill 102 M 3
Srah / An tSraith 95 E 6
Srahmore 94 D 6
Sráid na Cathrach/
  Milltown Malbay 83 D 9
Stack's Mountains 83 D 11
Staigue Stone Fort 76 B 12
Stamullin 93 N 7
Stewartstown 98 L 4
Stonyford 80 K 10
Strabane 101 J 3
Stracashel 100 H 3
Stradbally (Kerry) 82 B 11
Stradbally (Laois) 86 K 8
Stradbally
  (Waterford) 80 J 11
Strade 95 E 6
Stradone 97 K 6
Straffan 87 M 8
Straid (Antrim) 103 O 3
Straid (Donegal) 101 J 2
Straith Salach /
  Recess 88 C 7
Strandhill 96 G 5
Strangford 99 P 4
Strangford Lough 99 P 4
Stranorlar 101 I 3
Stratford 87 L 9
Strokestown 90 H 6
Stroove 101 L 2
Struell Wells 99 O 5
Suck 96 G 6
Suck (River) 96 G 6
Suir 85 I 9
Suir (River) 79 I 11
Summerhill 92 L 7
Sunderlin
  (Lough) 90 I 7
Swan 86 K 9
Swan's Cross
  Roads 97 K 5
Swanlinbar 91 I 5
Swatragh 102 L 3
Swilly 101 I 3
Swilly (Lough) 101 J 2
Swilly (River) 101 J 2
Swinford /
  Béal Atha na
  Muice 95 F 6
Swords / Sord 93 N 7
Sybil Head 82 A 11

T
Table Mountain 87 M 8
Tacumshane 81 M 11
Tacumshin Lake 81 M 11
Taghmon 81 M 11
Tagoat 81 M 11
Tahilla 76 C 12
Tallaght 87 M 8
Tallanstown 98 M 6
Tallow 79 H 11
Tandragee 98 M 4
Tang 90 I 7
Tara (Hill of) 93 M 7
Tarbert 83 D 10
Tarker (Lough) 97 L 5
Tarsaghaunmore 94 C 5
Tay 80 J 11
Tay (Lough) 87 N 8
Teelin 100 G 4
Temple of the
  Winds 99 P 4
Temple (The) 99 O 4
Templeboy 95 F 5
Templeglentan 83 E 10
Templehouse Lake 96 G 5
Templemore /
  An Teampall Mór 85 I 9
Templenoe 76 C 12
Templepatrick 103 N 3
Templetouhy 85 I 9
Tempo 97 J 4
Terenure 87 N 8
Termon /
  An Tearmann 101 I 2
Termonbarry 90 I 6
Termonfeckin 93 N 6
Terryglass 85 H 8
Thomastown /
  Baile Mhic
  Andáin 80 K 10
Thoor Ballylee 89 F 8
Three Castle Head 76 C 13
Thurles / Durlas 85 I 9
Tibohine 96 G 6
Timahoe (Kildare) 86 L 8
Timahoe (Laois) 86 K 9
Timoleague 78 F 13
Timolin 86 L 9
Tiobraid Árann /
  Tipperary 84 H 10
Tipperary /
  Tiobraid Árann 84 H 10
Tipperary (County) 84 H 10
Tobar an Choire/
  Tobercurry 95 F 5
Tobercurry /
  Tobar an Choire 95 F 5
Toberscanavan 96 G 5
Toe Head 77 E 13
Tollymore Forest
  Park 99 O 5
Tomhaggard 81 M 11
Toombeola 88 C 7
Toome 102 M 3
Toomyvara 85 H 9
Toormore 76 D 13
Toraigh /
  Tory Island 100 H 2

Torr Head 103 N 2
Tory Island /
  Toraigh 100 H 2
Tory Sound 100 H 2
Tourig 79 I 11
Tourmakeady /
  Tuar Mhic
  Éadaigh 89 D 7
Tower 78 G 12
Trá Lí / Tralee 83 C 11
Trá Mhór / Tramore 80 K 11
Trabane Strand 100 F 4
Trafrask 76 D 12
Tralee / Trá Lí 83 C 11
Tralee Bay 82 C 11
Tramore / Trá Mhór 80 K 11
Tramore Bay 80 K 11
Tranarossan Bay 101 I 2
Trean 88 D 7
Trillick 97 J 4
Trim /
  Baile Átha Troim 92 L 7
Trostan 103 N 2
Tuaim / Tuam 89 F 7
Tuam / Tuaim 89 F 7
Tuamgraney 84 G 9
Tuar Mhic Éadaigh /
  Tourmakeady 89 D 7
Tulach Mhór /
  Tullamore 86 J 8
Tulla 84 F 9
Tullaghan 96 G 4
Tullaghobegly 100 H 2
Tullaghogue 98 L 4
Tullamore /
  Tulach Mhór 86 J 8
Tullaroan 80 J 10
Tullig Point 83 C 10
Tullow / An Tulach 86 L 9
Tully 97 I 4
Tully Cross 88 C 7
Tully National Stud 86 L 8
Tullyallen 93 M 6
Tullycanna 81 L 11
Tullynally Castle 91 J 6
Tulsk 90 H 6
Turlough (Mayo) 95 E 6
Turloughmore 89 F 7
Turner's Rock
  Tunnel 77 D 12
Tuskar Rock 81 M 11
Twelve Pins (The) 88 C 7
Tynagh 89 G 8
Tyrella 99 O 5
Tyrone (County) 97 J 4
Tyrrellspass 91 J 7

U
Uachtar Ard /
  Oughterard 89 E 7
Uaigh /
  Owey Island 100 G 2
Ugga Beg
  (Lough) 88 D 8
Ulster American
  Folk Park 101 J 4
Union Hall 77 E 13

Unshin 96 G 5
Upper
  Ballinderry 98 N 4
Upperchurch 85 H 9
Urlingford 86 J 9

V
Valencia Island 76 A 12
Valley 94 C 5
Ventry 82 A 11
Ventry Harbour 82 A 11
Villierstown 80 J 11
Virginia 91 K 6

W
Ward 93 N 7
Waringstown 98 N 4
Warrenpoint 98 N 5
Water Garden
  (The) 80 K 10
Waterfoot or
  Glenariff 103 N 2
Waterford /
  Port Láirge 80 K 11
Waterford (County) 80 J 11
Waterford Harbour 80 L 11
Watergrasshill 78 G 11
Waterville /
  An Coireán 76 B 12
Wellington Bridge 81 L 11
Wesport Bay 94 C 6
Westmeath
  (County) 91 J 7
Westport /
  Cathair na Mart 94 D 6
Westport House 94 D 6
Wexford /
  Loch Garman 81 M 10
Wexford Bay 81 N 10
Wexford (County) 81 L 10
Wexford Harbour 81 M 10
Wheathill 97 I 5
Whiddy Island 77 D 12
White Park Bay 102 M 2
Whitechurch 78 G 12
Whitegate 78 H 12
Whitehead 103 O 3
Wicklow
  (County) 87 M 9
Wicklow /
  Cill Mhantáin 87 N 9
Wicklow Gap 87 M 8
Wicklow Mountains 87 N 8
Wilkinstown 92 L 6
Williamstown 96 G 6
Windgap 80 J 10
Windy Gap 98 N 5
Woodenbridge 87 N 9
Woodford 97 J 5

Y
Youghal / Eochaill 79 I 12
Youghal Bay 79 I 12

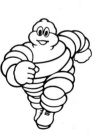

Notes

Travel with Michelin

Maps, Plans & Atlases

With Michelin's cartographic expertise you are guaranteed easy-to-read, comprehensive travel and tourist information. And you can also be confident that you'll have detailed and accurate mapping, updated annually to make this collection the best travel companion for any motorist.

Red Guides

Each of these 12 titles, revised annually, offer a range of carefully selected hotels and restaurants rated according to comfort; From the friendly farmhouse to the luxury hotel, there is something to suit everyone.
Titles: Benelux, Deutschland, España/Portugal, Europe, France, Great Britain & Ireland, Ireland, Italia, London, Paris, Portugal, Suisse.

Green Guides

With over 160 titles covering Europe and North America, Michelin Green Guides offer independent travellers a cultural insight into a city, region or country, with all the information you need to enjoy your visit.
Each guide includes recommended main sights with detailed descriptions and colour photographs, accurate plans, suggested routes and essential practical information.

In Your Pocket Guides

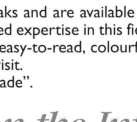

These handy pocket-sized guides are designed for short breaks and are available to destinations all over the world. Drawing on Michelin's acclaimed expertise in this field, they offer essential cultural and practical information in an easy-to-read, colourfully illustrated format, to help the reader make the most of any visit.
Titles available in English, "In Your Pocket" and French, "Escapade".

Michelin Route planner on the Internet

With Michelin's new website all you have to do is type in your start and finish points and your route is planned for you in a matter of seconds, with travel time, distances, road numbers, and tolls, for any destination in Europe
http://www.michelin-travel.com

Michelin Green Guide Collection

France

Atlantic Coast · Auvergne Rhône Valley · Brittany · Burgundy Jura · Châteaux of the Loire · Dordogne · France · French Riviera · Normandy · Northern France and the Paris Region · Paris · Provence · Pyrénées Languedoc Tarn Gorges

Great Britain

Great Britain · Scotland · Wales · The West Country · London

Other countries

Austria · Belgium Grand Duchy of Luxembourg · Berlin · Brussels · Europe · Germany · Greece · Ireland · Italy · Netherlands · Portugal · Rome · Scandinavia Finland · Spain · Switzerland · Thailand · Tuscany · Venice · California · Canada · Chicago · New England · New York City · Quebec · Washington DC

MICHELIN

First published 1990 by Manufacture Française des Pneumatiques Michelin
Société en commandite par actions au capital de 2 000 000 000 de Francs
Place des Carmes-Déchaux – 63 Clermont-Ferrand (France) – RCS Clermont-Fd B855200507
© Michelin et Cie, propriétaires-éditeurs 1998
ninth edition 1998

Great Britain: Based upon the Ordnance Survey with the permission of The Controller of Her
Majesty's Stationery Office © Crown copyright 39923 X.

Northern Ireland: All mapping covering Northern Ireland in this publication is based upon the
Ordnance Survey of Northern Ireland with the permission of the Controller of Her Majesty's
Stationery Office, Permit number 1073.

Republic of Ireland: All mapping covering the Republic of Ireland in this publication is based
upon the Ordnance Survey of Ireland by permission of the government. Permit number 6537.

In spite of the care taken in the production of this book, it is possible that a defective copy may
have escaped our attention. If this is so, please return it to your bookseller, who will exchange it
for you, or contact:

Michelin Tyre Public Limited Company
Tourism Department
38 Clarendon Road
WATFORD Herts WD1 1SX - U.K.
Tel (01923) 415000

The representation of a road in this atlas is no evidence of a right of way.

ISBN Hardback 2-06-112009-1 – ISBN Softback 2-06-112109-8 – ISBN Spiral 2-06-112209-4

Dépôt légal octobre 1997 – Printed in E.U. 10-97

Printed by Casterman